A HISTORY
OF REGULATORY
TAXATION

A HISTORY
OF REGULATORY
TAXATION

R. Alton Lee

The University Press of Kentucky

ISBN: 0-8131-1303-2

Library of Congress Catalog Card Number: 73-80460

Copyright © 1973 by The University Press of Kentucky

A statewide cooperative scholarly publishing agency
serving Berea College, Centre College of Kentucky,
Eastern Kentucky University, Georgetown College,
Kentucky Historical Society, Kentucky State University,
Morehead State University, Murray State University,
Northern Kentucky State College, Transylvania University,
University of Kentucky, University of Louisville, and
Western Kentucky University.

Editorial and Sales Offices: Lexington, Kentucky 40506

*For Marilyn, Edward and
Deborah; and to Michael
and the scholar he might have been*

Contents

Preface

The Founding Fathers constructed a system of government that has permitted, through a broad interpretation of powers, a growth and adaptation of governmental functions to new and changing conditions. The Constitution, according to strict constructionists, however, established a national government limited to the exercise of only those powers specifically delegated to it by the states; all the vast reservoir of governmental authority, except the enumerated powers given the central government, were to be exercised exclusively by the states. Despite this restrictive interpretation, the national government extended its control over an increasing number of social and economic areas in the late nineteenth century and into the twentieth. Congress accomplished this through enactment of statutes based on a broad construction of those functions specifically delegated to it—especially jurisdiction over United States mail, control of interstate commerce, and use of the taxing power. These laws, in effect, established a national police power in areas previously controlled, if at all, by the states and led to the regulation or abolition of commodities or activities not imagined by the framers of the Constitution in 1787.

My decision to investigate the development of a national police power through the use of the taxing power was predicated on a number of factors. On the one hand, the results of regulatory taxes can be interpreted to have been more significant than has use of the postal power for police purposes, and on the other, the taxing power can be examined in a single monograph while the history of the use of the commerce power to create a police power would require several volumes. In addition, the history of regulation through taxation, when compared to uses of the commerce or mail powers for the same purposes, is unique in illustrating the constitutional arguments, in Congress and the Supreme Court, over strict versus loose construction of the powers of the national government. The legislature and judiciary have rather uniformly followed a broad interpretation of the postal and commerce powers for regulation; these two branches of government have been inconsistent in construing the taxing power for police functions. Regulatory taxation provides an excellent example of a legislative-judicial struggle over public policy making.

Each of the topics studied in this book is important enough to warrant a monograph or several volumes in itself. Instead, the study has been narrowed to include only those developments that built a national police power through taxation and the contribution of these issues to that growth. In the attempt to synthesize the history of regulatory taxation it was necessary to omit consideration of various excise taxes, such as those on whiskey and tobacco, because their primary purpose is to raise revenue rather than to exert a regulatory effect on the product. Other specific social welfare taxes, of course, such as those on incomes and inheritances, require separate specialized treatment.

The evolution of the policy of regulatory taxation could be organized in various ways. I have elected to trace its development in a chronological manner, wherever possible, because it evolved primarily on a pragmatic basis. It falls readily into three distinct periods. From its inception, and continuing through the Progressive movement, Congress expanded this public policy primarily to assist agrarian interests by taxing "adulterated" foods and secondarily to institute reform of some social issues, namely, dangerous matches and drugs. This began rather tentatively, but when the Supreme Court sustained this policy as constitutional, it rapidly proliferated as a favorite congressional device to handle other social problems. In the second period, from World War I until the revolution in the Court brought about by President Franklin Roosevelt's appointees, a majority of the justices emphasized an interpretation of the limiting effects of the Tenth Amendment. This resulted in a restriction of congressional extension of the policy into areas the conservative justices considered reserved to state control. These included decisions on taxes on child labor, grain futures, the processing of agricultural products, and coal mining. With the broad interpretations given to the power to regulate interstate commerce by the Supreme Court after 1937, Congress increasingly used the commerce power to extend the national police power with a subsequent decline in the use of regulatory taxation. Finally, the libertarian majority on the Earl Warren Court, with its emphasis on protection of the individual's rights, questioned the registration features of regulatory taxes on firearms, gambling, and narcotics as violating the protection against self-incrimination. Because these taxes required registration of some type, the principal enforcement aspect of regulatory taxation was thus circumscribed and the evolution of this policy came full cycle—from first hesitant use by Congress in 1886 to doubt about its efficacy as a means of control almost a century later.

I should like particularly to thank John F. Davis, Clerk of the Supreme Court of the United States, for permission to use papers of the Supreme Court Library. In addition, I wish to express my gratitude to Irma Falck, Government Documents Division, and John Hagemann, Law Librarian, of the University of South Dakota Library staff, for their assistance in the research of this book. A grant from the University of South Dakota General Research Fund provided me with money to travel and to buy library materials. Philip Lagerquist and the staff at the Harry S. Truman Library were most helpful in providing research materials as were the staff of the State Historical Society of Wisconsin.

Fortunately, colleagues always seem to possess an uncanny faculty for detecting errors, both obvious and concealed, in fact and interpretation in one's writing. I should like to thank Professors Thomas Buckley of the University of Tulsa, Joseph Cash of the University of South Dakota, and John Ferrell for reading parts or all of the manuscript and calling attention to questionable points. As usual, President Gilbert C. Fite of Eastern Illinois University was most generous with his time, offering stimulation and suggestions for improving the study. His friendship and assistance have been invaluable, not only in this instance but over the years. I, of course, assume responsibility for weaknesses that remain, despite the efforts of these scholars. Finally, I must express appreciation to Gail Deibert for typing revisions of the manuscript and to my wife, Marilyn, for her excellent typing of the final copy.

1 Police Power
and the Taxing Power

Broadly defined, the police power includes governmental activity regulating and controlling issues concerning health, safety, morals, and the all-encompassing area of general welfare. The American constitutional system of federalism divides authority so that the national government has certain enumerated powers delegated to it by the people through the state governments. These are functions that, generally speaking, cannot be exercised effectively by the states acting individually and are powers other than those dealing with the police power per se. The framers of the Constitution sought to devise a system whereby an effective national government could be established while retaining most of the governing functions at the state level. Police powers were not given to the central government.

All powers, except those specifically delegated to the central government, were reserved to the states. To prevent any conflict or misunderstanding, the Tenth Amendment was added in 1791 which provided that "all powers not delegated to the United States, nor prohibited by it to the States, are reserved to the States respectively, or to the people." It was an accepted constitutional principle, at least until after the Civil War, that governmental regulations concerning health, safety, morals, and welfare were the exclusive province of the states. During the latter part of the nineteenth century and continuing to the present, however, there arose a host of new issues that stemmed from the economic, technological, and social advances of an emerging industrialized society. These problems required national regulation.

One of the characteristics of an emerging industrial society, "regardless of political form," is a substantial increase in the "range and scale of activities" of its government.[1] This was certainly true of the American experience. The Industrial Revolution brought new processes in foods and drugs which called for regulation to protect public health. Modern vehicular developments required control for proper use and public safety. The increased consumption of alcohol and narcotics, perhaps stemming in part from man's inability to cope with the modern world, created what many considered to be moral problems. The rise of organized crime, with a subsequent increase in gambling and the use by criminals of a variety of firearms, led to demands to restrict such activities on the basis of morals and public safety. In brief, a changing, complex, interdependent society created countless questions concerning its citizens' general welfare.

State governments generally proved to be inadequate to deal with these multitudinous problems, particularly as the issues became national in scope. When it became evident these questions required effective action, an increasing demand arose, particularly during the Populist and Progressive movements, that the national government exercise its powers to attack the problems. One historian has noted that during this period a significant change took place in the American political system in regard to regulatory legislation: a gradual "upward shift in decision-making" occurred, progressing from the local to the state to the national level and brought about largely through the efforts of nationally organized businesses that desired uniform control consistent with their national functions. As American business became increasingly national in operations and markets, it was obviously beneficial to industrial leaders to have a single uniform policy of regulation rather than a multitude of state and local restrictions.[2]

Businessmen and reformers, then, turned more and more to Washington for action. The national government, however, despite the general welfare clauses in the Constitution, would be limited in such activities unless Congress acted under a very loose construction of national powers—or a much

---

[1] Clark Kerr et al., *Industrialism and Industrial Man* (Cambridge, Mass., 1960), pp. 40–41.

[2] Samuel P. Hays, "Political Parties and the Community-Society Continuum," in *The American Party System*, ed. William Nesbet Chambers and Walter Dean Burnham (New York, 1967), p. 17. See also Samuel P. Hays, "The Social Analysis of American Political History, 1880–1920," *Political Science Quarterly* 80 (1965):389; Gabriel Kolko, *The Triumph of Conservatism* (Chicago, 1967) ; Robert H. Wiebe, *Businessmen and Reform* (Cambridge, Mass., 1962) ; Robert H. Wiebe, *The Search for Order* (New York, 1967). Glendon Schubert, *Judicial Policy-Making* (Glenview, Ill., 1965), p. 141, emphasizes that during this period conservative interests "shifted their major attention—successfully—to the control of the judiciary in general and of the United States Supreme Court in particular" to protect their vested interests.

broader interpretation than that to which it had previously adhered. The Supreme Court, moreover, would have to accept an expanded interpretation of congressional powers. Congress and the Supreme Court subsequently so liberalized construction of these clauses in the Constitution that in the process a major revolution in the traditional American constitutional system took place. The tremendous increase in the activities of the national government in the twentieth century resulted in a relative decline of functions of the states. Although state governments increased their activities and services, especially during and since the New Deal era, that expansion has not kept pace with the expansion of national government functions.[3] This greatly expanded nationalism was rooted, in large part, in a proliferating national police power.

Much of this change came through an expanded use of congressional power to regulate interstate commerce. Based on the broad interpretation of national control over interstate commerce enunciated by Chief Justice John Marshall in *Gibbons* v. *Ogden*,[4] Congress asserted control over numerous police power activities during the Progressive movement.[5] Beginning with the New Deal era, Congress used the commerce power even more extensively for regulation.

In a more remarkable development, Congress created a national police power through an expanded use of the taxing power. Article I, Section 8, of the Constitution delegates to Congress the "Power to lay and collect Taxes,

[3] If emphasis is placed on spending as an indicator of government activity, from a long-range viewpoint state government expenditures did not increase as rapidly in the 1930s as they did in the decade prior to the Great Depression or in the decade that followed it. An excellent brief account of state government activity in the 1930s can be found in James T. Patterson, "The New Deal and the States," *American Historical Review* 73 (October 1967) : 70–84.

[4] 9 Wheaton 1 (1824).

[5] See Felix Frankfurter, *The Commerce Clause under Marshall, Taney and Waite* (Chapel Hill, N.C., 1937) ; Charles Warren, *The Supreme Court in United States History* (Boston, 1926), vol. 2, chapt. 38; Robert E. Cushman, "The National Police Power under the Commerce Clause," *Minnesota Law Review* 3 (April 1919) :289; 3 (May 1919) :381; 3 (June 1919) :452. Congress used the power to control interstate commerce to assist states in suppressing lotteries which the Supreme Court upheld in 1903 (*Champion* v. *Ames*, 188 U.S. 321) ; the Pure Food and Drug Act of 1906 that regulated mislabeled and impure foods and drugs was held to be constitutional in 1911 (*Hipolite Egg Company* v. *United States*, 220 U.S. 45) ; the Mann Act of 1910, an attempt to suppress the white-slave traffic, was validated by the Supreme Court in 1913 (*Hoke* v. *United States*, 277 U.S. 308) ; the Webb-Kenyon Act forbade the shipment of liquor into dry states, which the Supreme Court sustained in 1917 (*Clark Distilling Company* v. *Western Maryland Railway Company*, 242 U.S. 311).

Duties, Imposts and Excises, and to pay the Debts and provide for the common Defence and general Welfare of the United States." This broad power is limited only by the requirement of uniformity, the stipulation that direct taxes be apportioned according to population, and the prohibition against levying duties on goods exported from any state.[6] The government's lack of power to tax had been a major weakness of the Articles of Confederation and, according to a nineteenth-century Supreme Court decision, had brought that government "to the verge of impotency." The necessity of giving the new national government ample power to raise revenue, and thus eliminate the reliance upon uncertain requisitions by states, this decision continued, "was a leading objective in the adoption of the Constitution," which helps account for the sweeping language in this clause.[7]

Thomas M. Cooley, who was probably the most noted authority on constitutional law in the latter part of the nineteenth century, wrote in regard to taxation, "no attribute of sovereignty is more pervading, and at no point does the power of government affect more constantly and intimately the relations of life than through the exactions made under it." In his classic work on taxation the conservative Cooley laid down the dictum, later sanctioned by the Supreme Court, that "the motives which have influenced the selection of objects for taxation, or determined the rate, [cannot] be inquired into for the purpose of invalidating it; proper motives in the legislature are always conclusively presumed." He further added that "the motives that influence the members of a legislative body raise questions between themselves and their constituents alone."[8] In exercising their power to tax, therefore, legislators are answerable only to a few constitutional limitations and to voters.

Significantly, as Cooley noted, the rate of taxation is not limited in any way. At least three schools of interpretation have emerged in relation to a loose or strict construction of the revenue powers of Congress.[9] Since 1787

[6] Article I, Sections 2, 8, and 9.

[7] *Veazie Bank* v. *Fenno*, 8 Wallace 533 (1869). Many expressions of this opinion can be found. See, e.g., Max Farrand, *The Framing of the Constitution of the United States* (New Haven, Conn., 1913), pp. 1–12; Merrill Jensen, *The New Nation* (New York, 1965), pp. 407–21; James Madison, *Notes of Debates in the Federal Convention of 1787* (Athens, Ohio, 1966), p. 7.

[8] Thomas M. Cooley, *Constitutional Limitations*, 6th ed. (Boston, 1890), p. 587; *A Treatise on the Law of Taxation*, 3d ed. (Chicago, 1903), 1:191.

[9] Robert E. Cushman, "The National Police Power under the Taxing Power of the Constitution," *Minnesota Law Review* 4 (March 1920) :250. The following three views of the extent of the taxing power are taken from this excellent article, pp. 247–81.

conservatives have maintained that the taxing power can be used only to raise revenue. This argument was used by John C. Calhoun and later by the Democratic party to oppose a high protective tariff. According to this viewpoint, Congress may impose taxes for purposes other than raising revenue, but only if they are directly connected with a delegated power, such as the commerce power. The tax must be supplemental to the principal power being exercised. A revenue law must only raise revenue. It cannot encroach in any way upon the reserved powers of the states.

Those who hold the middle-ground view argue that taxes can be used for purposes other than revenue but it is not an all-purpose grant of power. It is quite justifiable, according to this interpretation, to use the taxing power to help regulate commerce or to supplement the exercise of any other granted power. Taxes that help carry out regulations are approved. Yet this group believes that the taxing power is limited—although not as much as the strict constructionists—and insists that such power cannot be used to regulate objects outside the realm of delegated powers. To do so would be to usurp state authority and violate the Tenth Amendment; otherwise the reserved powers of the states would be meaningless and the intent of the Constitution to limit national powers would be ignored.

Finally, liberals or loose constructionists believe that because the wording in this grant of power is so sweeping, and specific limitations on the rate of taxation are not imposed, Congress may use the taxing power as an instrument to further the general welfare. Congress thus may use taxes not only to raise revenue, not only to regulate or to control, but to destroy harmful items that are beyond the scope of delegated authority in the exercise of a police power. In the absence of specific limitations, there is no reason to assume Congress is restricted in any way except by the constitutional prohibitions in regard to uniformity, apportionment, and the ban on export duties. Unless confined by such express limitations, the powers of Congress are complete and the purpose for which they are used is "policy" for which Congress is answerable only to the voters. Thus the taxing power can be used in any way that will promote the common defense or general welfare. Obviously, even advocates of this view would insist that the power to tax not be used to destroy private rights except when shown to be desirable for the general welfare. Taxes may be levied only for public purposes, such as is the case with all national powers, and cannot be exercised to achieve destruction of fundamental rights.

Throughout the history of the United States, congressional attitude has varied among these three viewpoints in terms of purpose and rate of taxation, depending upon the constitutional views of its members and the will of the people in regard to public policy. From the time that Alexander Hamilton's *Report on Manufactures* suggested protective tariffs in 1791 to the present, the taxing power has been used to achieve policies beyond the purpose of raising revenue. High rates have been levied on commodities such as liquor and tobacco with the intention of restricting their use because of the belief that they are "nonessential," or "harmful," or "sinful." The tax on cosmetics is another obvious example. Frequently these taxes accomplish the purposes both of raising revenue and of regulation. The tariff battles of the nineteenth century are good illustrations of the fluctuations of Congress over this policy, which served as the chief source of national revenue and also regulated or protected domestic products from foreign competition.

The government's power to tax has been given wide latitude in several Supreme Court decisions. The Revenue Act of 1867 contained a clause requiring the purchase of a national license before engaging in the business of selling liquor or handling lottery tickets. Several people were convicted for not purchasing such a permit and yet conducting these activities in violation of their state laws which forbade such businesses. In the famous *License Tax* Cases, the Supreme Court announced that the licenses themselves did not permit the purchaser to violate state laws, because Congress had specified that they were "special taxes" and not licenses. The issuance of such licenses could not be interpreted as granting a franchise as argued. The opinion further declared that this national tax was legitimate in states where these activities were condoned because "the power to tax is a very extensive power. . . . [I]t reaches every subject and may be exercised at discretion." [10]

An act of 1882 required a head tax of fifty cents for every person immigrating into the United States, to be paid by the ship captain. The law was challenged as being unconstitutional because it was not levied for the purposes of defense, the payment of debts, or the general welfare. The Supreme Court answered these objections by noting that it was not the taxing power that was being exercised. Rather, Congress was regulating foreign commerce that involved immigration and the head tax revenue was appropriated in advance to pay the costs of administering the law.[11] This decision helped establish the principle that the Supreme Court would uphold the

[10] 5 Wallace 462 (1867).
[11] *Head Tax Cases*, 112 U.S. 580 (1884).

levying of taxes if placed upon articles for the purpose of carrying out other congressional powers such as, in this instance, the regulation of interstate and foreign commerce.

On the other hand, the Supreme Court checked the power of Congress at times when little or no relationship could be shown between the taxing power and other constitutional functions as it did in the so-called *Coal Oil* Case. A section of the Revenue Act of 1867 placed a tax on naptha or other illuminating oils that were manufactured or sold if they were flammable at temperatures under 110° F.; it also contained an enforcement provision of fine and imprisonment if violated. The tax was repealed in July 1868, but the enforcement clause was retained in an effort to eliminate dangerous illuminants.[12] When this section was challenged, the Supreme Court agreed that "standing by itself, it is plainly a regulation of police" and therefore "it can have no constitutional operation."[13] Congress could not regulate such matters within the realm of the police power without exercising another power, such as taxing or regulating commerce. This doctrine was reiterated in the twentieth century when Congress, following repeal of Prohibition, proceeded to tax liquor dealers $1,000 annually in those states where liquor was forbidden. The Supreme Court announced that this violated the Tenth Amendment because the law was a penalty, not a tax, and such action was beyond national powers.[14]

The Supreme Court, however, generally endorsed congressional revenue measures. The stamp tax placed on the sale of stocks was questioned in 1901 in *Treat* v. *White*. The Supreme Court, referring to the stamp duty, declared that "the power of Congress in this direction is unlimited."[15] When opponents challenged the income tax clause of the Underwood tariff of 1913, the Supreme Court gave the revenue power an even broader interpretation. The power to tax, the Court said in this case, "is exhaustive and embraces every conceivable power of taxation."[16]

Chief Justice John Marshall had declared in *McCulloch* v. *Maryland* "that the power to tax involves the power to destroy."[17] Congress demonstrated the validity of this observation following the Civil War when it taxed out of existence all state bank notes. The effort to finance the Civil

---

[12] U.S., *Statutes at Large*, vols. 14, and 15.
[13] *United States* v. *Dewitt*, 9 Wallace 41 (1870).
[14] *United States* v. *Constantine*, 296 U.S. 287 (1935).
[15] 181 U.S. 264 (1901).
[16] *Brushaber* v. *Union Pacific Railway Company*, 240 U.S. 1 (1916).
[17] 4 Wheaton 316 (1819).

War and to establish a sound currency climaxed in an act of July 1866 which placed a tax of 10 percent on all notes of "persons, state banks, or state banking associations." A state bank challenged the law as being a direct tax that did not meet the requirement of apportionment according to population and that it violated the tax-exemption status of government by taxing a franchise granted by a state. The Supreme Court held the tax to be a constitutional exercise of power in *Veazie Bank* v. *Fenno* because this proscriptive tax was auxiliary to establishing a uniform national currency, a valid function of Congress.[18]

When Congress in 1909 levied a tax on corporations for the privilege of doing business, opponents argued that the tax could be exercised in such a way as to destroy state-chartered corporations. The Supreme Court, however, rejected the contention that the judicial branch provided a means of redress for excessive burdens of taxation. Rather, the High Tribunal said, "the remedy for such wrongs . . . is in the ability of the people to choose their own representatives."[19] Curiously, the Supreme Court handed down one of the most sweeping decisions on the taxing power in one of its most conservative phases, during the early New Deal era. The oleomargarine industry charged that a prohibitively high state tax on butter substitutes violated both the due process of law clause and the equal protection clause of the Fourteenth Amendment by destroying a legitimate business. But, in validating the tax, the Supreme Court pointed out that "from the beginning of our government, the courts have sustained taxes although imposed with the collateral intent of effecting ulterior ends which, considered apart, were beyond the constitutional power of the lawmakers to realize by legislation directly addressed to their accomplishment."[20]

By the latter part of the nineteenth century the power to tax had been established and used in a broad manner to raise revenue, to assist in carrying out other powers, and to regulate activities or commodities. Groups or interests who at this time wanted the national government to assist states in exercising control over, and help eliminate the problems arising out of, the emerging industrial society in the United States, could advocate using the taxing power when other exercises of control failed or were unfeasible. The earliest use of the taxing power in this manner had its origins in the efforts to curb artificial butter. When this successful tax measure was valida-

---

[18] 8 Wallace 533 (1869).

[19] *Flint* v. *Stone Tracy Company*, 220 U.S. 107 (1911).

[20] *A. Magnano Company* v. *Hamilton*, 292 U.S. 40 (1934).

ted by the judicial branch, Congress then attempted to tax out of existence numerous items that endangered the health, safety, morals, and welfare of the American public by increasing the rate of taxes imposed on these objects to prohibitive levels or by taxing them at a minimal rate in order to require registration and supervision. By the time of the Great Depression, the United States had not yet "succeeded in domesticating an unruly industrialism" and thus "as emergency succeeds emergency in the continuous process called history, an enlarged police power is likely to make provision for a revised public welfare."[21] This enlargement came, in part, through the taxing power.

The history of an expanding tax power illustrates change and reform and shows the flexibility of the American federal system and the way in which the powers of the national government can be increased through a loose interpretation of the "necessary and proper" and welfare clauses. As John Marshall also observed in *McCulloch* v. *Maryland* in the classic enunciation of broad construction: "let the end be legitimate, let it be within the scope of the Constitution, and all means which are appropriate, which are plainly adapted to the end, which are not prohibited, but consist within the letter and spirit of the Constitution, are constitutional."

In the development toward a broad construction of the taxing power to destroy "evil" items, two groups frequently proved to be stumbling blocks by adhering to a strict construction of the Constitution. One of these, Southern congressmen, continued the tradition of Jeffersonian Republicans and the states'-rights views of John C. Calhoun in efforts to deter the development of a national police power. The Supreme Court also occasionally proved negative to this development. In regard to the exercise of a national police power the Court at times decided that a particular type of destructive tax was not proper; in many other instances the Court held it to be valid and necessary. In all cases the decision depended upon the thinking of the justices in terms of the individual members' social values and constitutional principles.[22] If the justices agreed the problem was "evil" and should be

[21] Walton H. Hamilton and Carlton C. Rodee, "Police Power," in *Encyclopedia of the Social Sciences*, ed. Edwin R. A. Seligman and Alvin Johnson (New York, 1934), 12:192.

[22] Justice Felix Frankfurter noted that when a person is appointed to the Supreme Court he takes with him far more than his social and economic views. If he is "fit to be a Justice," Frankfurter argued, his outlook on the role of a judge "cuts across all his personal preferences for this or that social arrangement." To illustrate his point, he used the example of Justice Joseph Bradley, a corporation lawyer whose Court deci-

exterminated, the tax was upheld. If they believed the item was not "evil," the tax was struck down as an unconstitutional abuse of power. When regulatory taxes were invalidated by the Supreme Court, it was done through emphasis by the justices on "Dual Federalism." According to Edward S. Corwin this doctrine was grounded in the principle that the national government is one of enumerated powers only, and within thier respective spheres the national and state governments are "sovereign" and thus "equal."[23] The national government, therefore, cannot encroach upon the sovereign jurisdiction of states.

The story of the creation of a national police power through use of regulatory taxes provides a fascinating chapter in United States constitutional history. It demonstrates the activity of various interests which, either through altruistic or materialistic motives, contributed much to this aspect of constitutional development. It also substantiates the argument of political scientists who state that congressional lawmaking many times involves not pressure groups fighting it out with each other, but rather one pressure group achieving its wishes without organized opposition. Also, "a very large proportion of group activity is merely defensive or preventative."[24]

More important, it illustrates the fundamental importance of the American political system to the shaping of the legal system. Constitutional history is composed of far more than merely the activities of the judicial branch. The development of regulatory taxation illuminates the pitfalls of using this type of public regulation over an extended period of time and to attack disparate problems.[25] The use of taxation as an instrument of social control resulted in a legislative-judicial struggle over public policy. The policy in each case originated from public demand, was developed by Congress on the framework of previous regulations, and was subjected to review by a Supreme Court composed of an ever-changing membership and legal philosophy. The great power of the Supreme Court over political life

---

sions "were strikingly free of bias in favor of corporate power." Cited in Alan F. Westin, ed., *The Supreme Court: Views from Inside* (New York, 1961), p. 42. Justice Edward White is also a good example of this ability to be objective in regard to the oleomargarine tax.

[23] Edward S. Corwin, "The Passing of Dual Federalism," *Virginia Law Review* 36 (February 1950) : 1–24.

[24] David B. Truman, *The Governmental Process* (New York, 1955), p. 353.

[25] A United States circuit court judge described these as "habit-forming" statutes that were "missionaries of centralization and tend increasingly to destroy our inherited theories of local rule." Charles Merrill Hughes, "Covert Legislation and the Constitution," *Harvard Law Review* 30 (June 1917) : 801–11.

in the United States "has long troubled those interested in social progress."[26] The Court certainly played a major role, both positive and negative, in shaping the public policy of regulatory taxation.[27]

This legal history, however, is molded not only by political and judicial energies but also by social and economic forces. The history of the United States legal system, therefore, encompasses all aspects of American growth. The unique phase of constitutional regulation through taxation is an evolution which began with a seemingly innocuous tax on oleomargarine.

[26] Sidney Ratner, *American Taxation* (New York, 1942), p. 193.

[27] Schubert, *Judicial Policy-Making*, p. 157, notes that the Supreme Court is "activist when its decisions conflict with those of other political policy-makers, and the Court exercises restraint when it accepts the policies of other decision-makers."

2 *The Foundation Tax*

The Industrial Revolution and modern chemistry wrought fundamental changes in the production of food. Increasing technological expertise in the latter part of the nineteenth century made possible the manufacture of table foods from ingredients hitherto unused for such purposes, such as cotton-seed oil or animal fats, that closely resembled the genuine farm commodity. The manufacture of oleomargarine was an outstanding example of this trend.

As these products increased, a corresponding demand arose for the en-actment of legislation to curtail or to prevent adulteration of foods. When state governments found themselves powerless to halt many of the abuses— for example, the sale of oleomargarine as genuine butter—pressure groups turned to Congress for assistance, and from 1879 to the passage of the Pure Food Law in 1906 "exactly 190 measures to protect in some way the con-sumer of food and drugs appeared in Congress."[1] Several of these pertained to oleomargarine and received wide publicity through the organized oppo-sition of dairy farmers.

Oleomargarine was first developed when Napoleon III staged a contest for a palatable table food to ease contemporary food shortages caused by war. Hippolyte Megè-Mouriès won the prize from the French government in 1868 and patented his discovery of oleomargarine in the United States in 1873. Megè-Mouriès found that by extracting the oils from either hog or cow fat, and churning this oleo with skimmed milk, he could produce a white substance closely resembling butter in composition, food value, and appearance; hence the name oleomargarine. When a small amount of coloring was added to the compound to achieve the proper shade of yellow, the inexperienced eye was unable to detect the manufactured product from natural butter, which made oleomargarine a cheap substitute for the table spread churned from whole milk.[2] Oleomargarine increasingly appeared on the tables of laborers while the wealthy continued to purchase the more expensive butter. But the Frenchman's discovery began to be used in the United States in a period when American farm products were in heavy surplus, and dairy farmers strongly objected to any butter substitute which might depress prices even further.

Concurrently, technology was revolutionizing the dairy industry. During the 1880s the cream separator, using centrifugal force, came into general use and in 1890 the Babcock test was perfected to measure the butterfat content of milk. These innovations led to a flourishing new industry, commercial creameries, which increased production of dairy products and made this phase of agriculture more competitive.[3] These developments further split farmers who were already divided politically. Agriculturalists were still numerically superior to other groups but were not politically cohesive, in part because they lacked unity over means to achieve their objectives. As one agricultural historian has analyzed the situation, wheat farmers want high wheat prices while dairy farmers want cheap wheat for feed. Dairy farmers, of course, want good butter prices, but with the development of oleomargarine, their objectives would compete with cattle raisers and cottonseed producers who wanted the increased markets for their products.[4]

Oleomargarine producers soon began to use other, even cheaper, ingredients in its manufacture, and subsequent abuses developed in marketing the poorer quality, unwholesome, and even dangerous commodities. Some of these were sold as butter substitutes and labeled "Butterine" or "Suine"; others were fraudulently offered as pure butter. This occasional fraud, plus the increasing competition experienced by butter-makers, led to demands by the dairy interests to outlaw oleomargarine or at least to penalize it to the degree that butter could compete. One authority has

[1] Thomas A. Bailey, "Congressional Opposition to Pure Food Legislation, 1879–1906," *American Journal of Sociology* 36 (July 1930–May 1931) : 52.

[2] For the early development of oleomargarine production, see U.S., Congress, Senate, *Hearings on House Bill 9206*, Senate Reports (Serial 4235), 57 Cong., 1 Sess., 1901–1902, pp. 113–15; Edward Wiest, "The Butter Industry in the United States" (Ph.D. diss., Columbia University, 1916), pp. 214–26; Alton E. Bailey, *Industrial Oil and Fat Products*, 2d ed. (New York, 1951), pp. 272–74.

[3] John A. Garraty, *The New Commonwealth* (New York, 1968), p. 37.

[4] Gilbert C. Fite, "The Changing Political Role of the Farmer," *Current History* 31 (August 1956) :84–86. See also H. Clarence Nixon, "The Cleavage within the Farmers' Alliance Movement," *Mississippi Valley Historical Review* 15 (June 1928) : 22–23, which traces the division of the northern and southern alliances over the issue of regulating oleomargarine and compound lard.

noted that oleomargarine "created one of the most difficult social problems that society has ever been called upon to regulate."[5] In a short time European countries and the United States were forced to enact legislation to control the industry. Pressure for legislation concerning oleomargarine in America came particularly from the National Association for Prevention of Adulteration of Butter, organized in 1882 and replaced by the National Dairy Union in 1894.[6]

With dairy states pointing the way, the first such regulatory laws in the United States were passed in New York and Pennsylvania in 1877. Then in 1884 New York appointed a dairy commissioner to investigate and gather information concerning oleomargarine. This was an important development because other states soon adopted the idea of dairy and food investigating agencies.[7] Increased knowledge could improve regulations.

During the 1880s Harvey H. Wiley, chief of the Bureau of Chemistry in the Department of Agriculture, began his famous investigations which culminated in the Pure Food Law of 1906. In 1887 he published a study entitled "Foods and Food Adulteration." This report concluded that oleomargarine was being sold as butter, but stressed the fact that "if made carefully from the fat of a healthy animal," it was a wholesome nutritious food.[8] High quality oleomargarine was made only from animal oils. Vegetable oils, in addition to being too soft until hydrogenation (a process by which liquid oils are changed to solid fats) was developed early in the twentieth century, did not work well because they did not respond to treatments properly to remove their characteristic odors and flavors. But animal oils assumed the aromatic principles of the milk they were churned in and were used in more expensive oleomargarine.[9] Vegetable oils did not achieve a place of prominence in the manufacture of margarine until World War I during a shortage of animal fats.

[5] Wiest, "The Butter Industry," p. 241. Earl W. Hayter, *The Troubled Farmer* (DeKalb, Ill., 1968), p. 64, states that the controversy over the composition of oleomargarine "in length and bitterness . . . has few parallels in our history of food production." He has an excellent chapter on the "bogus butter" issue of the late nineteenth century.

[6] Martha Crampton Howard, "The Oleomargarine Industry in the United States: Its Development under Legislative Control" (Ph.D. diss., Columbia University, 1951), p. 30.

[7] Wiest, "The Butter Industry," p. 241.

[8] Oscar E. Anderson, Jr., *The Health of a Nation* (Chicago, Ill., 1958), pp. 71–72.

[9] U.S., Congress, Senate, *Hearings on House Bill 9206*, Senate Reports (Serial 4235), 57 Cong., 1 Sess., 1901, p. 59.

The issue first arose, however, not over the question of health, but over the competition which oleomargarine presented to pure butter. It was commonly believed that if the housewife had a choice between butter and oleomargarine, at nearly equal prices, she would choose butter. So during the 1880s many dairy states enacted laws controlling the manufacture and sale of oleomargarine. By 1890 only Arizona, Arkansas, Kentucky, North Carolina, Tennessee, Utah, Washington, and Wyoming had not passed such legislation. At this time Maryland, Maine, Minnesota, Michigan, New York, Pennsylvania, and Wisconsin prohibited its manufacture and sale; New Hampshire required it to be colored pink. The remaining states merely compelled it to be labeled by its true name.[10] Some of these labeling laws, however, particularly in the dairy states, were "ingeniously contrived to create prejudice in the minds of purchasers." One, for instance, required the term "adulterated butter" to be used not only on the package but also on each container of oleomargarine consumed in hotels, restaurants, and other public eating establishments. Another required not only a printed label but also a verbal notice to purchasers of what they were buying.[11]

The artificial coloring of oleomargarine was the chief practice about which the dairy interests complained. It was useless for the substitute-butter people to point out that farm women, when churning butter, had for years added carrots to their product to give it additional color and that butter manufacturers had taken a cue from oleomargarine-makers to color artificially their "pure" commodity to give it additional eye appeal. The natural color of butter varies with the seasons; it is at its most golden hue in the spring months when the cow is grazing on new grass and dandelions. Thus the epitome of color was reached in June—color which the carotene (precursor of Vitamin A) would achieve. Many authorities pointed out, quite correctly, that when properly made, oleomargarine was cleaner, purer, and of more uniform quality than the average butter of that day when many creameries were atrociously filthy. But to the dairyman, the adding of annatto or other coloring to butter was a legitimate way to please the eye of the buyer; artificial coloring of "bogus buttter" was a fraud. Overlooking their own practices, they asked: If it is not a deception then

10 U.S., Congress, House, *Report of Commissioner of Internal Revenue for Fiscal Year Ending June 20, 1890*, House Executive Document 4 (Serial 2851), 51 Cong., 2 Sess., 1890, pp. 184–88. See also report on these state laws from Department of Agriculture printed in the *New York Times*, May 31, 1886.

11 *Nation* 71 (December 27, 1900) :502–3.

why color it to imitate butter? This reasoning accounted for the law of New Hampshire which required coloring oleomargarine pink.

In turn, butter-makers came under sharp criticism. "It is a notorious fact," stated one contemporary journal, "that the farming community, alive to the cheapness of the products simulating the dairy, purchase the inferior grades in large quantities *and mix with butter*, which they return to the market as the latter product solely." This same account noted that two-thirds of the butter sold "in the large cities of the West is of this character."[12] Also, it was pointed out, in the early 1890s the United States and Canada were "invaded with agents" selling a chemical that claimed to increase the yield of butter churned from milk. Whole milk contains casein (a fat from which cheese is made) and butterfat. Quality cheese is relatively free of butterfat and good butter should contain no casein or other nitrogenous elements. The agents were selling this chemical, labeled Black Pepsin, for two dollars per ounce to farmers. It was a preparation of salt, annatto, and "a small quantity of rennet," costing about three cents and which, when added to milk, retained a certain amount of casein resulting in a greater quantity of butter. But the dairy interests, with a great deal of publicity, convinced much of the public that the greatest fraud was on the part of "bogus butter" and staged a nationwide campaign to restrict its production.

In early 1886 the National Butter, Cheese, and Egg Association issued a circular to county, state, and national legislators and to the people generally, pointing out the danger "fraudulent imitations of butter" presented to dairy products. The pamphlet noted that oleomargarine establishments in the United States were valued at $2 million, while dairy investments totaled over $3 billion. It appealed for legislation to suppress "imitations of dairy products" not sold under their true names.[13] That same month the *New York Times* headlined a convention of dairy farmers in New York City, representing twenty-six states, with the caption "Farmers Discussing the Best Way to Fight Bogus Butter." This convention resolved to establish a committee "to formulate and urge upon Congress legislation for the suppression or regulation of oleomargarine." The resolutions called for a minimum tax of ten cents per pound on the manufacture and sale of the product to achieve this purpose.[14] In the meantime congressmen were for-

[12] See *Scientific American* 69 (July 15, 1893):34. See especially Hayter, *The Troubled Farmer*, pp. 68–71, for descriptions of country-made butter during this period.
[13] *New York Times*, February 12, 1886.

mulating plans to suppress the industry. Pro-dairy congressmen decided the best approach would be the one proposed by the dairy convention: to tax oleomargarine; outright prohibition might create too many constitutional obstacles.

Several bills were introduced during the first session of the Forty-ninth Congress, especially in December 1885 and January 1886, either to prevent the sale of imitation butter or to tax it heavily. Those bills involving a tax were referred to the Committee on Ways and Means chaired by Democrat William H. Hatch of Missouri. This congressman had long championed agricultural causes, authoring, among other significant measures, the Hatch Act of 1887, which established state agricultural experiment stations, and the law that raised the Department of Agriculture to cabinet status in 1889. On March 29, 1886, Hatch recommended, and the House approved, that the tax bills be referred to the Committee on Agriculture. This was a highly unusual procedure about which opponents complained later because Ways and Means was to consider all revenue measures.[15] On April 28 the Committee on Agriculture recommended H.R. 8328, written by the National Dairymen's Association, as a substitute for all the tax proposals.[16] The bill sought to levy a rather high tax on oleomargarine. One month later debate began in the House of Representatives on the measure. Before this, however, supporters and opponents of the bill subjected Congress to a barrage of petitions. Most of the supplications against the proposal came from livestock exchanges, because of the vested interests in oleo oil and lard, and most of the favorable opinions came from dairy states.[17]

William L. Scott, Democrat of Pennsylvania, introduced H.R. 8328 on the floor of the House, stating the bill was vital to "one of the chief industries of the country." In less than ten years, he declared, oleomargarine had reached the point where it was displacing one-fifth of "the purest product of the dairy," and yet its ingredients were "acknowledged to be not only offensive in their original character to human taste but positively injurious to the public health." The oleomargarine industry had grown so vast, Scott explained, that state legislatures were powerless before it; so an appeal had

---

[14] Ibid., February 19, 1886; *Congressional Record*, 49 Cong., 1 Sess., 1886, 17:4865.

[15] *Congressional Record*, 49 Cong., 1 Sess., 1886, 17:2891.

[16] Ibid., p. 3931. The statement of authorship was made by Warner Miller, who favored the tax, in the Senate, ibid., p. 7073.

[17] These petitions are listed in ibid., 9:71.

been made to Congress for laws in order that butter-makers could be "placed upon at least an equal footing with their dangerous competitors." Because it cost from seven to nine cents to manufacture a pound of "bogus butter," he noted, the proposed tax of ten cents would allow the "genuine" to compete with the "imitation." When opponents claimed that the tax would be unconstitutional, Scott answered that sufficient power existed to act under the general welfare clause. Whiskey was taxed at a rate of ninety cents per gallon "with the avowed object of restricting its sale," he observed, so certainly it was in the public interest to stop this "piracy." [18]

Albert J. Hopkins, Republican of Illinois, also leading the fight for the tax, discovered that some congressmen believed ten cents was too high. "If any were actuated by honest motives" and wanted to lower the rate to five cents or two cents, Hopkins said, he would be agreeable; he just wanted to abolish "the deception and fraud." Annual production of butter was 1.6 billion pounds at that time while oleomargarine had reached the yearly rate of 200 million pounds. Inasmuch as other industries were protected by a high tariff, he insisted, the dairy industry also deserved protection. The question of constitutionality was not involved, Hopkins declared, but only the issue of policy, and it was always good policy "to do right." Because "all kinds of filthy fats . . . of animals dying from all kinds of diseases" are used in the manufacture of oleomargarine and its consumption thus led to "insanity, Bright's Disease and many of the ailments that undermine the strongest and most robust," this legislation, he said, was vital. Finally, Hopkins answered the argument that "bogus butter" was a cheap food for the poor with an eloquent appeal to laborers: "Has it come to this in America, that the laboring man must live on adulterated foods? Must his wife and family use for the pure butter of our dairies an artificial butter, the compound of diseased hogs and dead dogs? Let the rich and prosperous man, these new converts to the poor man's rights, pay the laboring man better wages, so he can live upon wholesome food." [19]

Southern states'-rights advocates rushed to the rescue of laborers in the urban areas. John Reagan, Democrat of Texas and famous for his efforts in establishing the Interstate Commerce Commission, argued that the objective of the measure must be to raise revenue for the law to be valid. Because the purpose of this tax was to destroy a product, he insisted, it would be invalid because the Constitution does not authorize Congress "to destroy

---

[18] Ibid., pp. 4865–67.
[19] Ibid., pp. 4868–69.

any product or to outlaw any article." States may do so if desirable, Reagan declared, but Congress cannot "because the power was not delegated to it by the people." Democrat Nathaniel Hammond of Georgia agreed with Reagan that this proposal would be an invasion of state police power and would result only in making butter "dearer" and the cheap substitute "meaner." Hatch finally ended Reagan's interruptions with the comment that the Texan's brain was in "such a condition that it could not entertain any other idea than interstate commerce." Thus, Hatch declared, if an angel brought Reagan "straight from the throne the plan of salvation . . . he would unhesitatingly reject it as unconstitutional unless he was allowed to amend it with his interstate commerce bill."[20]

Reagan's argument on the constitutionality of the measure was cleverly answered by William Hepburn, Republican of Iowa. According to the Texan, Hepburn said, if the bill prohibited the manufacture of oleomargarine in 1887, it would become unconstitutional. But in 1888, the price of butter would subsequently rise to twenty-five or thirty cents because of the demand that would result. The manufacturers of the "bogus article" could then compete and would resume production. According to this argument, he concluded, the bill would be a constitutional tax in 1886, unconstitutional in 1887, and again constitutional in 1888, not because of its provisions "but because of the price of butter! [*laughter*]." Hepburn further noted that every congressman had "his desk fairly well weighted down" with petitions and resolutions from livestock associations, boards of trade, and other groups, but he was relieved that this opposition to the measure emanated "from a single house in Chicago"—the Armour Company—and thus did not have widespread support.[21]

Republican Stephen Millard of New York warned opponents of the measure not to anticipate a Supreme Court decision on the constitutionality of such a tax. Rather, he said, the bill should be enacted and then "if Mr. [Philip] Armour and his friends believe the measure to be unconstitutional they have their remedy." He noted that in 1880 the United States exported 39,236,658 pounds of butter; in 1885 this amount had dropped to 21,683,148, or a decline of nearly 50 percent in five years. On the other hand, 19,844,256 pounds of oleomargarine were exported in 1880 compared to 37,000,000 in 1885, much of which was sold as genuine butter. "It is no wonder," Millard concluded from these statistics, "that Hungary

[20] Ibid., p. 4870; for Hatch's remark, see p. 5204.
[21] Ibid., pp. 4902–3.

and Germany have closed their ports against the American farmer." [22]

Iowa Republican David B. Henderson presented a lurid analogy of the manufacture of oleomargarine. While butter was mentioned in the Bible, he said, the first reference he had found to imitation butter was in Shakespeare. He then quoted several stanzas from the Fourth Act of *Macbeth* in which the witches threw poisoned entrails, bat wool, dragon scales, goat gall, and all manner of vile ingredients into a cauldron for their brew. This passage reminded him of what a witness had said earlier when testifying on oleomargarine production. According to the witness, dead animals including hydrophobic dogs that had been killed, were rendered and used to manufacture " 'pure' oleo oil." Henderson's rendition of *Macbeth* was followed by "great laughter and applause." He, too, noted that Armour had sent agents to exchanges throughout the country to persuade them to submit petitions against the bill. [23]

Lewis Beach, Democrat of New York, emphasized the inadequacy of state regulations. How, he asked, could state laws deal with the problem when manufacturing took place in one state and the product was retailed nationwide? Although Beach believed national legislation was necessary, he hesitated to use a "questionable" taxing power to handle the issue. Instead, Beach introduced a substitute measure which would require oleomargarine to be colored with alkanet "or some other harmless pigment" to give the commodity "a well-defined pink color." In this manner, he chortled, "we hoist these oleomargarine fellows with their own petard," because the only way they could "sell their stuff" was to imitate yellow butter. [24]

One of the congressmen representing the Chicago area, Republican Ransom Dunham, denied that imitation butter was being made from various kinds of diseased animals. He introduced affidavits from the Armour, Swift, and Fairbanks companies, the nation's three largest packers, which described their process of making oleomargarine. They affirmed that they processed only healthy animals in a sanitary method and used only good hog leaf lard to produce Butterine. In both products the same coloring material was added that dairymen used to color butter. At certain times, especially during cold weather, a small quantity of cottonseed oil was added to soften the texture of the product. Dunham then informed Beach that he

[22] Ibid., pp. 4894–95.
[23] Ibid., p. 4909.
[24] Ibid., pp. 4911–12.

cared not if the requirement were to color oleomargarine "pink or red or sky-blue"–the manufacturers were not trying to deceive consumers–but that the motive behind this tax proposal was simply to raise the price of butter.[25]

Opponents adopted the strategy of offering facetious amendments to kill the proposal. Democrat John Findlay of Maryland wanted to prohibit shipment of oleomargarine to "any point included in Her Majesty's East Indian possessions inhabited by the Parsees or fire-worshippers" and extend the provisions to include sausage–an amendment which the Chair ruled out of order. Reagan of Texas offered an amendment to apply the tax to watered milk, adulterated butter, ancient eggs, sanded sugar, glucose syrup, or artificial honey, all of which were being sold to the public at this time. But the House ruled the motion out of order by vote of 131 to 32. Mississippi Democrat Henry Van Eaton's amendment would have taxed manufacturers of poultry incubators $10,000 per year and a tax of one dollar for each pullet and two dollars per rooster hatched by artificial means in order to protect "the great American hen" as well as the "great American cow." [26]

Because states'-rights congressmen had called attention to the opposition of laborers to a tax on cheap food, Congressman Hatch asked Terence V. Powderly, Grand Master Workman of the Knights of Labor, then in convention at Cleveland, to send him a telegram which he subsequently read on the floor of the House. Powderly emphatically stated that the assembly had instructed him to report that no person had been authorized by the Knights to speak for the organization on the issue "either in the affirmative or the negative." The Knights of Labor were taking no position on the question, he said. Apparently Edwin Dodge and George Stearne of Chicago, Armour agents, were unsuccessful in their efforts to induce the Knights to oppose the tax.[27]

Despite Olin Wellborn, Democrat of Texas, describing the tax as "un-American" and Arkansas Democrat Clifton Breckinridge quoting the Supreme Court case of *United States* v. *DeWitt*, which struck down the 1867 naptha law, a bill to tax oleomargarine at five cents per pound passed the House by vote of 177 to 101.[28]

[25] Ibid., pp. 4915–16.

[26] Ibid., pp. 4982, 5008, 5011.

[27] Ibid., pp. 5074–75. The *Washington Evening Star*'s account of the Knights' convention is reprinted in ibid., p. 5125.

[28] Ibid., pp. 5156, 5159, 5213.

The same arguments for and against the measure emerged in the Senate which were presented in the House. In addition, Senator Richard Coke, Democrat of Texas, quoted Cooley's *Constitutional Limitations* to show that any use of a tax, other than for revenue, was "tyrannical and unlawful." Also, Republican John Ingalls of Kansas called attention to the fact that Senator Warner Miller, Republican of New York, the bill's sponsor, was a dairyman himself and that Hatch in the House had a like vocation— implying that business reasons motivated their desire to tax oleomargarine. Miller replied that he spent ten dollars to experiment in dairy improvements for every one dollar he received from his investment and denied that the proposed measure would help him financially.[29]

On July 20 the Senate voted to cut the tax to two cents a pound and the bill passed by the close vote of 33 to 28. The House accepted this change three days later and on August 2 President Grover Cleveland signed the bill into law.[30] When he affixed his signature, however, Cleveland gratuitously sent a message to Congress explaining his support of the law. The constitutionality of the proposal had been much debated, the president said, and this suggested it should be vetoed. But because Cleveland did "not feel called upon to interpret the motives of Congress" in passing the bill, he had approved the measure. If oleomargarine could not "endure the exhibition of its real character," which this law would require, he insisted, "the sooner it is destroyed the better, in the interest of fair dealing."[31]

The law required manufacturers of oleomargarine, oleo, oleomargarine oil, butterine, lardine, suine, and neutral oils to purchase an annual license for $600, wholesalers $480, and retailers $48 per year to operate their businesses. Each had to file annual reports with the Bureau of Internal Revenue and affix stamps on all such commodities, paying a revenue of two cents per pound, except that which was to be exported. Imports of the above-mentioned commodities would be taxed at the rate of fifteen cents per pound and the commissioner of Internal Revenue was authorized, with the approval of the secretary of the treasury, to "make all needful rules and regulations for . . . carrying into effect" the provisions of the law.[32]

As one contemporary scholar noted, the 1886 tax marked the beginning

29 Ibid., pp. 7084, 7151.

30 Ibid., pp. 7202, 7272, 7402, 7875.

31 Ibid., p. 7920; James D. Richardson, *Messages and Papers of the Presidents* (Washington, D.C., 1913), 7:4992–94.

32 U.S., *Statutes at Large*, vol. 24.

of "a new era in . . . the sphere of sumptuary legislation." [33] Based upon the evidence presented in the congressional debates, the only justification for passage of this law would be to compel the truthful labeling of oleomargarine and thus prevent any possible fraud being imposed on consumers. A case could have been made for a close inspection of the manufacturing process but, if so, facts and logic would call for an extension of the same principle to apply to the manufacture of butter where conditions were certainly as bad, according to contemporary descriptions, as in the "bogus butter" industry.

The effects of the oleomargarine laws were immediate and varied. The number of oleomargarine manufacturers declined from thirty-two in 1887 to twenty-one in 1890 (ten of these were in Illinois and Connecticut), and production totaled only 32,844,950 pounds in the latter year compared to the 1886 high of 200,000,000 pounds. [34] As might be expected, opponents challenged the tax law and some of the state statutes, with several cases reaching the Supreme Court. The Pennsylvania law, which completely prohibited the manufacture or sale of oleomargarine, was attacked as being a violation of the due-process clause of the Fourteenth Amendment. In *Powell* v. *Pennsylvania* the Supreme Court answered the appellee's argument that if the law were valid the state could destroy any product, by accepting the principle that it was a question of "public policy" and within the power of state legislative action. And, the Court added, "the possibility of abuse of legislative power does not disprove its existence." [35] So the statute was declared to be valid in prohibiting the sale of interstate oleomargarine in Pennsylvania.

The Powell case was determined by the Morrison Waite Court. The rest of the oleomargarine cases were heard by a Court headed by Melville W. Fuller who received his appointment from Cleveland in 1888. Fuller had been a Chicago corporation lawyer who at one time counted as a client, among others, Philip Armour. He was highly successful in his law practice and, by hard work and aggressive individualism, amassed considerable personal wealth before joining the Court. He was a close friend of Cleveland

[33] Henry C. Bannard, "The Oleomargarine Law: A Study of Congressional Politics," *Political Science Quarterly* 2 (December 1887) : 546.

[34] U.S., Congress, House, *Report of Commissioner of Internal Revenue for Fiscal Year Ending June 30, 1890*, House Executive Document 4 (Serial 2851), 51 Cong., 2 Sess., 1890, pp. 177–79.

[35] 127 U.S. 678 (1888). Arnold M. Paul, *Conservative Crisis and the Rule of Law* (New York, 1960), pp. 31–35, has a good discussion of this case.

and this, coupled with Republicans sensing victory in the election of 1888, led to charges of "cronyism" and that such an important appointment should not be made by a potential "lame duck" president.[36] In 1895 Fuller wrote two of the most important decisions handed down by his Court—one that emasculated the Sherman Antitrust Act and the other that struck down the income tax.

Justice Stephen Field was one of the dominant members of both the Waite and Fuller courts. This justice, a brother of David D. Field who was a leader of the New York bar, was the epitome of nineteenth-century individualism. He followed the gold rush to California in 1849 and quickly established a legal and political career on the frontier. He served on the Supreme Court for thirty-four years and, during the latter part of the nineteenth-century, was primarily responsible for the Supreme Court's elevating the public policy of laissez-faire to a constitutional doctrine. His nephew, David Brewer, soon came under the sway of his uncle following his Court appointment in 1890 to replace Stanley Matthews. Field was invariably supported in his constitutional positions by Samuel Blatchford, Matthews, and later Brewer, ex-railroad lawyers who were strongly pro-business, and former lower court judge Henry Brown. These ultraconservative justices, with Fuller, dominated the Supreme Court during the 1880s and 1890s. John Marshall Harlan was many times the lone dissenter during this period until joined occasionally by Edward White after 1894. Tests of the oleomargarine laws would place the conservative justices in the difficult position of sustaining the right of a manufacturer to do business or supporting the individualistic farmer who was the epitome of the American traditions.

Six years after the Powell case a dealer challenged the Massachusetts law of 1891 that forbade the sale of artificially colored oleomargarine within the borders of that Commonwealth. His attorney argued that this prohibition violated the national revenue law. By placing a tax on oleomargarine, Congress had recognized it as an article of interstate commerce and

---

[36] William F. Swindler, *Court and Constitution in the Twentieth Century*, 2 vols. (Indianapolis, Ind., 1969–1970), 1:31. Many of the ideas and discussions of justices in this and succeeding chapters are taken from this excellent study. Material on the background and thinking of the justices can also be found in a provocative article, John R. Schmidhauser, "The Justices of the Supreme Court: A Collective Portrait," *Midwest Journal of Political Science* 3 (February 1959) :1–55. Rocco J. Tresolini, *American Constitutional Law* (New York, 1959), has a helpful appendix containing brief biographies of some of the more important justices.

national law would take precedence over state statutes. The Supreme Court rejected this contention with Chief Justice Melville Fuller and Justices Stephen Field and David Brewer dissenting. The majority of the justices reasoned that it was within the powers of the state to suppress fraud and deception in the sale of imitation butter and the national law, even though the tax was paid, did not authorize the violation of state statutes. The dissenting justices agreed with the plaintiff's argument that the 1886 law was designed to protect the public from fraud and thus it should take precedence over the Massachusetts act.[37]

In 1892 one provision of the 1886 tax was tested. A Boston wholesale dealer had not kept proper records as required by the commissioner of Internal Revenue concerning oleomargarine that he bought and sold. He was convicted of violating Section 18 of the act for knowingly or willfully refusing to fulfill the requirements of the law. The Supreme Court, however, reversed his conviction on the grounds that the bookkeeping requirement found in Section 5 applied only to manufacturers. Because the law he supposedly violated was merely a stipulation extended to wholesalers by the Internal Revenue commissioner, this did not therefore constitute anything "required by law," the High Court said, and so could not carry criminal penalties.[38]

Authorities also arrested Israel C. Kollock, a Washington, D.C., grocer, and charged him with selling to a certain Florence Davis one-half pound of oleomargarine as butter because the package was not marked as required by the commissioner of Internal Revenue. He appealed his conviction to the Supreme Court on the ground that it was unconstitutional to allow the commissioner to determine what constituted criminal offense. Chief Justice Fuller, speaking for the Court, decided that the criminal offenses were "fully and completely defined by the act and the designation by the Commissioner of the particular marks and brands to be used was a mere matter of detail." In a significant passage, Fuller announced that, although the law might operate in such a manner as to prevent deception, "its primary object must be assumed to be the raising of revenue." The 1886 tax was similar to the revenue laws for stamps on packages of cigars, tobacco, and "spirits" and therefore was found to involve "no unconstitutional delegation of

---

[37] *Plumley* v. *Massachusetts*, 155 U.S. 461 (1894). Willard L. King, *Melville Weston Fuller* (New York, 1950), p. 239, observes that this decision, in effect, overruled Fuller's opinion in *Leisy* v. *Hardin*, which accounts for his dissent in this case.

[38] *United States* v. *Eaton*, 144 U.S. 677 (1892).

power." Kollock's appeal for a writ of habeas corpus was denied.[39]

Finally, the Original Package Doctrine of the *Brown* decision of 1827 clouded the legal aspects of the oleomargarine laws. The John Marshall Court fashioned the constitutional doctrine that goods in interstate commerce could not be regulated by states until broken down from the original package and inserted in the stream of intrastate commerce.[40] This principle created problems after the Civil War when many states voted to prohibit the sale of intoxicating beverages. According to the Brown opinion, liquor could be imported from a wet state in interstate commerce and sold in the original package, a principle which the Supreme Court upheld in *Leisy* v. *Hardin* in 1890.[41] That same year, Congress passed the Wilson Act which subjected liquor to the laws of the state, upon arrival at its borders, thus permitting dry states to intercept the importation of alcoholic beverages in any form.[42] This statute was upheld the following year by the Supreme Court on the basis of supremacy of national laws over interstate commerce.[43] The same basic issue, dealing with the state laws prohibiting sale of oleomargarine, produced the case of *Schollenberger* v. *Pennsylvania*.[44]

Despite the Pennsylvania statute prohibiting the sale of oleomargarine, the Oakdale Manufacturing Company of Providence, Rhode Island, shipped to a Philadelphia wholesaler, who had purchased a national license, a forty-pound tub of oleomargarine. The wholesale dealer subsequently sold that tub in the original package to James Anderson and was convicted of violating the state law. Justice Rufus Peckham, speaking for the majority on the Court, held that, although a state could regulate the sale of oleomargarine, as long as the product was not unhealthful it could not be completely excluded because the 1886 tax had recognized it as a commodity in interstate commerce. For precedents, Peckham cited the *Brown* and *Leisy* decisions.

Peckham carefully differentiated between this case and the issue raised in the Powell litigation which dealt with the question of Fourteenth Amendment due process rights. Justice Peckham noted that a state could exercise its police power to control or even to ban the manufacture and sale of a

---

[39] *In re Kollock*, 165 U.S. 526 (1897).
[40] *Brown* v. *Maryland*, 12 Wheaton 419 (1827).
[41] 135 U.S. 100 (1890).
[42] U.S., *Statutes at Large*, vol. 26.
[43] *Wilkerson* v. *Rahrer*, 140 U.S. 572 (1891).
[44] 171 U.S. 1 (1898).

product that was completely intrastate in nature. But it is beyond the power of a state to prohibit "absolutely" the entry of an article of interstate commerce. This would violate the rights of citizens of other states which were obtained through the national commerce power. He also distinguished this case from the Plumley decision. A state had the power to prevent fraud and could inspect goods in interstate commerce to enforce this. But the right to protect its citizens did not extend to the power to prohibit entry of goods in interstate commerce.

The *Plumley* decision had prompted several states to prohibit the entry of artificially colored oleomargarine; by 1898 twenty-six states passed such laws and the number increased to thirty-two by 1902.[45] But with the Schollenberger opinion, a state could not interfere with interstate commerce by prohibiting the sale of oleomargarine imported from another state. This decision led to demands to extend the provisions of the Wilson Act to include imitation butter, which was later accomplished.

The successful validation of the 1886 tax by the Supreme Court established and confirmed the principle that Congress could, and would, tax certain products in this manner. Congressmen from the dairy states of New York, Pennsylvania, Iowa, and Illinois were able to push the bill through Congress over the protests of states'-rights congressmen from the South. This was a major victory because as farm prices dropped sharply in the 1890s agricultural interests sought to persuade Congress to build on this foundation of the taxing power by extending the principle to other "adulterated" commodities to help bolster agrarian income. Soon after the enactment of the 1886 oleomargarine tax, farmers were successful in having a prohibitive tax placed on another fraudulent food, mixed flour, but were unsuccessful in restricting adulterated lard.

45 Howard, "The Margarine Industry," p. 76.

3 *Impure Food Taxes*

The battles over the next two adulterated commodities that agricultural groups sought to have taxed evolved into a major struggle between proponents of the taxes and Southern states'-rights congressmen. These proposals, one involving cottonseed oil and the other dealing with flour, were of vital interest to the South. Southerners were concerned not only because their region produced cottonseed and consumed flour but also because they viewed such expanding national regulatory legislation as an invasion of states' rights. Congressmen south of the Mason-Dixon line took the lead in opposing what they considered an alarming encroachment into the realm of police power over food—a function they considered as reserved to the states by the Tenth Amendment.

The first of the proposals, dealing with mixed lard, could have affected the attempts of the "New South" to industrialize. Before the Civil War, cottonseed was regarded not only as useless but as an annoyance necessitating disposal. But after 1865 Southerners found new uses for cottonseed and their attitude toward it changed radically. One eminent historian of the postwar South points out that cottonseed "was viewed variously as trash in 1860, fertilizer in 1870, cattle feed in 1880, and table food in 1890."[1] As scientists discovered new techniques to convert cottonseed oil into food oils in the 1880s and the residue bulk used as cattle feed, cottonseed became increasingly important to the Southern economy. At the same time Northern farmers began criticizing the use of cottonseed oil to adulterate or to replace "pure" dairy foods.

Because cotton seed is toxic when ingested, it could not be used as a food substance until feasible oil-pressing machines were developed. In the 1850s such machinery was constantly improved so that by 1860 there were seven active cottonseed mills in the South. During the Reconstruction period the number of mills rose to twenty-six in 1870 and then mushroomed to 533 by 1929. In 1871 only 4 percent of the crop was crushed; by 1914 around 80 percent was processed. During the early years the oil was used to some extent in the manufacture of soap but most of it was exported to Europe, especially France and Italy. There it was processed, in some instances mixed with olive oil and then reexported to the United States as olive oil. Italy, which received 40 percent of the cottonseed oil exported during the 1870s, soon found its olive growers demanding protection from the American product, because it lessened the demand for their crop. In 1881 Italy more than doubled its tariff on American cottonseed oil and the next year there were no exports of the oil to that country.[2]

Fortunately for Southerners, technicians were finding other ways to use cottonseed oil. The process of hydrogenation was of great importance because it allowed this oil to be used in the manufacture of oleomargarine and other table foods. The value of cottonseed oil increased proportionately —its commercial value rose from $1,590,000 in 1874 to $46,950,575 in 1899 and to $334,950,000 in 1947.[3]

A new technique brought about the manufacture of compound lard. Prior to the Civil War refined lard was produced by pressing some of the oil out of regular lard and this commanded a higher price. Then in the 1880s chemists found that when regular lard was mixed with beef stearine (the remains of beef fat after extracting the oil or oleo), or cottonseed oil, the result was similar to the firmness achieved with refined lard. Because cottonseed oil was three cents a pound cheaper than lard and beef stearine was two cents a pound less at this time, the enterprising lard manufacturer could, and did, place on the market a compound lard which was sold as "refined lard" with greater profits to himself. By 1890 some 320 million pounds, or over half of the 600 million pounds of lard produced annually in the United States, was of the compound variety. The public first obtained general knowledge of lard adulteration in August 1883 when the Chicago

---

[1] John Samuel Ezell, *The South since* 1865 (New York, 1963), p. 144.

[2] Alton E. Bailey, ed., *Cottonseed and Cottonseed Products* (New York, 1948), pp. 23–26.

[3] The figures for 1874 are from ibid., pp. 27–28; those for 1899 can be found in U.S., *Census of Agriculture, 1945* (Washington, D.C., 1947), 2:428; the amount for 1947 was determined from the tables in U.S., Department of Agriculture, *Agricultural Statistics, 1953* (Washington, D.C., 1953), p. 123. In 1949 Congressman Thomas B. Abernathy of Mississippi, stressing the importance of cottonseed oil in table foods, declared that in the previous year 21.8 percent of the oil went into shortening, 35.3 percent was used for margarine, and almost all the remainder went into mayonnaise, salad oils, and salad dressings. U.S., Congress, House, Committee on Agriculture, *Hearings on Oleomargarine*, 81 Cong., 1 Sess., 1949, p. 19.

Board of Trade published the results, including the charges and evidence, of a trial it held concerning the questionable activities of a Chicago meat packer. This report indicated that "cottonseed oil, oleo stearine, tallow, bench-cuttings, floor-scrapings, heads, feet, marrow-bones, guts, etc.," were found in the lard tanks of Chicago packinghouses.[4] The nature of the "etc." was not indicated.

In many cases the manufacturers of compound lard neglected to label it as such and instead continued to print on the packages descriptions like "Pure Refined Lard" or "Prime Family Lard." As production of this type of lard increased, demands grew, particularly from hog-raisers and refined lard manufacturers, that so-called counterfeit lard be labeled truthfully and that restrictions be placed on the "fraud." Despite the millions of pounds involved, regulation would affect few manufacturers because about 90 percent of the production took place in Illinois and Missouri in the plants of Armour and Fairbanks companies. Swine growers became so disturbed in Illinois that in July 1889 the state legislature passed an act requiring compound lard to be labeled as such.[5]

This false labeling had become a national problem by 1890 due to the importance of lard in American exports. Much of the lard exported by the United States was of the compound variety, and European countries were becoming concerned over this deception. Congress was already alarmed over the fact that Germany, France, Switzerland, Italy, Denmark, Roumania, Turkey, and Portugal had recently prohibited importation of American hams and bacon for fear of trichinae, and Denmark had prohibited the importation of American lard except that which was refined. The export of large amounts of compound lard to England had resulted in that country's prosecuting its tradesmen for selling an adulterated product. The effect of this publicity caused lard imports in England to drop from 4,000–5,000 cans per week to 200 cans per week.[6] It was also pointed out that because French farmers were unable to compete with Americans in pork production, ten years previously France had used the excuse of trichinae to protect its markets by banning American pork. During the 1880s there was a duty of one cent per pound on cottonseed oil coming into France while lard entered free. This differential, claimed the French, served as an induce-

---

[4] U.S., Congress, House, Report 970 (Serial 2809), 51 Cong., 1 Sess., 1889, p. 2. Hereafter cited as House Report 970.

[5] *Congressional Record*, 51 Cong., 1 Sess., 1890, 21:8956–68.

[6] House Report 970, pp. 3–4.

ment for Americans to convert the oil into "prime family lard and unload it upon the French before they discovered the trick." In 1890 the United States minister to France, Whitelaw. Reid, was trying to get the pork ban lifted and it was argued in Congress that a law controlling compound lard would help him in this effort.[7]

Pure lard manufacturers decided that the artificial product should be penalized in order to equalize the competition. They enlisted the support of Alexander Wedderburn of Alexandria, Virginia, who was the editor of a Grange newspaper, to assist in the campaign to handicap the artificial product. Wedderburn, described by opponents as "a demagogue pure and simple," used his newspaper to inundate Grangers with descriptions of the problem of compound lard and the necessity of congressional action in order to build pressure for restrictive legislation. Apparently Wedderburn became a little too enthusiastic about the project. He got a post office established, obtained the appointment of one of his employees as postmaster, and was soon charged with sending out his anti-compound lard circulars in the form of newspapers at one-eighth the postal rate he should have paid. When the *New York Sun* exposed this activity, Democrat James B. Morgan of Mississippi introduced a resolution in the House of Representatives which was adopted on August 17, 1890, calling for an investigation of the episode. The Department of Agriculture, whose staff sympathized with hog farmers, had intervened on Wedderburn's behalf and persuaded the Post Office Department to set aside its criminal proceedings against him. So the House resolution asked the postmaster general to submit the pertinent papers to the lower house.[8] But congressmen were still awaiting the documents when the lard bill was debated. Wedderburn later became a special agent for the Department of Agriculture investigating adulteration of foods.

Because the oleomargarine tax had been successful, proponents of restrictions on compound lard decided to use the same approach. Republican Edwin H. Conger of Iowa introduced a bill which was assigned to the House Committee on Agriculture, following the precedent established with the oleomargarine bill in 1886. The Committee on Agriculture held hearings, debated, delayed, and then in an emergency session, the majority voted to report a measure to the House known as the Conger bill.

The majority report of the committee not only recommended H.R. 11568 to the House as a revenue measure but declared that the Conger bill

[7] *Congressional Record*, 51 Cong., 1 Sess., 1890, 21:9083.
[8] This episode is detailed in ibid., pp. 9077, 9087, 9095.

was necessary to compel the branding of compound lard that was made and sold as pure lard "so that consumers may be advised of the nature of the article they purchase." Second, the bill would assist pure lard manufacturers in "the unfair competition of an imitation article." Finally, it would relieve "to some extent the existing depression in the farming industry caused in part by the displacement of a large and increasing amount of the pure fat of the hog by a spurious substitute."[9] This bill would place the manufacture and sale of lard under the supervision of the commissioner of Internal Revenue. Any lard made from products other than that "exclusively from the fresh fat of slaughtered swine" would be regarded as compound lard. Manufacturers of such products would have to pay $96 per annum, wholesalers $24 a year, and retailers $1.92 for a special license to do business. Compound lard would have to be marked, stamped, or branded as such "in a conspicuous place" and a tax of two mills per pound was proposed with a tax of two cents per pound on all such imported lard.[10]

Because the Conger bill was designed to help hog raisers and its detrimental effects would be felt chiefly by producers of cottonseed oil, the ensuing fight in Congress over the proposal was labeled "The Hog vs. the Negro." Opponents of the measure, led by cottonseed oil processors, argued that because of the operation of the Southern tenant system the landlord controlled all agricultural products in one manner or another through mortgages and liens. The lone exception was cottonseed which, because it had previously been considered worthless, was by tradition still left with the tenant. It constituted the only item of worth for the Negro tenant farmer and sale of his cottonseed gave him a little cash for some of "the comforts and really many of the necessaries of life."[11] If compound lard were taxed, the burden would filter down to the tenant Negro. Any benefits of the measure, the second minority report on H.R. 11568 concluded, would accrue "not to farmers, but to big packing houses."[12] So the measure became an issue between the cottonseed oil processors on the one hand piously appealing for help for the Negro and, on the other, packinghouses purportedly trying to assist farmers in raising the price of hogs.

[9] House Report 970, p. 2. The first report was dated March 21, 1890; the second report was dated July 30, 1890, House Report 2857 (Serial 2815), with minor changes in such things as fines.

[10] The bill was reprinted in *Congressional Record*, 51 Cong., 1 Sess., 1890, 21: 8894–96.

[11] Ibid., p. 8968.

[12] House Report 970, Minority Report of John Wilson, p. 7.

The majority report of the Committee on Agriculture stressed the issue of falling hog prices. A table was inserted in the *Congressional Record* showing that the average price of hogs had dropped from $6.75 in 1883 to $4.71 in 1890. The document attempted to connect this with the manufacture of compound lard by pointing out that in 1890 total cottonseed oil production was 28 million gallons or 210 million pounds valued at $10 million. It was noted that 70 million pounds were used in manufacturing compound lard and the total value of this amount would equal $3.5 million, a sum, it was argued, which should be going to hog raisers. While the sale was important to the South, the report admitted, "no trade has a right to rise on the ruins of its fellow, wrought, not by legitimate competition in a fair field, but by cunning and the subtle devices of the wicked." To bolster further the argument that the Conger bill would not really adversely affect the Southern Negro, the majority report reprinted a letter from W.H. Nelson, Master of the Tennessee State Grange, to A. J. Wedderburn. In it Nelson stated that a tax of five cents, or even ten cents, per gallon on cottonseed oil would not be detrimental to Southern tenant farmers. This was true, he asserted, because the price of cottonseed was "fixed" by the Cottonseed Oil Trust, formed in 1884, at around eight to ten dollars per ton. The trust had found that when it offered a lower price, competition arose from cotton growers who had small mills and the seed was then used for fertilizer and stock feeding. Protests from the South against the Conger proposal, he concluded, were "all gotten up in cities, towns, or country stores." No cotton farmer, Nelson insisted, had "at any time signed any such paper, unless he saw . . . a pecuniary profit in some way other than in the price of cottonseed or else he did it through a most shameful ignorance or indifference." [13]

The first minority report, opposing the Conger bill, had a different set of statistics. According to these figures, cottonseed oil constituted 5 percent of the value of the cotton crop, or $12 million annually, and half of this went into the manufacture of compound lard. Because cottonseed brought from ten to sixteen dollars per ton, the price would be "materially affected" if half the market were cut off. The same table on hog prices was included, but the minority concluded that this decline resulted basically from corn values. When corn was plentiful and cheap, as in the immediate preceding years, larger amounts were fed to swine and hog production increased, which reduced pork prices correspondingly. This report determined, therefore, that because compound lard was now being correctly labeled and

[13] Ibid., Majority Report, pp. 4–8.

cottonseed oil and beef stearine were as healthful as lard, a tax could not be justified.[14]

House debate on the bill was actually rather brief, considering the importance of the constitutional principle involved in this use of the taxing power and despite parliamentary maneuvers to delay voting. Marriot Brosius, Republican of Pennsylvania, chairman of the Committee on Agriculture, introduced the measure to the House Committee of the Whole by quoting testimony from Harvey H. Wiley, chief of the Bureau of Chemistry of the Department of Agriculture, on samples of lard that contained cottonseed oil. He had reprinted in the *Congressional Record* excerpts of letters from European countries on the subject. One, dated November 15, 1887, came from Antwerp warning the Chicago Board of Trade and the New York Produce Exchange that exports of fraudulent compound lard must stop or Americans would lose the Belgian market. A letter from Hamburg expressed the hope that Congress would halt the sale of compound lard before it became necessary for the Reichstag to prevent its importation as had been done with pork. A letter from the United States consul at Nantes warned that the French were considering a tax of thirty francs per kilogram on American adulterated lard to protect their domestic product. Finally, Brosius inserted a statement made during committee hearings. An official declared that if the Fairbanks Company wanted to put only 20 percent pure lard in their "refined lard," they saw no fraud involved and considered it "perfectly fair to do it," which to Brosius constituted an attitude needing changing.[15]

William E. Mason, Republican of Illinois, the chief spokesman for the compound lard manufacturers, opposed the Conger bill because the national government did not need the revenue. He complained that Brosius and the majority of the Committee on Agriculture had suddenly changed their minds, called a quorum at 4:00 P.M. on a Saturday, and voted to report the bill immediately, thus leaving no opportunity to offer amendments in the committee. He urged that Congress attack the problem through the commerce power by prohibiting the shipment of goods in interstate commerce unless "marked for what they are." Two days later Mason described the problems concerning the inquiry into Wedderburn's postal activities. He told his colleagues he had been trying to get access to the necessary documents from the Post Office Department "for a week . . . and was informed

14 Ibid., Minority Report, pp. 4–23.
15 *Congressional Record*, 51 Cong., 1 Sess., 1890, 21:8898.

they could not be furnished to me until after the Conger bill had been voted upon." He charged that friends of the bill were causing the delay in the Wedderburn investigation.[16]

Charles Stewart, Democrat of Texas, observed that the Conger bill was the "first fruit of a great error," referring to the oleomargarine law. Although the 1886 tax was the most "outrageous perversion of the taxing power . . . that has ever been perpetrated by Congress," this measure, he said, was "far worse." At least, he argued, the earlier law gave farmers some protection while this one did not. Stewart noted that everyone quoted John Marshall's dictums when advocating revenue measures, but even the great chief justice "never once conceived that the taxing power could be used for the purpose of preventing or suppressing fraud. That discovery was made by that distinguished body of constitutional expounders, the Committee on Agriculture," he sarcastically commented. If compound lard was injurious to health, Stewart declared ,"the remedy should be found in the police powers of the States, and not in Congress." The framers of the Constitution, he insisted, "never once thought of conferring upon Congress the taxing power for any such purpose." He concluded that the "flood" of favorable petitions that apparently were worrying many congressmen were "precisely alike and must have emanated from the same source" so they could be safely ignored.[17]

Democrat William McAdoo of New Jersey called attention to a meeting held in Atlanta on March 19, 1890, at which representatives from the Alabama, Arkansas, Florida, Georgia, Louisiana, Missouri, North Carolina, Tennessee, and Texas chapters of the National Farmers Alliance and Industrial Unions endorsed resolutions opposing the Conger bill.[18] William C. Oates, Democrat of Alabama, reported he had hundreds of petitions from Negroes asking for defeat of the lard bill to protect their cottonseed. In a refutation of the statement by the Master of the Tennessee Grange, Oates declared that the farmers knew what they were signing, calling attention to the affidavit attached to one of the petitions. The document, "sworn to by a U.S. Commissioner," affirmed that the person gathering signatures had either read the petition to or had the signers themselves read it before signing and thus they were aware of what they were doing.[19]

16 Ibid., pp. 8956–58, 9095.
17 Ibid., pp. 8966–68.
18 Ibid., pp. 9087–88.
19 Ibid., p. 8968.

John H. Rogers, Democrat of Arkansas, made the most passionate appeal to Republicans on behalf of the Southern Negro. He noted that the Republican party boasted of freeing the Negro and "then whacked everything he is interested in." As examples, Rogers listed the recent cut in the duty on rice and the removal of sugar from the protected list. When Republican Elijah Morse of Massachusetts interrupted him with the observation that a bounty of two cents per pound had been placed on sugar, Rogers replied that this money went to the planter and the Sugar Trust. He further observed that Republicans refused to lower the revenue on tobacco, had raised the duty on cottonties over 300 percent leaving the Negro at "the mercy of the bagging trust," and had lowered the protection of cottonseed oil by 75 percent. What the Republicans were trying to do to the Negro, he complained, was "to put one arm around his neck and 'honey-fugle' him" for his vote and "to put the other arm down into his pocket up to the elbow and take out his hard earnings."[20]

Both Southern and Northern opponents of the lard tax emphasized that laborers, especially the Knights of Labor, had indicated opposition to the Conger bill through petitions because compound lard gave them a cheaper food than pure lard. Conger cast some doubt on the authenticity of this sentiment by reading an editorial from the Saint Louis German newspaper *Tageblatt*. According to this account, the Fairbanks Company of Saint Louis obtained signatures on such labor petitions by requiring the "little girls in its employ" to canvass houses for signers with the threat of discharge if they failed to return "with a satisfactory number." Being familiar with the situation and "out of sympathy for the poor children," many laborers, including members of the Knights, signed the petitions.[21]

Despite their appeals, opponents of the Conger bill found themselves outnumbered, so they resorted to parliamentary maneuvering to obstruct the measure. Several members discovered that by answering roll call there would be a quorum to do business and then they would wander off to cloakrooms so there would not be a quorum when a vote was called. To defeat this tactic Republican Joseph Cannon of Illinois introduced a resolution calling upon the House sergeant-at-arms to arrest all members not "officially excused." The debate over this resolution resulted in two congressmen engaging in "a personal difficulty" during which "blows were passed." Finally, the Conger bill passed the House on August 28, 1890, just prior to

[20] Ibid., pp. 9092–93.
[21] Ibid., p. 9080.

adjournment, by vote of 126 to 33, with 167 not voting.[22] Only eleven of the thirty-three negative votes were Southern, and five of these were Kentuckians. Because the Republicans sponsored the Conger bill and the party had the necessary votes, many of the Southerners apparently deemed it useless to take a recorded stand on the issue and refrained from voting.

Algernon Paddock, Republican of Nebraska, chairman of the Senate Committee on Agriculture and Forestry, reported the bill with the recommendation that it be considered along with his Pure Food measure. It was passed over on December 15, 1890, and again on March 3, 1891, just before final adjournment of the Fifty-first Congress and thus never became law.[23] The use of cottonseed oil in foods continued to increase and by 1912 179 million pounds were used for cooking purposes and 446 million pounds went into compound lard for a total of two-thirds of the food oils consumed in the United States.[24] The Conger bill might therefore, if enacted, have seriously retarded the use of cottonseed oil and subsequently the growth of this important Southern industry.

Although the compound lard tax was defeated, Southerners were unable to prevent the taxing of mixed flour. By the time the United States declared war on Spain, flour millers had discovered various way of adulterating their product with cheaper ingredients. A. J. Wedderburn, now a special agent investigating food adulteration for the Department of Agriculture, sent out a questionnaire hoping, apparently, to receive answers from honest millers about the widespread practice of mixing flour. The returns indicated that from 10 to 40 percent of the wheat flour then produced was mixed with corn starch or corn flour. One miller responded that almost 50 percent of the flour sold in Tennessee, Alabama, Georgia, Florida, and South Carolina was mixed with these ingredients. A Saint Louis millers' committee recommended to Wedderburn that this practice be halted by Congress and enclosed a proposed law, patterned after the oleomargarine tax, to accomplish this purpose.[25]

In the meantime the Department of Agriculture was publishing reports

22 Ibid., pp. 9278, 9283.

23 Ibid., 51 Cong., 2 Sess., 1890, 22:450, 3909.

24 Bailey, *Cottonseed*, p. 35. In 1950 margarine and shortening alone used 418 million pounds and 549 million pounds of cottonseed oil respectively. U.S., Department of Agriculture, *Agricultural Statistics, 1958* (Washington, D.C., 1959), pp. 139–40.

25 U.S., Congress, House, Committee on Agriculture, "Adulteration of Wheat Flour," Dr. H. W. Wiley, Report to the Secretary of Agriculture, 55 Cong., 2 Sess., 1898, House Report 309 (Serial 3679), pp. 4–14.

on food adulteration. In 1898 a report on "Cereals and Cereal Products" was released. In this report cereals "came off very well," but it was noted that corn meal was occasionally used in wheat flour and sometimes alum was added to whiten the bread. Although bread was made with certain chemical leavening agents which "retained questionable mineral residues," no evidence was found that chalk, terra alba, or other substances were being used as claimed.[26] Because corn flour was worth from $1.50 to $2.00 per barrel and wheat flour from $4.50 to $5.00 per barrel, it is easily seen that a 40 percent mixture of corn flour would be lucrative to manufacturers, although fraudulent, if the ingredients were not labeled.

Corn flour was mixed with wheat flour after a process of sulphur fumes and hot water, which produced sulphuric acid, had broken down the kernel. The outer edge of the kernel, or bran, was then scarped off leaving the starch in a semi-liquid form. This was then dried and ground. Unfortunately, there was no purification process to remove the residue sulphuric acid. An even more questionable practice in the flour industry came with the discovery that mineraline, a white clay of North Carolina, could be ground up and mixed with flour, giving it a whiter texture. Proponents of a bill in Congress that would regulate the mixing of flour reprinted advertisements in the *Congressional Record* from companies which offered to demonstrate how to mix mineraline with flour. These circulars advised using only an 18 percent mixture for high-grade wheat flour; one could use from 25 to 30 percent for a low-grade product. One advertisement from the York Manufacturing Company in North Carolina offered a mixer free of charge with the purchase of mineraline. The machine, it was announced, would "distribute completely any proportion desired and costs nothing to attach." The ad called attention to the fact that one could realize a profit of $400 to $1,600 for each carload of mineraline used, depending, of course, on the percentage of mixture. As mineraline became more commonly used, the price of "flourine," as the product was sometimes labeled, rose correspondingly. A quotation of prices from the Glucose Sugar Company of Chicago, a major company producing corn flour, indicated that on November 2, 1897, flourine was $1.22 per hundredweight; by May 25, 1898, it had advanced to $1.50.

These advertisements also demonstrated that flourine was directed largely toward the Southern trade. One called attention to the fact that flour

[26] Oscar E. Anderson, Jr., *The Health of a Nation* (Chicago, Ill., 1958), pp. 121–22.

was judged by the consumer according to its color and by using mineraline the miller could "meet competition," noting especially that "for all Southern trade flourine is used extensively." This same circular described the mixing process as merely conveying the ingredients twenty to twenty-five feet, by which time it would be "thoroughly mixed."[27] As this practice of mixing flour increased, so too did a corresponding demand to regulate the industry.

A bill, patterned after the oleomargarine tax, was introduced in the 1898 session of Congress but was ignored in the flurry of congressional activity over the current war with Spain. Advocates of the measure developed a stratagem to push the proposal through Congress; it was attached to the War Revenue Act of 1898. The Dingley Tariff of 1897 was deemed inadequate to finance the war effort so on April 27 Nelson Dingley, Republican of Maine, introduced a measure to levy additional internal revenue taxes. When the bill reached the Senate, William Mason submitted the Mixed Flour Act as an amendment. This was necessary because revenue measures can originate only in the House, although the Senate can amend such bills if the changes are germane to the proposal. Mason explained that because the flour bill had become bogged down in the House, his Committee on Manufactures instructed him to report the Senate flour proposal as an amendment to the revenue bill.[28]

In offering his amendment to Dingley's bill, Mason explained that the flour measure was necessary because from 75 to 80 percent of the flour sold was adulterated. "No civilized country in the world . . . gives so little protection to the consumers of food and drink as . . . this country," Mason said. He admitted the bill was drawn up by the National Board of Trade, but its purpose was not to strike at legitimate business in any way. Rather, the main reason for enacting the law would be "to give notice to the people who consume flour of what they are buying when they buy it," or to force honest labeling. He submitted statements from the Winter Wheat Millers' League, Southwestern Wheat Millers' Association, Millers' National Association, and the state millers' associations of Illinois, Iowa, Kansas, Kentucky, Michigan, Minnesota, Missouri, Nebraska, and Pennsylvania, all endorsing the proposed tax.[29]

There was almost no debate on the mixed flour proposal. Apparently

[27] *Congressional Record*, 55 Cong., 2 Sess., 1898, 31:5349, 5346, 5350, 5522, 5721.
[28] Ibid., p. 5349.
[29] Ibid., p. 5346.

there was little objection to forcing the correct labeling of mixed flour. The Senate accepted Mason's amendment by a vote of 41 to 29, with 19 not voting. Six Southern senators voted for it, nine against it, and six did not vote.[30]

Joseph W. Bailey, Democrat of Texas, was one of the few Southern opponents to protest when the amended revenue bill was discussed in the House of Representatives. He objected to the tax as being an invasion of the state police power. If Congress invaded this realm in the case of flour, he argued, the same could be done with meat, lard, "or everything that people eat." The national government had to stop this increasing intervention somewhere, he lamented, "or else there is a place for falling off."[31]

Despite Bailey's objection, the House accepted the Senate addition on June 9 and William McKinley signed the measure into law on June 13, 1898.[32] The law required that all wheat flour mixed with any other ingredient be labeled "Mixed Flour" in black letters at least two inches high. It required manufacturers of such products to pay twelve dollars per annum for a license and a tax of four cents per 196-pound barrel, except that which was to be exported.[33] The small license fee and tax served the purpose of bringing mixed flour under national government surveillance and thus force labeling. An amendment in 1901 permitted a 5 percent maximum mixture of other ingredients in flour and the product could still remain outside the purview of the law, but the next year this was repealed. Ironically, the Mixed Flour Act was born in one war and expired in another. The Revenue Act of 1942 repealed the law which by that time was useless, because the practice of mixing flour had vanished.[34]

It would seem logical that Southern congressmen, while opposing the compound lard bill for economic reasons, would have favored the mixed flour tax for the purpose of protecting Southern consumers. In both cases, however, Southerners opposed any invasion of state police power or any expansion of central authority. Both these measures were Republican-sponsored so Southerners were joined by those Northern Democrats with an interest to protect. They opposed the lard bill as well as the flour act. That the interests of constituents dominated the thinking of some congressmen is

---

[30] Ibid., p. 5525.

[31] Ibid., p. 5725. On the other hand, Bailey was an ardent avocate of a national income tax. For his role in getting Senate approval of the Sixteenth Amendment, see Sidney Ratner, *American Taxation* (New York, 1942), pp. 284 ff.

[32] *Congressional Record*, 55 Cong., 2 Sess., 1898, 31:5727, 5904.

[33] U.S., *Statutes at Large*, vol. 30.

[34] Ibid., vols. 31, 32, and 56.

demonstrated by Mason of Illinois leading the opposition to the lard tax and sponsoring the flour measure.

In regard to adulterated lard, it can also be concluded that, in this case, two powerful trusts came into conflict over vested interests. While a Meat Trust per se never materialized, by this time the industry was dominated by Armour, Fairbanks, and Swift who were able to achieve the same results through cooperation that they could through a formal trust. Little evidence was presented which demonstrated the unhealthful aspects of compound lard; basically it was an issue of fraudulent labeling and both the Cottonseed Oil Trust and the meat packers had an interest in this product. Thus, in the case of compound lard, the tax and government supervision never became law. Mixed flour, on the other hand, presented not only a fraud but a health danger through the use of mineraline and sulphuric acid and, in a period of concern over pure food, was brought under national control and regulation and eventually disappeared as a problem.

Two years before passage of the mixed flour bill, however, dairymen were successful in having another fraudulent dairy product taxed. In 1896 the principle of a regulatory tax was applied to filled cheese, and this adulterated commodity was gradually eliminated. Also, a short time later dairymen were able to persuade Congress to tax artificially colored oleomargarine at a prohibitive rate. The emergence of these two taxes constituted the next phase in the development of a national police power.

4   *Adulterated Dairy Products*

By the 1890s the issue of adulterated, or filled, cheese proved to be a major dairy problem, particularly when it affected foreign markets, and efforts to restrain production of this food were effective. The process, becoming widespread by the mid-1890s, was a simple one: after removing the butterfat from whole milk, the skimmed milk was then heated and lard or neutral vegetable oils, or both, were then injected into the liquid. Quality cheese was composed of water, milk, and casein of approximately equal thirds, but filled cheese consisted of 70 percent milk and 30 percent other ingredients such as lard or neutral oils and rennet, salt and coloring. Critics pointed out that this product cost about three cents per pound to make, wholesaled for seven to eight cents, and retailed for ten cents. Good cheese retailed for about eleven cents or approximately the same price. Thus filled cheese could not be justified even on the grounds of being a cheap food for laborers as had been maintained in the case of oleomargarine.[1]

Yet, it was argued, filled cheese hurt the production of pure dairy cheese in at least two ways. By 1896 critics estimated an annual production of some 20 million pounds of the adulterated commodity which in turn cut off the market for about half of the pure cheese. More important, however, was the increasing complaint from European importers that the sale of filled cheese, if continued, would eventually ruin the highly favorable reputation of American cheese and result in the loss of these foreign markets for all American cheese, good or bad. Such a possibility prompted the dairy interests to seek restrictive legislation from Congress.

The National Dairy Union, formed for the purpose of fighting "counterfeit butter and cheese," held its annual meeting in Washington, D.C., January 10–12, 1895. W. D. Hoard, editor and publisher of *Hoard's Dairyman*, the nation's most popular dairy newspaper, was elected president at this meeting. The organization passed a resolution requesting Congress to license the manufacture and sale of filled cheese in the same manner it regulated oleomargarine and to place a tax of two cents per pound on the commodity. This was necessary, the resolution stated, because the increasing production of fraudulent cheese had reached "such vast proportions that it has greatly injured, and threatens to utterly destroy, the legitimate manufacture and trade in genuine full cream cheese." Hoard then used his influential newspaper to promote a filled cheese tax, calling upon all dairymen to contribute one dollar to the National Dairy Union for a campaign fund.[2]

The issue had not really become important until the year of Hoard's presidency. Before that time only a small amount of filled cheese was manufactured. But in 1895, some 12 million pounds of filled cheese were produced, and from January to April 1896 about 18 million pounds were manufactured. This amount was produced chiefly by 200 manufacturers, but the matter had reached such proportions in some dairy areas that in 1895 Wisconsin had enacted a law prohibiting its manufacture. Yet filled cheese manufacturers in other states, such as Illinois, continued production, labeling their commodity "New York Pure Dairy Cheese" or "Wisconsin Full Cream Cheese," which in turn hurt sales of the pure product.[3] Some Chicago producers even had railroad receipts altered to show that their misbranded cheese was shipped from a Wisconsin station. The executive committee of the Wisconsin Dairymen's Association then instituted an educational program, with a "liberal sum" of money, to advertise to foreign dealers that Wisconsin forbade the production of filled cheese. Wholesalers, therefore, should negotiate directly with Wisconsin producers to avoid being sold the fraudulent product.[4]

In his annual report of 1895, the secretary of agriculture called attention to the loss of markets in England for American cheese as a result of exporting filled cheese. He noted that when the issue over the increased importation of low quality cheese arose in Great Britain, there was no refuting the fact that the United States was exporting an inferior grade. In contrast, the secretary said, the Canadian government cabled an immediate denial that its cheese was filled, all of which resulted in "an excellent advertise-

[1] *Congressional Record*, 54 Cong., 1 Sess., 1896, 28:3792.
[2] *Hoard's Dairyman* 25 (January 25, 1895) : 786–89.
[3] *Congressional Record*, 54 Cong., 1 Sess., 1896, 28:3794–95, 3832.
[4] *Hoard's Dairyman* 26 (May 10, 1895) :219; 26 (September 27, 1895) :619.

ment for Canadian Cheese" in the British Isles to the detriment of American sales.[5] Tables in the 1896 report of the secretary of agriculture illustrate vividly how the exportation of filled cheese had reduced American sales in Great Britain. According to these figures, American exports of cheese dropped from a total of 82,100,221 pounds in 1892 to 37,777,291 pounds in 1896; of these totals, American sales of cheese to England in the same years fell from 70,201,769 to 29,801,334 pounds, or well over a 50 percent decline.[6]

To counteract this development, in 1896 the National Dairy Union sent its newly elected president, W. H. Hatch, now a retired congressman, and two other lobbyists to Washington to work for a tax on filled cheese.[7] Samuel A. Cook, Republican of Wisconsin, introduced a bill in the first session of the Fifty-fourth Congress to restrict filled cheese production by taxation. In introducing his proposal, Cook quoted a letter from the Wisconsin governor and declared that when he had been governor of Wisconsin previously he had received similar letters from foreign countries asking for a curtailment of the fraudulent commodity. Filled cheese, Cook observed, had resulted in a decline of nearly 40 percent in sales of American cheese to English markets alone, a figure that was actually too low, thus necessitating his proposed legislation.[8]

Charles H. Grosvenor, Republican of Ohio, answered protests that the recommended tax would hurt the cheese industry by pointing out that the 1886 oleomargarine law had not curtailed production of that food. The results instead, he said, were a reduction in the number of such factories, but an increase in the amount manufactured, and also a "greatly improved" quality in the "bogus butter." He concluded, therefore, that a tax on filled cheese would not hurt the industry but would merely require a truthful labeling of the product. To buttress his argument for the need for the proposal, Grosvenor inserted a report in the *Congressional Record* from Harvey H. Wiley to Charles Dabney, assistant secretary of agriculture. The report, dated March 5, 1896, stated that the sample of filled cheese Dabney had sent Wiley to be analyzed contained 5.44 percent ash, 22.25 percent casein, 34.02 percent fat, "almost exclusively stearine," 31.09 percent

---

[5] *Report of the Secretary of Agriculture Containing the Message and Documents Submitted to Congress,* 54 Cong., 1 Sess., 1895 (Washington, D.C., 1896), pp. 24–25.

[6] Ibid., 54 Cong., 2 Sess., 1896, p. 590.

[7] *Hoard's Dairyman* 26 (January 24, 1896) : 960.

[8] *Congressional Record,* 54 Cong., 1 Sess., 1896, 28:3792.

water, and 7.2 percent sugar and other "undetermined" ingredients.[9]

James A. Tawney, Minnesota Republican and a member of the sub-committee that had studied the problem of filled cheese, argued that the proposed tax was an improvement over the oleomargarine measure. The 1886 tax, he noted, was so high that manufacturers and dealers, rather than pay, assumed the risk of incurring the penalties for violating the law; the present proposal called for lower rates so that the law could be "more rigidly enforce[d]." While Nelson Dingley, Republican of Maine, would use the taxing power in this manner only under "extraordinary conditions" and then only where "the interest to be protected is of great moment, and where the State legislation is powerless," he declared, the filled cheese problem justified the exercise of such national power.[10]

Opponents of the tax proposal became quite concerned over this unique exercise of the taxing power. Benton McMillan, Democrat of Tennessee, pointed out that because of widespread violations the oleomargarine law was not working as promised and therefore regulation through the taxing principle should not be further extended.[11]

Franklin Bartlett, Democrat of New York, cited the Supreme Court cases of *Wilkerson* v. *Rahrer* and *Plumley* v. *Massachusetts* to prove that control over such commodities really belonged in the realm of state police power.[12] The *Wilkerson-Rahrer* case upheld the Wilson Act of 1890 which empowered states to forbid the importation of liquor into their states in interstate commerce if they desired.[13] The Plumley decision affirmed the power of a state to prohibit the sale of colored oleomargarine within its borders, despite Congress's having recognized that product as an item of interstate commerce by levying a tax on it.[14] Based on these decisions, Bartlett reasoned that the power to control such commodities was within the reserved powers of the states under the Tenth Amendment and Congress should not attempt to intervene by trying to control filled cheese.

The bill passed the House, however, on April 11 by a vote of 160 to 58,

[9] Ibid., pp. 3832, 3847.

[10] Ibid., pp. 3836, 3873.

[11] Ibid., p. 3835. McMillan, like Bailey of Texas, was a strict constructionist on the taxing power but a strong advocate of an income tax. For his key role in enacting the income tax clause in the Wilson-Gorman tariff of 1894, see Sidney Ratner, *American Taxation* (New York, 1942), pp. 172ff.

[12] *Congressional Record*, 54 Cong., 1 Sess., 1896, 28:3876–77.

[13] 140 U.S. 572 (1891).

[14] 155 U.S. 461 (1894).

with 136 not voting. Congressmen from the dairy states of Iowa, Michigan, Minnesota, New York, Pennsylvania, and Wisconsin were quite solidly behind the measure, indicating this was a bipartisan effort. Sixty-two representatives from these states voted for the bill, thirty-five abstained, and only four voted against the proposal. Charles N. Brumm of Pennsylvania was the only Republican from these states voting against the bill; the other three were Democrats.[15]

When the measure was discussed in the Senate more than a month later, opponents of the bill tried to kill it by adding an amendment that would increase the tax on beer by seventy-five cents per barrel. This was defeated by a vote of 27 to 34.[16] To justify the cheese tax, Minnesota Republican Senator Knute Nelson quoted the Supreme Court decision in *Veazie Bank* v. *Fenno* which upheld the prohibitive tax on state bank notes. The opposition insisted that the bank decision rested on the currency power, not the taxing power.[17]

George G. Vest, Democrat of Missouri, argued that the taxing power could be used only to support the interstate commerce power or currency powers and thus could not be used as an auxiliary to a police power which is reserved to the states. Vest claimed that the dairy industry was sending "threatening letters and circulars" to senators and representatives demanding a vote for the tax or "you will hear from us at the election." He received, he complained, a half dozen of these missives "by every mail," and under such pressure "the Constitution amounts to nothing."[18] *Hoard's Dairyman*, however, noted that Vest resided in Kansas City and assumed that his opposition was based on "local packing house sentiment" rather than the wishes of his statewide constituency.[19]

Despite Vest's opposition, the bill passed the Senate 37 to 13, with 39 not voting, and President Grover Cleveland signed it into law on June 6, 1896.[20] Not one senator from the above-mentioned dairy states voted against the measure although four of the twelve abstained from voting. Filled

[15] *Congressional Record*, 54 Cong., 1 Sess., 1896, 28:3886. It should be noted that, although Illinois had a strong interest in dairying at this time, most of the filled cheese was manufactured in this meat-packing state. With pressure from the meat-packing interests, most Illinois congressmen opposed this tax.

[16] Ibid., pp. 5712, 5777.

[17] Ibid., pp. 5716–17.

[18] Ibid., p. 6089.

[19] *Hoard's Dairyman* 27 (May 22, 1896) :268.

[20] *Congressional Record*, 54 Cong., 1 Sess., 1896, 28: 6103, 6291.

cheese was defined as "all substances made of milk or skimmed milk, with the adulteration of butter, animal oils or fats, vegetable or any other oils, or compounds foreign to such milk, and made in imitation or semblence to cheese." Manufacturers of such a product had to pay $400 per annum, wholesalers $250, and retailers $12 for licenses to operate their businesses. The law required filled cheese cartons to be labeled as such with two-inch black letters and levied a tax of one cent per pound on it. The act placed a duty of eight cents per pound on all imported filled cheese.[21] Again, as with oleomargarine, the low tax achieved the purpose of labeling and control.

As might be expected from experience with the oleomargarine tax, attempts were made to evade the law. The next year W. A. McKnight, representing the Liverpool and Manchester chambers of commerce, came to the United States to persuade the national government to tighten up enforcement of the statute. Filled cheese exported to England was correctly labeled, McKnight noted, but the manufacturers "cunningly placed a surplus wrapper around the cheese" which was "removed when received in Great Britain, thus leaving the imitation . . . to be palmed off as pure American cheese." Manchester health officials had reported a fatal case of poisoning from such cheese, so enforcement of the law was necessary before England took steps to ban all American cheese. Because most of the filled cheese was manufactured in the Chicago area, McKnight traveled there to address the Chicago Produce Board. He warned the board that its members must report violators of the Filled Cheese law so that "the confidence of the foreign consumer will gradually return [to pure American cheese]."[22]

The Filled Cheese Act was tested in the national courts as being an unconstitutional tax, reaching the Supreme Court in 1904 in the case of *Cornell* v. *Coyne*.[23] Litigants in this case insisted that the tax of a penny per pound paid on filled cheese that was to be exported violated the constitutional prohibition against levying duties on exports. The High Court rejected this argument, observing that the tax was not a duty in this sense but was merely a levy on the "manufacturing of articles in order to prepare them for export." Justice John Marshall Harlan, joined by Chief Justice Melville Fuller, dissented, declaring that Congress had exempted the domestic tax on tobacco manufactured for export and this was a similar question. Because a provision of the Filled Cheese Act applied to cheese stamps, the existing

21 U.S., *Statutes at Large*, vol. 29.
22 *New York Times*, May 19 and 28, 1897.
23 192 U.S. 418.

laws relating to tobacco stamps, Harlan reasoned, Congress therefore must have intended to exempt export cheese from the tax as it had exempted export tobacco. The law remained on the statute books, however, being re-enacted in 1926 and again in 1954.[24] A report in 1901 indicated that the problem was nearly eliminated by that time. In that year, only 1,305,459 pounds of filled cheese was made and most of this was exported.[25]

The dissatisfaction of dairy farmers with the oleomargarine tax was closely associated with the filled cheese issue. The problem of competition from "fraudulent" butter continued to plague butter-makers, and in every session of Congress from 1886 to 1902 various bills were introduced to amend the original oleomargarine revenue law. Some proposals sought to repeal the tax, but most of them aimed at subjecting oleomargarine to state laws. Three bills to achieve the latter objective were introduced in the Fifty-sixth Congress and five in the Fifty-seventh. In addition, charges were made of widespread violations of the 1886 statute. By 1900 oleomargarine production had climbed back to more than 100 million pounds annually (43 percent of this was in Illinois), or an increase of 137 percent over that of 1887, and the number of manufacturers had risen back to thirty-two.[26] But, as noted in Congress during debates on other food taxes, the tax on licenses was so high that many oleomargarine dealers ran the risk of violating the law rather than purchase the permit.

By 1902 an additional problem had come to public attention: the practice of renovating rancid butter. Butter deteriorated when it was stored for a long time, or when it became too warm in grocery stores without adequate refrigeration. In the mid-1890s a new process was introduced widely by which this sour butter was accumulated from small retailers, renovated, and then sold, not under its true name of "process" butter, but as the fresh dairy product. The procedure included melting the mass, which permitted the curd and brine to settle. The broth and scum on top and the curd and brine at the bottom were removed, air was blown through the remaining butter-fat to remove odors, and it was then churned with milk and rapidly cooled with icewater. After allowing it to ripen for a few hours, the excess milk was worked off, and salt was added for flavor. The fraud of selling process butter and oleomargarine as pure butter became so widespread that a magazine

---

[24] *United States Code Annotated*, 26 ss 4831.

[25] U.S., Congress, Senate, *Statistics of Oleomargarine, Oleo Oil and Filled Cheese, 1900 and 1901*, Senate Document 168 (Serial 4231), 57 Cong., 1 Sess., 1901, pp. 9–10.

[26] Ibid., pp. 6–7.

article was published describing this process of renovation and suggested a simple test to be performed in the kitchen to detect the good from the bad. The housewife merely had to boil a spoonful. If it boiled "noisily" and "sputtered" it was process butter or oleomargarine; if it boiled quietly and produced very little foam it was pure butter.[27]

The extensive production of process butter plus widespread violations of the oleomargarine law, and the subsequent increase in its production, prompted dairy interests around 1900 to intensify their pressure on Congress for even more discriminatory legislation against imitation butter. There was, however, disagreement on the best course of action. William W. Grout, Republican of Vermont, proposed a new bill in Congress in 1900, but problems of approach developed when the National Dairy Union wanted a ten cent per pound tax and Grout, instead, wanted to authorize states to prohibit importation of oleomargarine. The Plumley decision of 1894 showed no need for the Grout proposal but then the Schollenberger doctrine was announced four years later which struck down the Pennsylvania prohibitory law. Adams discussed this with Grout and Tawney and they decided to combine the two proposals.[28] Grout's revised or new measure would subject oleomargarine to state laws and provide for a new program to help butter manufacturers. It proposed lowering the tax on uncolored oleomargarine to ¼ cent per pound but raising the levy to ten cents per pound on the artificially colored product.[29]

The House Committee on Agriculture held hearings for three months on the proposal with the National Dairy Union presenting favorable testimony for the measure and representatives from the cottonseed oil, meat packers, and stockgrowers interests expressing adverse views. The committee reported the bill favorably to the House, in part because, its sponsors explained, the states were powerless to control the industry. By this time thirty-two states had forbidden the manufacture and sale of colored oleomargarine and West Virginia (in 1891) and South Dakota (in 1897) had joined New Hampshire in requiring it to be colored pink. Despite these efforts, it was estimated that four-fifths of colored oleomargarine was being sold illegally.[30]

[27] *Scientific American* 52 (August 10, 1901) : 21412.
[28] U.S., Congress, Senate, *Hearings on House Bill 9206* (Serial 4235), 57 Cong., 1 Sess., 1901, pp. 295–96.
[29] *Congressional Record*, 56 Cong., 1 Sess., 1900, 33:133.
[30] Ibid., pp. 134–37.

Grout distributed twenty samples of oleomargarine to congressmen and showed them how to lift carefully the enclosing flap of the package to see, cleverly concealed, the label and stamp required by law. The illegal profits from this fraud the previous year, he said, amounted to $15 million. Grout then discussed the Plumley decision, noting the dissent by three justices. If a majority of the Court ever reversed this precedent, he warned, the section of his bill giving priority to state laws would be necessary.[31] He had overlooked the Schollenberger decision, which necessitated the provision.

In contradiction to Grout's claim of widespread violations of the law, Illinois Republican William Lorimer quoted the testimony of the Bureau of Internal Revenue which indicated that there were relatively few breaches of the revenue measure. Rather than raise the tax rate, Lorimer endorsed the Agriculture Committee's minority report which proposed that manufacturers be required to stamp each piece of oleomargarine in sunken letters, as well as labeling the wrapper and box, to prevent possible fraud. Republican James Wadsworth of New York also opposed the Grout bill. He submitted testimony showing oleomargarine to be pure and healthful and argued that Charles X. Knight, secretary of the National Dairy Union, and W. D. Hoard, its current president, had written the tax clause. They then, he claimed, distributed in his and many other congressional districts, a circular depicting an oleomargarine manufacturer dressed in prison garb and giving money to a congressman with the implication that the imitation buttermakers were bribing Congress not to pass the bill. This, he declared, was "a cowardly attack—by innuendo—upon the integrity" of congressmen who had dared to oppose the dairy lobby.[32]

Willis Bailey, Republican of Kansas, too, indicated that there had been considerable pressure on Congress from the dairy industry and also from oleomargarine people. He stated that the National Livestock Association, in its annual convention at Fort Worth, endorsed a resolution condemning the Grout bill. Moreover, when the Committee on Agriculture began hearings, it was "flooded with petitions" from all over the country, but all of these were printed in Chicago by the National Dairy Union. In opposing the measure, Bailey cited the testimony of Harvey Wiley that oleomargarine was a wholesome food and that butter-men hurt themselves by coloring their product. Instead, Wiley suggested, butter should be left uncolored and the consumer would then have no difficulty distinguishing it from oleo-

31 Ibid., pp. 141–42.
32 Ibid., pp. 145–48, 138–39.

margarine. Bailey observed that the national government had consistently used the taxing power in the past to protect American industry, but the Grout bill, if passed, would mark the first time that this power would be used to protect one domestic industry against another. This, he said, would be "a perversion" of the taxing power.[33]

Despite these protests the Grout bill passed the House by vote of 197 to 92 and was sent to the Senate.[34] The Senate Committee on Agriculture reported it without amendments, but it was continually set aside in the upper house, never debated, and died. Although Grout did not return to the Fifty-seventh Congress, his proposal, still known as the Grout bill, was again introduced in 1902 by Republican Edward S. Henry of Connecticut.

The National Association of Dairy and Food Commissioners met in Buffalo on October 17, 1901. They appointed a committee on legislation which met the following January and adopted a resolution calling for a tax of ten cents per pound on artificially colored oleomargarine to prevent fraud.[35] This endorsement of the Grout bill resulted in its being reported favorably by the House Committee on Agriculture. Debate then followed with the same arguments, pro and con, that had been used in Congress since 1886 over the use of the taxing power. One congressman, however, noted that in observing the positions of congressmen on the measure this time, it was less a constitutional issue than a question "of locality."[36]

It had been thought previously that only the manufacturer could color oleomargarine because it had to be heated for the process. The House Committee on Agriculture was invited to visit such a factory in the Capital where they saw oleomargarine colored "in a few minutes, without much difficulty, and without any heating process whatsoever." This convinced many members of the committee that the new method, when it became known, could easily be used to advantage by wholesalers and retailers under the present law, if they were not already doing so.[37]

Proponents of the Grout bill called attention to the fact that, in addition to the National Dairy Union, the presidents of the National Grange and the Women's Industrial and Patriotic League endorsed the measure, as well as 136 editors of farm newspapers. They also played up the known cases of

[33] Ibid., pp. 152–55.
[34] Ibid., p. 186.
[35] U.S., Congress, Senate, *Hearings on House Bill 9206* (Serial 4235), 57 Cong., 1 Sess., 1901, pp. 284–85.
[36] *Congressional Record*, 57 Cong., 1 Sess., 1902, 35:1359.
[37] Ibid., p. 1266.

fraud in the oleomargarine business. Letters from William J. Moxley and Braun & Fitts, large oleomargarine manufacturers, were inserted in the *Congressional Record* which informed retailers that these companies would pay all fines and costs for them to violate the 1886 tax and the state prohibitory laws until they were struck down by the courts as unconstitutional. An official of the Hammond Company in Indiana had recently been arrested for offering the Michigan food commissioner "a standing bribe" to let him sell his product in violation of Michigan law. Walter P. Wilkins, president of the Standard Butterine Company of Washington, D.C., was currently under indictment for fraudulently removing all distinguishing labels and marks from oleomargarine before shipping to distributors. His brother, Joseph, had been convicted for committing a similar offense in the Philadelphia railroad yards. The attorney general had advised President William McKinley against pardoning Joseph Wilkins because he had been a "persistant violator of oleomargarine laws." In 1902 Joseph was the manager of Braun & Fitts, apparently demonstrating to that company how simple it was to remove stamps and labels.[38] Although it was not mentioned in the debates, the Armour Company also made headlines at this time. During his third month in office, Governor Theodore Roosevelt of New York received an offer from Armour to settle its $1.5 million fines imposed for selling oleomargarine as butter for $20,000, which was "flatly refused."[39]

Opponents argued that if the Grout bill were enacted the price of cattle would drop two dollars per head, the price of hogs twenty cents each, and cottonseed oil twenty cents per gallon because the demand for these products would be reduced. They also insisted that the proposal would assist a trust then forming in the creamery business. An Associated Press newspaper article of January 20, 1902, with a Topeka, Kansas, dateline reported that Charles Pattison and John Parks, who owned the Kansas Creamery Trust, had traveled to New York City and had obtained $18 million to form a national creamery trust. The Grout bill, then, would materially aid this giant trust, it was argued. All arguments, however, were to no avail. The motion to recommit the Grout bill lost by a vote of 117 to 162 and the measure passed the House.[40]

When the proposal reached the upper house, senators spent much time

---

[38] Ibid., pp. 1528, 1531, 1618, 3463–64.

[39] William Henry Harbaugh, *The Life and Times of Theodore Roosevelt* (New York, 1966), p. 119.

[40] *Congressional Record*, 57 Cong., 1 Sess., 1902, 35:1547, 1605–6, 1659–60.

debating whether or not the tax would hurt the laboring man. By this time contemporary journals were voicing opinions on the issue. The *Outlook*, soon to become a muckraking magazine, called attention to the 222,788 pounds of oleomargarine shipped into New York in 1899, despite the state's prohibitory law. Although it cost only half as much to make oleomargarine as butter, this imitation butter was being sold at pure butter prices. If this could be stopped and the product sold for what it was, this journal concluded, it could furnish "the poor man who cannot well afford to buy butter with a wholesome substitute for half the price." The Grout bill, therefore, was objectionable because it would merely raise oleomargarine prices.[41] The *Nation*, the long-established magazine of liberal opinion, was certain the proposed tax would "fall with greatest severity on the laboring classes in the cities." The Grout bill was "spoilation"; this journal sorrowfully concluded that the bill would pass because "the butter-makers have the votes" and this was more important than the merits of the proposal.[42]

When Senator William B. Bate, Democrat of Tennessee, presented the minority report of the Committee on Agriculture on the Grout measure, he included testimony from various labor organizations, including the United Mine Workers and the Amalgamated Association of Iron and Steel Workers. These unions argued that butter retailed for thirty-five cents and oleomargarine for twenty cents per pound; if the Grout bill became law, they claimed, butter prices would rise to fifty cents.[43]

Texas Democrat Joseph W. Bailey led the states'-rights opposition. He argued that, if the bill passed, Congress would soon be asked to abolish electric streetcars for the benefit of horses and ban all cotton made to look like wool. "Once enter upon this kind of legislation," he warned, "and . . . it will end only after the Congress of the United States has become a kind of board to settle the rivalries between competing manufacturers . . . according to the power and influence of the rivals."[44] But the only major change the Senate made in the House version was to include a tax on adulterated butter. The bill passed the Senate by vote of 39 to 31; the House concurred in the change on April 24, and President Theodore Roosevelt signed it into law on May 9, 1902.[45]

[41] Harry B. Mason, "The Urgent Need of Pure Food Reform," *Outlook* 65 (June 16, 1900) : 402.
[42] *Nation* 71 (December 27, 1900) : 503.
[43] *Congressional Record*, 57 Cong., 1 Sess., 1902,, 35 : 3198–99.
[44] Ibid., p. 3558.
[45] Ibid., pp. 3614, 4642, 5232.

Oleomargarine was now taxed at ¼ cent per pound if uncolored and ten cents per pound if artificially colored. A tax of ten cents per pound was also levied on adulterated butter with a ¼ cent duty on renovated butter. The distinction between the latter two categories was based on *adulterated butter* being the term used to describe the process of refining various "lots or parcels" of rancid butter by acids or other chemicals, while the renovated type was process butter.[46]

The 1902 tax, because of its discriminatory differential rates on colored and uncolored oleomargarine, was tested in the Supreme Court in one of the most important cases in the constitutional history of this period. In *McCray* v. *United States*, an Ohio retailer appealed his conviction for paying only ¼ cent per pound tax on colored oleomargarine.[47] He based his defense on the fact that, in making the oleomargarine, butter was included which had been artificially colored with Wells-Richardson Improved Butter Color; thus his product was not artificially colored according to the law but had a natural color from the inclusion of butter. McCray also contended that the prohibitory tax would destroy the oleomargarine industry and thus deprive these people of property without due process of law and that it was an unconstitutional invasion of police powers reserved to the states.[48]

The Supreme Court that heard this case was almost entirely different in membership from the one that decided the earlier oleomargarine questions. Fuller was still the chief justice, and John Marshall Harlan remained on the Court. The other seven members of the Bench had been appointed since the *Powell* v. *Pennsylvania* decision.

David Brewer very quickly came under the influence of his famous uncle, Stephen Field, and adopted his constitutional views on laissez-faire and individualism. Henry Brown had several years experience as a district judge prior to his nomination. Rufus Peckham, a Cleveland appointee, was a vigorous exponent of laissez-faire and is best known for writing the decision in *Lochner* v. *New York* in 1905 which forbade states establishing maximum hours of work for bakers. Joseph McKenna, McKinley's only appointee to the Supreme Court, was a faithful party man who consistently supported Republican principles of the period, including laissez-faire.

Two of Theodore Roosevelt's appointees participated in the McCray

---

[46] U.S., *Statutes at Large*, vol. 32.

[47] 195 U.S. 27 (1904). For the importance of this case see Loren P. Beth, *The Development of the American Constitution, 1887–1917* (New York, 1971), pp. 156–57.

[48] *McCray* v. *United States*, Appellate Case #18952, Record Group 267, National Archives.

case. William Day, a former secretary of state and circuit court judge, possessed an odd mixture of conservative and liberal constitutional views. Although he dissented in the Lochner case, he wrote the first child labor decision. Oliver Wendell Holmes, Jr., who became a famous dissenter from the conservative opinions of his colleagues, was a primary exponent of judicial self-restraint. While he was no ardent champion of social reform, he was always willing to allow governmental intervention in social and economic matters if it were policy determined by the people's representatives.[49]

Associate Justice Edward White, who delivered the opinion in the Mc-Cray case, had been appointed by Cleveland. There is some question about Cleveland's reasons for choosing him. White was a leading Southern senator who opposed certain regulatory taxes, including the original 1886 oleomargarine measure before the rate was lowered by the Senate.[50] He also opposed one of Cleveland's major programs, the Wilson-Gorman tariff of 1894. Allan Nevins believed Cleveland concluded that White's elevation to the Supreme Court during the tariff battle "would temporarily weaken the protectionists" in their opposition to his lowering of the tariff rates. But other factors could have been considered. White also was a proponent of a national income tax, which was included in the 1894 tariff, and he dissented when it was declared unconstitutional in 1895 in *Pollock* v. *Farmers' Loan and Trust Company*. This could have influenced Cleveland's thinking as well as White's quoting a message of Cleveland when he argued against a grain futures prohibitory tax in the Senate. In any case, White was a Louisiana sugar planter, a Democrat, an ardent states'-rights senator and a champion of Dual Federalism. His position on the latter was expressed in 1895 when he joined the majority in the famous *Sugar Trust* Case (*United States* v. *E.C. Knight*), which incorporated this principle into constitutional law.

The solicitor general defended the oleomargarine tax by citing the *Kollock* decision that the 1886 tax was a revenue measure and the *McCulloch* v. *Maryland* dictum that "the power to tax involves the power to destroy." He further called attention to the *License Tax* Cases and *Veazie Bank* v. *Fenno* precedents that if the taxing power is used oppressively, resort must be made to the voters and not to the courts.

Justice White's opinion accepted the solicitor general's reasoning. White

[49] William F. Swindler, *Court and Constitution in the Twentieth Century* (Indianapolis, Ind., 1970), vol. 1, chaps. 1–3.

[50] Allan Nevins, *Grover Cleveland* (New York, 1933), p. 571. White's position on these taxes, while a senator, is presented in the next chapter.

asked, and answered, two questions: 1) did McCray artificially color his oleomargarine within the meaning of the law, and 2) was the 1902 tax constitutional? He disposed of the first point by noting that the act declared that anyone "who shall *add to or mix*" any coloring into oleomargarine would be held liable for paying the higher levy. In this case, the product was artificially colored, regardless of the method used, and therefore subject to the larger duty.

The more important issue, the question of the act's constitutionality, received much more attention from the High Tribunal. White cited the *Kollock* case of 1897 to substantiate the concept that the judicial branch cannot restrain a lawful legislative function on the basis that "a wrongful purpose or motive has caused the power to be exercised." In significant terminology the opinion concluded that "on their face they levy an excise tax" and therefore the taxes could not be "judicially restrained because of the results to arise" from their collection. White referred to *Spence* v. *Merchant* in which the Supreme Court determined that "the power to tax may be exercised oppressively upon persons." But legislatures that do so are answerable not to the courts but to the voters who elect the members.

Justice White insisted that courts never declared laws unconstitutional merely because "it appeared to the judicial mind that the particular exercise of constitutional power was either unwise or unjust." To do so, he said, would be an encroachment upon the principle of separation of powers and "a mere act of judicial usurpation."

One of his most pertinent observations was that the concept that the taxing power was restricted by the Fifth and the Tenth amendments rested on the assumption that the courts can inquire into the motives of Congress. He noted that the Supreme Court had already determined that the deceptive nature of oleomargarine permitted states to prohibit its manufacture which did not violate the due process clause of the Fourteenth Amendment. Based on the same premise, he declared, the Fifth Amendment due process clause does not limit the power of the national government to tax.

As long as the tax did not take property without due process of law it would be regarded as public policy and thus valid. But, the Supreme Court opinion warned in a prophetic observation, if the legislature abused the taxing power to the point where it "was plain to the judicial mind that the power had been called into play, not for revenue, but solely for the purpose of destroying rights," the Court would have to strike this down as "an arbitrary act." If Congress attempted to destroy fundamental rights, which are beyond the reach of national power, through prohibitory taxation, this would constitute "the exercise of an authority not conferred," warned White, the former Southern states'-rights senator.

Chief Justice Fuller and Justices Brown and Peckham dissented, with no written opinion, making the outcome a six-to-three decision.[51] In this same year and again in 1909 the Supreme Court affirmed the validity of the ten-cents-per-pound tax on colored oleomargarine despite the defendants' argument that an infinitesimal amount of palm oil was used in the manufacture of the product which "naturally" colored it yellow.[52]

Robert E. Cushman, in analyzing the McCray decision, quoted Senator Edward White's criticism of the 1886 oleomargarine tax when he was in the Senate. Cushman decided that White regarded the original prohibitive tax of ten cents per pound as "objectively unconstitutional," but when the rate was reduced in the final bill it was "objectively constitutional." Yet eighteen years later, Justice White found the ten cent tax to be constitutional. Cushman concluded that the change in White's constitutional views stemmed from his changed position. As a justice of the Supreme Court, White would endorse the traditional presumption of constitutionality of a law unless it was clearly demonstrated otherwise; also he abided by the normal principle of judicial self-restraint on constitutional questions of public policy.[53]

By 1945 oleomargarine was a misnomer because the industry used almost no animal fats or oils. Cottonseed oil and soybean oil, through improved processes of hydrogenation, constituted 98.4 percent of the postwar margarine.[54] Also by this time margarine, being cheaper than butter, was more desired by the housewife during the butter shortage of the war years and the postwar inflationary period. Homemakers were becoming increasingly annoyed with the kitchen chore of mixing the coloring pellet into the spread to save $9\frac{3}{4}$ cents per pound. So a major drive was initiated during

[51] John Barker Waite, "May Congress Levy Money Exactions, Designated 'Taxes,' Solely for the Purpose of Destruction?" *Michigan Law Review* 6 (February 1908) : 277–93, answers his title negatively and notes that "if this decision is correct, it marks a fresh score for the federal government against the strict constructionists and states rights opponents."

[52] *Cliff* v. *United States*, 195 U.S. 159 (1904) ; *Moxley* v. *Hertz*, 216 U.S. 344 (1909).

[53] Robert Eugene Cushman, "The National Police Power under the Taxing Clause of the Constitution," *Minnesota Law Review* 4 (March 1920) :247–81; White's quote is at p. 277.

[54] Alton E. Bailey, *Industrial Oil and Fat Products* (New York, 1951), pp. 279–80.

the Truman administration to repeal the discriminatory tax. It now became an intraparty struggle. Democratic Senator Hubert Humphrey of Minnesota led the butter lobby, fighting to continue the tax, while Democratic Senator J. William Fulbright of Arkansas sought to have it repealed. As usual, congressmen received petitions and other propaganda from both sides. The League of Women Voters, the National Association of Margarine Manufacturers, consumer leagues, and operators of rest homes advocated repeal, while the American Butter Institute, the National Creamery Association, the National Cooperative Milk Producers Association, and various state dairy organizations sought to ward off the attack.[55] Successfully appealing to consumer and labor votes, the Democratic platform of 1948 strongly endorsed "repeal of the discriminatory taxes on the manufacture and sale of oleomargarine."[56]

In pursuance of this promise H.R. 2023 was introduced in the next session of Congress. It passed the House by the overwhelming vote of 287 to 89.[57] The bill was ignored in the Senate in a flurry of debate over the Fair Deal programs and was not discussed until the next session of Congress. Humphrey led the Senate opposition to the bill in 1950, warning of a giant international cartel, Unilever, Limited, that could monopolize the margarine business if the discriminatory tax were repealed. He claimed that the margarine lobby had spent $6.4 million in 1947 and $5.9 million in 1948 in a massive effort to convince the housewife that margarine should be colored at the factory. Fulbright countered with the point that, while six companies controlled 60 percent of the margarine industry, eight dairies controlled 71 percent of the milk in the United States. Butter, he noted, could be misleadingly colored yellow; margarine made from cottonseed oil was naturally yellow and had to be bleached white to avoid the heavy tax. He also pointed out that the public "clamoring" for repeal consisted of 90 percent of the nation's newspapers and most of the radio commentators as well as labor and church groups. The Senate passed the bill 56 to 16 and President Truman signed it on March 16, 1950.[58]

The new law repealed national taxes on oleomargarine but required

[55] For examples of this literature see Files of Senator J. Howard McGrath, Proposed Legislation-Senatorial, H.R. 2023, 81 Cong., Harry S. Truman Library, Independence, Mo.

[56] Kirk E. Porter and Donald Bruce Johnson, comps., *National Party Platforms, 1840–1964* (Urbana, Ill., 1966), p. 434.

[57] *Congressional Record*, 81 Cong., 1 Sess., 1949, 95:3728–29.

[58] Ibid., 81 Cong., 2 Sess., 1950, 96:56–63, 559, 4128.

truthful labeling and margarine could be packaged only in one pound containers or less. If margarine was served in a public establishment the proprietor must notify the customers of such by a sign and serve it in a triangular shape or have its true name stamped on it. Any suggestion that it was a dairy product in any way would be misleading, according to the act, and could lead to action by the Federal Trade Commission.[59] Before Truman signed the bill, the Bureau of the Budget sent a copy to the departments involved—the Federal Security Agency, the Federal Trade Commission, the Department of Agriculture, and the Treasury Department—for analysis. All these agencies responded favorably to the bill. The Federal Security Agency, however, raised the question of inspecting eating establishments to enforce the regulations. It was pointed out that it would require $4 million to inspect the half-million eating places in the United States once a year, compared to the cost of $5 million annually to enforce regulations on all other food, drugs, and cosmetics. The necessary inspection, this agency believed, injected the national government into an area "which, for reasons of comity or constitutional doubt, has heretofore been reserved for control by the States and local authorities under their police powers."[60]

When the 1950 repeal was passed, sixteen states still had discriminatory legislation against oleomargarine. Finally, on May 4, 1967, Wisconsin became the last state to repeal its law and permit the manufacture and sale of colored oleomargarine, although it is heavily taxed.[61] Thus ended the eighty-one year struggle of the oleomargarine business for survival.

Throughout this long battle two elements of argument can be discerned. First it was a continual constitutional argument between states'-rights congressmen and loose constructionists and thus cut across party lines. The strict constructionists feared any extension of national powers. Once the first discriminatory tax was passed others followed. But it was the unique interpretation of the taxing power that startled and frightened them. The loose constructionists, however, believed they were justified in broadly interpreting the national taxing power to control fraud and deception and even, some thought, a health menace posed by some of these products.

Second, it was a continual struggle between two powerful lobbies to protect their interests. For eighty-one years the dairymen were the more

[59] U.S., *Statutes at Large*, vol. 64.
[60] Report of the Bureau of the Budget on H.R. 2023, March 14, 1950, White House Bill File, Truman Papers, Truman Library.
[61] *New York Times*, May 5, 1967.

powerful. In terms of principle, the strict constructionists command respect for their interpretation of the constitutional system. The latter groups, the lobbies, are merely expressions of practical politics within the system. Most important, out of this struggle emerged the principle that Congress would use the taxing power for prohibitive purposes and the Supreme Court would sustain it. When the taxing power was next used to help agriculture, it resulted in a prohibitive tax on grain futures.

5 The Effort
to Tax Grain Futures

As prices of farm products fell rapidly in the 1890s farmers decided, perhaps erroneously, that futures were contributing to the decline. Buying and selling in futures had begun during the Civil War era as a result of the agricultural, transportation, and communications revolutions of the period. For as agricultural production expanded enormously and water and railway transportation provided access to burgeoning urban markets in industrial centers, along with the telegraph permitting rapid communication, new techniques were needed to handle the increase in volume and to adjust to new developments in marketing. The middlemen handling agricultural products gradually evolved the vehicle of "time contracts" or futures to facilitate marketing in the new industrialized society.

Wheat is harvested in the summer and cotton is picked in the fall, for example, yet wheat millers and cotton spinners need constant supplies of raw materials throughout the year in order to keep their mills in continuous operation and to assure a regular flow of finished products to markets. Merchants met this need by developing futures as a method of marketing commodities for the producer and the manufacturer. These agreements, at first verbal but in later years formalized into written contracts by produce exchanges, were promises to deliver to the processor certain quantities of the raw product at particular dates in the future at agreed upon prices. Many times these contracts were made before the crop was harvested or even planted.

As the process for dealing in futures developed, manipulators sought to take advantage of the system. When contracts, promising delivery in certain months in the future, were signed by a person who did not yet have physical possession of the crop, the seller attempted to keep the details secret so as not to affect the future price of the commodity. But the contracts of major operators many times became known in the business world and enterprising speculators would then attempt to corner the supply of the product and thus force up the price at which the futures seller (selling short) had to pay to obtain the article to complete physical delivery. So the practice of options emerged as a form of insurance by which the seller could choose the day of the month for delivery. The manipulators could not hold a corner for very long, certainly not for thirty days, because of storage, interest, and other costs and because of competition. Options would help prevent corners and also assist the seller by permitting him to purchase at the lowest price possible.

Along with the development of futures markets came the practice of "hedging" by which both buyers and sellers protected themselves against future price fluctuations.[1] After making the futures contract they immediately negotiated an opposite contract. The buyer contracted to sell the commodity in the same month at the same price as he actually had contracted to buy and the buyer did the reverse. Obviously, the miller who bought wheat had no intention of selling it but if the price fell before his contract to buy came due, he could sell his hedge and then buy at the lower price. The hedger had no intention literally of completing his hedging contract. Usually the parties to these contracts settled them not by physical delivery but by cash settlement of the difference in contract price and current market price. Often a hedger sold his contract to another hedger. The exchange, through its clearinghouse, settled these contracts by a process of cancellation called "ringing out." These practices were often carried to excesses, especially by unscrupulous speculators, and financial abuses by exchanges led to some 330 bills being introduced in Congress from 1884 to 1953 to control futures trading.[2]

Futures markets came from the need to shift the price risk of physical ownership.[3] These risks are shifted from hedgers to speculators who buy

---

[1] Erwin A. Gaumnitz, ed., *Futures Trading Seminar* (Madison, Wis., 1960–1966), 3:4, 15, states that futures first began in the United States in 1867 and hedging started in the 1880s. Stanley Dumbell, "The Origin of Cotton Futures," *Economic History* 1 (May 1927) : 259, notes that futures evolved along with improved communications. He points out that selling cotton "in transit," which was the forerunner of futures, began in New York City in 1851 soon after the development of the telegraph.

[2] Gaumnitz, *Futures Trading Seminar*, 1:17–19.

[3] Harold S. Irwin, *Evolution of Futures Trading* (Madison, Wis., 1954), pp. 50–60; Julius B. Baer and Olin Glenn Saxon, *Commodities Exchanges and Futures Trading* (New York, 1949), pp. 197–250, is excellent on hedging.

and sell futures contracts, gambling that future prices of the commodities will fluctuate to their advantage. Hedgers, on the other hand, are not concerned with price fluctuations because they are protected through their time contracts. A processor will normally hedge, both on raw materials and on the finished product. A typical flour miller would normally carry a two-month supply of wheat; yet bakers want assurance of flour six months in advance. So the miller buys wheat months in the future and hedges it to protect against price rises. At the same time he sells flour in futures to the baker and buys a hedge in flour futures to protect himself against a drop in flour prices. By this means he is protected, although not absolutely, against price fluctuations either way and makes his profit through milling operations. Because he operates on a narrow margin of profit, he does not wish to take risks. He thus shifts the risk to the speculator who is willing to gamble.

This, of course, is the simplified procedure.[4] It becomes much more complicated when the processor faces a market with twenty to thirty grades of cotton or many grades of wheat. His mill grinds a certain grade of wheat to produce a certain quality of flour. Thus he must also, through time contracts, guarantee availability of his grade of wheat and quality of flour to maintain his reputation. The same holds true for the cotton industry.

A typical transaction by a cotton merchant will suffice to illustrate these operations. Assume that middling (average grade), one-inch staple cotton is selling at 10.5 cents in January on the spot (cash) market while May futures is selling at 10 cents. Company A contracts to sell and deliver to Company B in May at 13 cents, a price that includes costs of transportation and a profit. A hedge is then made to purchase the cotton in May at 10 cents. Before delivery date the company is able to buy the grade of cotton at 9.5 cents or a half-cent below the price when the contracts were made in January. But in the meantime the price of May futures declined to 11 cents or a two-cent drop. The company buys the physical cotton for delivery and closes out the hedge by paying the difference of two cents per pound. The company lost 1.5 cents per pound, or realized only one cent for costs and profit. This illustrates that hedges are not perfect, but the company has

---

[4] The problem of congressmen attempting to control futures is well exemplified by "Sockless" Jerry Simpson of Kansas. He campaigned in 1896 on the issue of abolishing futures. When asked later why he failed to carry out his promise on this in Congress, he replied, "I found out a whole lot of things about the grain market I did not know when I was making those speeches before." Quoted in *Congressional Record*, 67 Cong., 1 Sess., 1921, 61:1312, by the current congressman from Simpson's congressional district, Jasper "Poly" Tincher.

minimized its risks. If the cash price difference had been one cent cheaper instead of half a cent, and the future price had declined one cent, instead of two, the company would have realized a total profit, including costs, of its expected 2.5 cents. On the other hand, the gambling speculator won by betting correctly that the spot market would not decline as much as the futures price. If the reverse had happened, he would have sustained a serious loss. It is of considerable consequence that an estimated 75 to 90 percent of these speculators lose significantly.[5]

Many economists are convinced that futures markets, operated legitimately, tend to keep prices higher for the producer than would a pure cash, or spot, market.[6] If the processor were not protected by his time contract he would be forced to pay lower prices to the producers in the crop-moving period to protect against the risk of a price decline months later and to make provision for storage costs. But in searching for explanations of low prices in the 1890s many farmers, and congressmen representing rural constituencies, concluded that futures speculators were at least part of the agricultural problem. When the annual wheat and cotton crops were sold ten or even twenty times over each year, this lent credence to the belief of the uninitiated farmer that speculation in futures resulted in either higher prices for consumers or lower prices for farmers than would occur in a cash market system. Agrarians soon became convinced that more and more of their hard-earned profits fell into the hands of manipulators who did not till the soil but who made huge profits, from the sweat of farmers, by dealing in futures. As one congressional committee report stated, these "speculative gamblers . . . toil not, neither do they spin, and yet gather a golden harvest" from the fruits of farmers' toil.[7]

With an increase in agricultural agitation, bills began to appear in Congress to control futures. In 1887 two measures were presented to the House to restrict futures dealings. These proposals were sent from the Committee on the Judiciary to the Committee on Agriculture which recommended they be tabled. The committee agreed that "the demoralizing effects of these gambling transactions are destructive to public morals" and voted unan-

---

[5] Gaumnitz, *Futures Trading Seminar*, 3:23. Abba P. Lerner, *Everbody's Business* (New York, 1961), chapt. 6, makes the important point that speculators are "socially useful" because they improve the use of resources so long as they do not become "socially harmful" in achieving corners and monopolies.

[6] Irwin, *Evolution of Futures Trading*, pp. 63–69.

[7] U.S., Congress, House, Report 1321 (Serial 2811), 51 Cong., 1 Sess., 1890, pp. 1–2.

imously that they should be suppressed by law. But the committee could find "no grant of power in the constitution for congressional action" because these contracts involved the "question of morals" which was in the province of state-reserved powers. And, the committee added, the jurisdiction of the states in these matters "is ample and exclusive."[8]

Then in 1890 Congressman Benjamin Butterworth, Republican of Ohio, introduced a measure, based on the principle of the 1886 oleomargarine law, to tax dealers in futures and options.[9] It was reported out of committee but never came to a vote. According to one authority, however, this proposal "served to stir up interest in the subject" and in the next Congress "a determined effort was made" to tax futures.[10] By this time farm prices were declining rapidly and the Committee on Agriculture reversed its position concerning the power of the states being "ample and exclusive."

Several measures to regulate futures were introduced in the first session of the Fifty-second Congress, and the House Committee on Agriculture reported H.R. 7845. The committee strongly urged passage of this bill not only to raise revenue but also to "relieve the producer of the destructive competition" resulting from trading in futures and short selling. Enactment of the measure, the committee report stated, would reinstate that "free action which has been destroyed by the practice of 'short selling' " through which prices were determined even before the planting of crops. This legislation, the committee declared, would "restore to the producer an honest market and such prices as will follow the unfettered operation of the law of supply and demand." The proposal would require a $1,000 license fee of all dealers in futures and would place a five-cent-per-pound tax on all cotton, hops, pork, lard, and bacon futures, and a twenty-cent-per-bushel tax on wheat, corn, oats, rye, barley, grass seed, and flax seed futures.[11]

When William Hatch introduced the measure on the floor of the House, he noted that the trading procedures which the bill sought to eliminate were not opposed by any board of trade representatives appearing before his Committee on Agriculture during the hearings. The rules of all the nation's boards of trade officially forbade these proceedings, he said. The problems

[8] U.S., Congress, House, Report 4141 (Serial 2675), 50 Cong., 2 Sess., 1888, pp. 1–2.

[9] *Congressional Record*, 51 Cong., 1 Sess., 1890, 21:706.

[10] G. Wright Hoffman, "Governmental Regulation of Exchanges," *Annals of the American Academy of Political and Social Sciences* 155 (May 1931):48.

[11] U.S., Congress, House, Report 969 (Serial 3045), 52 Cong., 1 Sess., 1891, pp. 1–2.

arose after the public doors were closed on their business activities in the early afternoons, he observed, after which "millions and millions of wind products" were bought and sold unofficially by the members of these boards.[12] In arguing for the proposal, Edward H. Funston, a Kansas Republican, referred to John Marshall's famous dictum in *McCulloch* v. *Maryland*: "That the power to tax involves the power to destroy." He bluntly stated that in this instance he wanted to abolish trading in "wind" commodities. "I do not disguise the fact that all we want to do is to destroy this system," he declared, "which has been ruining the agricultural interests of the country."[13]

States'-rights congressmen immediately protested this enlargement of national power. Hilary A. Herbert, Democrat of Alabama, opposed the measure because it invaded the police power reserved to the states to regulate contracts between citizens. The bill, Herbert intoned, "sets the most dangerous precedent that can possibly be conceived." Charles Boatner, Louisiana Democrat, agreed, calling it "a vicious prostitution of the taxing power to accomplish a purpose admittedly beyond the lawful jurisdiction of Congress." Isidore Rayner, Democrat of Maryland, insisted the bill would destroy "every conception of State sovereignty, and if carried to its legitimate conclusions will gradually extinguish all the well-defined distinctions" that had been erected between the national government and "the rights of every State to legislate within the domain of its own jurisdiction."[14]

Minnesota Democrat James Castle described proponents of the bill as "simply the cat's-paws of a syndicate of elevator operators" who wanted to achieve monopoly over the grain markets. These few entrepreneurs would then be able to force down the price of wheat, he declared, as they were able to do eight years previously, before the current futures trading in wheat and flour had fully developed. Debate was quite brief and, despite these objections, the House passed the bill that same day by vote of 167 to 46 with 116 not voting.[15]

H.R. 7845 was then sent to the Senate where it was reported favorably by the Committee on Judiciary. The minority on the Senate committee, however, objected to futures being taxed as this was a "perversion" of the

---

12 *Congressional Record*, 52 Cong., 1 Sess., 1892, 23:5073.
13 Ibid., p. 5077.
14 Ibid., p. 5074.
15 Ibid., pp. 5075, 5077–78.

taxing power. The problem, the minority stated, should be handled instead through the power to control interstate commerce.[16]

Senate opposition to the Hatch bill was voiced by George Vest, Missouri Democrat. Vest declared that if he could vote for this proposal he should be able to vote for Congress to "take into its exclusive control all the police powers of the country and exclude the states entirely." He could not support the measure because his party opposed "using the revenue or taxing power of the country as a police power." He noted that the Pillsbury flour interests had sent lawyers to testify before congressional committees for the proposal and had "deluged" congressmen with petitions to pass the bill. The measure was necessary, the company representatives had argued, in order to help the "downtrodden and oppressed farmer." But, Vest suggested, the company was actually motivated by the desire to lower the price of wheat they purchased.[17]

Democratic Senator Edward White of Louisiana delivered the most significant speech opposing the Hatch bill. He argued that because these were contracts the national government could no more regulate them than any other state-controlled contracts for marriage, divorce, property titles, or wills. This was an unconstitutional use of the taxing power, he insisted. White noted that he was as much opposed to lotteries as anyone. Yet when his Louisiana constituents had pressed him to introduce a bill in Congress to tax them out of existence, he refused, saying, "Great as is this evil, there is an evil yet greater, and that is the disruption and the destruction of our Government by calling upon the Federal Government to do an illegal, and unconstitutional thing."

Senator White presented a very concise, elaborate argument in terms of a law being "objectively constitutional" yet "subjectively unconstitutional." He agreed that if the futures tax became law, the Supreme Court would hold it to be constitutional "because we have breathed into this law a living lie, because we will have declared that our purpose is to tax for revenue, when every line and every letter of the bill says the bill is not an exercise of the taxing power at all, but an attempt to destroy the very framework of the Constitution by going into the State and doing that which the Federal Government confessedly has no power to do."

To substantiate his distinction between "objective" and "subjective" constitutionality, White quoted Grover Cleveland's message concerning the

[16] U.S., Congress, Senate, Report 893 (Serial 2915), 52 Cong., 1 Sess., 1891, p. 1.
[17] *Congressional Record*, 52 Cong., 1 Sess., 1892, 23:6437–41.

1886 oleomargarine tax: a tax is objectively constitutional if it raises revenue, but subjectively unconstitutional if it operates to destroy. The same principle applied to a tax on futures contracts, White insisted.[18] This speech, couched in elaborate constitutional rhetoric, was generally regarded as having prompted Cleveland to appoint White as an associate justice of the Supreme Court in 1894.[19]

The Hatch bill was passed over several times and was finally reconsidered in the second session of the Fifty-second Congress. At this point Senator William D. Washburn, Republican of Minnesota and member of a prominent flour-manufacturing family, called attention to the various interest groups that were trying to delay a Senate vote on the bill. He read into the *Congressional Record* a telegram sent to him from New Orleans. The person sending this message noted that the many telegrams being sent to senators from "cotton speculators and cotton-speculating towns" asking for a delay in voting, resulted from a plot to exaggerate reports of a small cotton crop and "unload at higher prices" before "innocent outsiders" discovered there was a plentiful supply of cotton for that year. Early passage of the futures bill, Washburn declared, would "interfere with their plans," which prompted these dilatory activities.[20]

Democrat James George of Mississippi delivered a lengthy speech describing how commodities exchanges could affect farm prices. He stated that speculators had managed to stimulate "a considerable agitation against the antioption bill down South." Whenever these people wanted to increase this unrest, he said, they merely reported that consideration of the Hatch bill was destroying cotton prices. When they desired to perform a similar operation in the West, these manipulators maintained that the uncertainty over passage of the measure was responsible for the decline in wheat and corn prices. Actually, he declared, whenever it was generally believed probable that the bill would be enacted, speculators "deliberately forced down prices"; then when it was periodically reported that the measure would fail, they allowed prices to rise slightly, only to repeat the process.[21]

Senator William Peffer, the famous Kansas Populist, agreed that pressure from special interests was causing the prolonged Senate delay in voting on the proposal. He observed that futures speculators had defenders in

---

18 Ibid., pp. 6516–19.
19 U.S., Congress, Senate, Report 508 (Serial 8525), 64 Cong., 1 Sess., 1925, p. 74.
20 *Congressional Record*, 52 Cong., 2 Sess., 1892, 24:85.
21 Ibid., p. 164.

"every great city and in every line of business." These economic groups enjoyed special advantages due to a long list of previous legislation designed
to assist them and were "parts of one stupendous wrong which has grown
up under our vicious laws." This wrong, vested interest, he warned, resulted
in all the special interests rushing to the rescue of any of the parts that might
be injuriously affected by proposed reform legislation.[22]

Major opposition to the Hatch bill again came from Senator White. He
argued that futures markets were necessary in the system of marketing.
Contrary to farmers' beliefs, White insisted, futures contracts did not
interfere with the operation of the law of supply and demand, but rather
permitted the producer to receive higher prices. To prove this, he cited
statistics on production and sales of cotton over a period of years, both
before and after cotton futures were developed.

White objected to the measure specifically because it would legalize
futures and options but make such contracts taxable if negotiated through
an organized exchange. This, he declared, was a "flagrant and . . . outrageous example of class legislation. I say let us bear in mind the elementary
conception of American freedom. Let us adhere to them, and let us not
follow every jack o' the lantern which leads us to give up the faith and the
hope of our fathers. Our principles are everlasting, for they are true. If the
methods of dealing [in futures] are condemned, strike them down, but do
not go further and strike at persons and places [boards] of exchange by a
discrimination as unjust as it is unamerican."[23]

Fearing passage of the bill, White proposed an amendment to include
dealing in flour futures which was accepted. The Senate also deleted the
House provisions on grass seed and flax seed. The measure then passed the
Senate January 31, 1893, by vote of 49 to 29.[24] When it was returned to
the House, the flour change proved the major stumbling block to its
approval.

Democrat William J. Coombs of New York and other opponents of the
futures tax emphasized that flour millers were pressuring Congress to pass
the bill without the flour futures addition so that they would then be able
to set flour prices. Coombs had reprinted in the *Congressional Record* a

[22] Ibid., p. 298.

[23] Ibid.. p. 315; his lengthy speech is in ibid., pp. 930–52.

[24] Ibid., p. 995. Cedric B. Cowing, *Populists, Plungers, and Progressives* (Princeton, N.J., 1965), p. 22, analyzes the vote on this bill and notes that the "anti-speculator"
tier of states (North Dakota, South Dakota, Nebraska, Kansas, Texas) had a 100
percent favorable vote in the House and 77.7 percent in the Senate.

news story of the recent formation of the Spring Wheat Millers' Association. This organization held meetings in December 1892 which resulted in "nearly every mill from Duluth to Boston" joining the combination which, if the Hatch bill became law, could then control flour prices for the nation, without the check upon them provided by futures speculators. This threat of monopoly was sufficient. The House refused, by vote of 172 to 124, to suspend the rules and accept the Senate version, which required a two-thirds vote, and the two houses were unable to agree upon a compromise version.[25]

The next year Hatch introduced a new measure to tax futures and options. His bill, debated in June 1894, proposed a license fee for futures dealers and would compel delivery of the products or the seller would be taxed. This tax would amount to the difference between the contract price and the current spot market price of the commodity which, he hoped, would eliminate the transactions in "wind" products. Again he omitted flour futures and again the opposition raised the specter of the Flour Trust. Congressmen called attention to the omission of flour futures in both this and the 1893 proposal, noting the relationship between the Pillsbury milling interests and the Washburn milling company. Opponents suggested that Hatch had omitted flour futures in order to gain the support of Senator Washburn of Minnesota for his bill. An amendment to add flour futures to the measure then easily won acceptance and the proposal passed the House 150 to 89.[26] It was reported in the Senate but never debated. The Democrats lost control of Congress in the elections of 1894 and, although they repeatedly introduced bills to tax futures during the next few years, none was debated in either house.

The next year two bills were introduced in the first session of the Fifty-fourth Congress, one to prevent and one to tax futures and options. In every session of Congress thereafter, through the Sixty-second Congress, one or more bills were submitted to prohibit, to tax, to prevent gambling in futures, or to deny dealers in futures access to the means of interstate communications. The first session of the Sixtieth Congress marked the high point in the number of such bills with a total of fourteen. None of these measures, however, was reported out of committee until 1910.[27]

Evidence seems to indicate that the early attempts to tax grain futures failed in part because proponents of the idea could not agree on their ap-

[25] *Congressional Record*, 52 Cong., 2 Sess., 1892, 24:2355, 2357–58.
[26] Ibid., 53 Cong., 2 Sess., 1894, 26:6481, 6724.
[27] The result of this proposal will be traced in the next chapter.

proach. The question of whether to exercise the congressional power to tax or to control the problem through the use of the interstate commerce power helped to frustrate this first effort to regulate futures trading. In addition, party discipline was involved. The measure was sponsored by Democrats who controlled the House at that time, yet the leadership was unable to persuade enough Southern states'-rights Democrats of the necessity of voting for the bill.

Returning agricultural prosperity in 1897 ended the "first period of anti-speculator agitation" in Congress.[28] During consideration of the Hatch bills, Senator Peffer undertook a major study of the current agricultural depression. His report of 1894 was submitted to the Senate by the Committee on Agriculture and Forestry in early 1895. Peffer decided that futures and options constituted one of the significant causes of depressed farm prices particularly because they "injuriously affected" wheat prices. His report demanded that futures and options "be abolished and prohibited under heavy penalties."[29] But despite this report Congress took no action on futures until World War I.

Congress and the public again became concerned over futures contracts during the presidency of Woodrow Wilson. In 1914 cotton futures were taxed and in the Sixty-fifth Congress several bills were introduced to tax or to prohibit all types of futures. Then with United States entry into the war necessitating a significant increase in revenue, the House Ways and Means Committee recommended taxing grain futures contracts.[30] In October 1917 Congress enacted the War Revenue Act which contained a host of nuisance taxes, including a minimal levy of two cents per $100 on all futures.[31] The wheat provision in the Food Control Act of 1917, however, prohibited futures dealings in wheat and it was not until July 1920 that the Chicago Board of Trade resumed trading in wheat futures.[32]

Congressional concern over grain futures following World War I was expressed in a resolution directing the Federal Trade Commission to investigate the futures markets. The resulting intensive study by the FTC was

[28] Cowing, *Populists, Plungers, and Progressives*, p. 24.

[29] U.S., Congress, Senate, Report 787, "Agricultural Depression: Causes and Remedies" (Serial 3288), 53 Cong., 2 Sess., 1894, pp. 33–35, 102.

[30] U.S., Congress, House, Report 45 (Serial 7252), 65 Cong., 1 Sess., 1917, p. 8.

[31] U.S., *Statutes at Large*, vol. 40. This tax was lowered to one cent per $100 in the Revenue Act of 1924; ibid., vol. 43.

[32] For the debates on this measure see Cowing, *Populists, Plungers, and Progressives*, pp. 80–84.

the most thorough one yet made of the grain trade and was published in seven volumes from 1920 to 1926. This investigation concentrated on the operations of the Chicago Board of Trade because this market handled "six-sevenths of the future trading of grain in the United States."[33] The report stressed the necessity of futures markets for hedging purposes; this in turn required the presence of speculators willing to buy and sell these contracts. "Measures looking to the elimination of merely gambling and other injurious or incompetent elements in futures trading," the report continued, however, "would probably not injure the market but would rather, on the whole, increase its efficiency." In the final volume, published in 1926, the FTC urged "administrative supervision along the lines of present grain futures legislation."[34] Congress, with the prodding of the farm bloc, had enacted the legislation referred to in 1921 and 1922.

When wheat futures trading resumed in 1920, a bill was introduced in Congress that December to tax these contracts. The House Committee on Agriculture heard eighty witnesses, took 1,070 pages of testimony, and unanimously recommended enactment of a futures tax sponsored by two Kansas Republicans, Arthur Capper in the Senate and Jasper "Poly" Tincher who then represented the district in Kansas that had elected "Sockless" Jerry Simpson to Congress during the Populist Crusade. The measure, it was reported by the committee, had the approval of the secretary of agriculture, the grain trade in general, and farmers and their organizations, including the National Grange, the Farmers' Union, and the American Farm Bureau Federation. The bill, the committee declared, would not affect the "legitimate hedge," but would "absolutely destroy manipulation" in the grain trade.[35] Capper's Senate Committee on Agriculture and Forestry also recommended the proposal. The Senate report noted that speculators required a fluctuating market for successful operations while producers needed a stable one. The measure would stabilize grain markets and also "eliminate . . . some of the undesirable practices of professional speculators."[36]

When Tincher introduced his bill on the floor of the House he described the committee hearings on the measure, noting that representatives of grain

[33] Federal Trade Commission, "Future Trading Operations in Grain," vol. 5 of *Report on the Grain Trade* (Washington, D.C., 1920), p. 43.

[34] Ibid., 7:2, 9, 279.

[35] U.S., Congress, House, Report 44 (Serial 7920), 67 Cong., 1 Sess., 1921, p. 2.

[36] U.S., Congress, Senate, Report 212 (Serial 7918), 67 Cong., 1 Sess., 1921, p. 4.

exchanges had always previously resisted such legislation. This time, "much to our surprise," Tincher said, the exchanges favored his proposal and "it rather frightened" him. He asked the first produce-board witness the reason for the switch and received this reply: "We have promised you repeatedly that we would eliminate the evils occurring in the grain exchanges —we get home and some of us eliminate the evils, but some little exchange will not and we eventually have to come back to that evil in order to protect our own exchange."[37] Apparently the major exchanges were now willing to accept national controls in order to force conformity upon smaller and, to them, irresponsible boards.

Republican Edward Voight of Wisconsin informed his colleagues that the committee had considered use of the interstate commerce power but had decided instead to use the taxing power to regulate grain exchanges because of the intrastate nature of many of the transactions. The committee, therefore, "had recourse to the taxing power which, as is well known, includes the power to destroy."[38]

Tincher's measure sought particularly to abolish the practice of "puts" and "calls." *Indemnity* was a synonym used by the trade for these terms. These indemnities were the privilege a speculator purchased for, say five dollars per thousand bushels, that would permit him the option of buying wheat at a certain price before the market closed the following day. A "put" was purchased in hopes that the price would advance. If it did not, the speculator forfeited his privilege money. A "call" was the reverse—an option to sell. When asked if the proposed prohibitive tax on these activities would be constitutional, Texas Democrat Marvin Jones responded that Congress possessed "the taxing power absolutely." His interrogator then posed the obvious sequential question of why the proponents did not just prohibit these activities outright. If that approach were used, Jones replied, "a constitutional question might arise" but the Supreme Court had "allowed us to go a long ways in the taxing power," so he believed this was the "wiser method."[39]

In the following day's debate Tincher described the "flood of telegrams" congressmen had received the previous day, opposing his measure, as being "the same old propaganda." They were "all in the same language" and some were "forgeries," Tincher insisted, because they were "ostensi-

---

[37] *Congressional Record*, 67 Cong., 1 Sess., 1921, 61:1313.
[38] Ibid., pp. 1323–24.
[39] Ibid., p. 1316.

bly" signed by grain trade representatives who had testified favorably for his bill when it was in committee. The House then passed his measure by vote of 269 to 69.[40]

Capper sponsored the bill in the upper house and, in introducing it to his fellow-senators, "summarized the evils in the marketing system" which the proposal sought "to correct." These evils, Capper said, were a) market manipulation by large operators; b) promiscuous and unrestricted speculation in foodstuffs; c) dissemination of false crop information; d) gambling in indemnities or "puts" and "calls"; and e) arbitrary interference with the law of supply and demand. That these "evils exist and should be eliminated," Capper declared, "is not challenged," so this measure would place responsibility "upon the boards of trade to correct the evils." Capper answered the question of constitutionality of the proposed tax by declaring that in the case of "McRae [*sic*] v.the United States, . . . the Supreme Court . . . expressly said that the power of Congress to tax is its broadest power; and that the courts would not inquire into the reason for the use of the power." He was advised, he said, "by able lawyers that the proposed law is entirely constitutional."[41] The Senate approved the measure without a roll call vote and President Warren G. Harding signed it on August 24, 1921.[42]

The Future Trading Act of 1921 regulated boards of trade selling wheat, corn, oats, barley, rye, flax, and sorghum. It placed a tax of twenty cents per bushel on indemnities or "puts and calls," "bids," "offers," or "ups and downs" to be paid by the seller. This heavy tax would effectively destroy this practice. Section 4 levied an identical tax on all futures contracts unless the seller had physical possession of the commodity or the contracts were made by or through a member of a board of trade designated by the secretary of agriculture as a "contract market." The law regulated these contract markets by prohibiting them from disseminating false crop or price reports or manipulating prices and forcing them to accept agricultural cooperatives as members. The secretaries of agriculture and commerce and the attorney general were empowered to suspend or revoke the designation of "contract market" if any board of trade violated these regulations.[43]

The Future Trading Act was soon challenged and a case reached the

40 Ibid., pp. 1371, 1429.
41 Ibid., pp. 4763, 4764.
42 Ibid., pp. 4771, 5864.
43 U.S., *Statutes at Large*, vol. 42.

Supreme Court the next year. In *Hill* v. *Wallace* the high court declared Section 4 to be an unconstitutional abuse of the taxing power because it clearly sought to regulate exchanges, which was a state prerogative, and not to raise revenue.[44] Tincher and Capper immediately introduced bills in Congress to reenact the measure under the power to control interstate commerce. The House committee report recommending Tincher's bill noted that from May 15 (the date of the Hill decision) to May 31, 1922, May wheat contracts dropped thirty-two cents and yet there was no visible sign of an increased supply of wheat nor any favorable crop report during that time. This decline, the report concluded, resulted from speculators feeling "perfectly free to manipulate, as they evidently did."[45] The Senate committee report called attention to the Supreme Court suggestion in *Hill* v. *Wallace* that "if Congress should find that they [boards of trade contracts] are conducted under such conditions as to obstruct or burden interstate commerce they are subject to the regulatory power of Congress." The committee had found them to be an obstruction and, the report continued, "the Supreme Court attaches great importance to congressional findings." Because of the sharp drop in wheat prices following the Hill decision, the report emphasized that there was "an urgent demand for Federal supervision of the boards of trade."[46]

Congress quickly passed the Grain Futures Act of 1922, which declared that activities of boards of trade were of public interest and a problem of interstate commerce.[47] The power to control interstate commerce was invoked to establish the same regulations and to prohibit the same practices as those contained in the tax law of the previous year. Thus, after three decades of effort, agrarian congressmen were successful in controlling grain futures and eliminating the most flagrant abuses in futures markets, although not through the taxing power. In the meantime attempts were made, through the taxing power, to assist Southern farmers in controlling cotton markets.

[44] 259 U.S. 44 (1922). The constitutionality of this and the child labor tax will be considered in detail in Chapter 9.

[45] U.S., Congress, House, Report 1095 (Serial 7957), 67 Cong., 2 Sess., 1922, p. 2.

[46] U.S., Congress, Senate, Report 871 (Serial 7951), 67 Cong., 2 Sess., 1922, pp. 4–8.

[47] U.S., *Statutes at Large*, vol. 43. For a good study of the operation of this law prior to the New Deal, see William R. Johnson, "Herbert Hoover and the Regulation of Grain Futures," *Mid-America* 59 (July 1969) : 155–74.

6 *The Taxation of Cotton Futures*

When the effort to tax futures failed in the 1890s, congressmen representing farmers continued the struggle. None of the numerous bills introduced in Congress in the following decade, however, were reported out of committee until the Taft administration. During this period congressmen focused their attention on cotton futures and especially on the New York Cotton Exchange. The increased interest in the cotton futures markets resulted from a major investigation of the cotton exchanges of the United States, following a poor cotton crop.

A bad storm in the Gulf of Mexico area occurred in 1906 which caused an unusually large amount of low-grade cotton to be marketed that year. Such a development should have brought a significant drop in prices on the lower grades of cotton for futures contracts, but the New York market artifically held these prices up which, of course, hurt merchant hedgers. This situation aroused congressmen from cotton districts, and the House of Representatives passed a resolution requesting the Bureau of Corporations to make a systematic study of cotton markets. Instructions given the bureau called for an investigation of the causes of price fluctuations in cotton. Specifically, the House wanted to know if these price gyrations resulted from dealing in cotton futures contracts or if speculators were able, through "conspiracies," to manipulate prices. A year later Herbert Knox Smith, chief of the bureau, submitted his findings.

The report, dated May 4, 1908, was the most thorough investigation yet conducted by a public agency concerning futures contracts and constituted a major reference for several years for reform-minded congressmen. The 648-page study outlined the procedures used by exchanges regarding classification, or grading, of cotton and the determination of "difference" in futures contracts. After discussing the process and necessity of hedging by merchants, the Smith report concluded that futures contracts were vital in the marketing and processing of cotton in order to eliminate as nearly as possible the price risks of cotton merchants and spinners. The role of speculators in this process was justified on the grounds that these people were willing "to take a large share of this risk."[1]

The report noted that dealing in cotton futures arose as a result of the Civil War and postwar developments. During and immediately after the war huge profits could be made in cotton because of the demand and the un-certain supply. With these conditions the spinner, contracting to sell finished goods, did not want to depend on widely fluctuating daily prices yet also could not buy his entire stock at once. At the same time the seizure of a blockade runner with a load of cotton was a major event, due to the shortage of raw cotton; when news of a capture arrived in port, enterprising spec-ulators would promise to sell the cotton "to arrive," hoping to be able to purchase the confiscated cargo. Then with the successful laying of the trans-Atlantic cable in 1866, speculators in Liverpool, the world's largest cotton market, began in 1868 to contract sales of cotton "to arrive" follow-ing news of the departure of a cargo of cotton from the United States. The practice of dealing in cotton futures arose out of the postwar economic chaos of the South. Although several cotton exchanges were subsequently estab-lished in the United States to handle futures contracts, only those in New Orleans and New York survived into the twentieth century.

These two exchanges, the Bureau of Corporations found, had developed different procedures for marketing cotton. While the report emphasized the necessity of futures and hedging, particular features of the system, espe-cially certain practices on the New York Exchange, were condemned. The New York system of grading cotton and the method of fixing difference par-ticularly received sharp criticism.

The hedging process, it was noted, was complicated by the grading systems used. While each spinner used a different grade, of course, "even running" cotton, or all cotton of the same grade, was desirable for his operations. "Even running" lots of cotton, then, commanded a higher price than mixed grades. The spot merchant, as a result, tried to sell his "even running" cotton in the spot market and use the futures market to dispose of his mixed grades. Spinners, using the futures market, were faced with the

[1] U.S., Congress, House, Document 912 (Pts. 1 and 2), 949 (Pts. 1 and 2) (Serial 5322), 60 Cong., 1 Sess., 1907. No. 949 is basically an elaboration of No. 912.

problem of receiving mixed lots and usually cotton of the lower grades. When the Smith investigation was initiated, the New York Exchange used thirty grades for classifying cotton; when the report was submitted in 1908, both the New York and New Orleans markets used eighteen classifications. The grading was conducted by a special committee of the exchange and paid for by the seller. The grade of cotton was based upon the length of fiber, its lack of deterioration, and the amount of dirt, trash, or discoloring in it. Futures contracts were based upon a minimum of 50,000 pounds or 100 bales of 500 pounds each; the contracts were written for one grade using the "middling," or average, grade of cotton as the basis. Because of climate, soil, weather conditions, care in picking, ginning, and a host of factors, cotton varied widely in grades. Thus, under the minimum contract, a spinner would receive a wide variety of cotton, even with the use of only eighteen classes. Spinners, therefore, usually tried to buy in the spot market to see what they were getting and used the futures market to hedge.[2]

Because of the changes in transportation during the Industrial Revolution, the New York Cotton Exchange underwent a transformation in the latter part of the nineteenth century. Early in its career the New York market, with its great port, was a major spot market for New England spinners. Then as railroad mileage multiplied, New Englanders were able to obtain cheaper "through" rates from Southern spot markets, so the New York Exchange gradually declined as a spot market. The increasing wealth of the South, following the economic devastation of the war and Reconstruction, a subsequent decrease in dependence on Wall Street banks for financing, and an increase in textile milling in the South, contributed to this decline. In time the New York Exchange carried just enough spot cotton to meet the minimal demands for physical delivery. And as this market became increasingly a futures market, these few deliveries diminished in number.

Because it cost approximately $1.50 per bale to ship the cotton from the South to New York, the Exchange tended to hold the grades selling most cheaply to make up this difference in transportation costs, compared with the New Orleans market which handled more spot transactions, less futures, and better grades of cotton.[3] Although no public records were kept, a senator alleged in 1914 that the New York market at that time had annual

    [2] Ibid., 912, p. vi.

    [3] Ibid., 949, pp. 49–51. Harold D. Woodman, *King Cotton and His Retainers* (Lexington, Ky., 1968), pp. 270–79, discusses some of the developments giving rise to cotton futures.

sales of 200,000 bales of spot cotton and 300 million to 400 million bales of futures.[4] Because of its wide range of classifications, its significant activity in cotton futures, and the low grades attracted to the North, it was generally believed in the Cotton Belt that the New York Exchange contributed much in depressing cotton prices. The futures price of these lower grades were usually quoted at least one cent below the spot price, and because it was important in the cotton futures market, prices in the South tended to follow the New York quotations. It was not unusual for delivery on a cotton contract to include twenty different grades; thus the spinner sought to protect himself by bidding a cent or more under the spot price in his futures hedging contract.

Although actual delivery of the minimum contract of 100 bales sometimes involved twenty grades, the contracts were written to call for only one grade, so the classification committee averaged the grade of the lot. The spinner, forced to protect himself on delivery of wide variations in grades, accordingly bid lower on futures contracts than he would for spot cotton. To improve this situation, the Smith report, among other suggestions, recommended that each bale be graded, a procedure opposed by the exchanges because of the cost involved. The report also suggested the elimination of the sale of the lowest grades of cotton, which would force the farmer to take better care in picking, and the insertion of a clause in cotton contracts calling for a premium to be paid on "even running" deliveries of lots. In exercising his option, the seller had to notify the buyer three days prior to delivery in the contract month and the New Orleans market was given a five-day notification. The report further recommended that the seller be required to notify the buyer at the same time of the grade to be delivered so the buyer could provide for disposal of the delivery if it were undesirable for his purposes.[5]

The other major criticism directed at the New York market involved its method of determining the "difference" in futures contracts. All contract prices were based on the middling grade, yet the seller might be forced to deliver a lower grade, or a higher one. Under these contracts the buyer had to accept delivery when the seller "put" (announced delivery), regardless

[4] *Congressional Record*, 63 Cong., 2 Sess., 1914, 51:5524. The Smith report noted that in the 1870s the New York spot market sold 500,000 bales or 15 percent of the crop; current New York spot sales of 200,000 bales represented only 2 percent of the annual crop. Document 912, p. 23.

[5] U.S., Congress, House, Document 912, p. v; 949, pp. 209; 912, p. viii (Serial 5322), 60 Cong., 1 Sess., 1907.

of grade. The amount of money or differential between the contract price and the price of the grade delivered was labeled "difference." If a grade lower than the contract was delivered, the price was "off" (below) the price of "basis" (middling) and the buyer settled the contract accordingly; if the grade delivered was higher than "basis," the price was "on" (above) and the buyer had to pay the "difference." Thus if the buyer contracted at ten cents for "basis" and received strict low middling, a lower grade, worth nine cents, the contract was settled for nine cents or one cent "off"; if he received middling fair, a higher grade priced at eleven cents, the price was "on" one cent. This difference was decided by a committee of the exchange.

The New Orleans Exchange determined "difference" on a daily basis according to the commercial price of cotton. This "commercial difference" was more advantageous to the seller because it most accurately reflected the current prices determined by the supply and demand. The New Orleans committee on difference met daily, ascertained the price that day on each grade of cotton on the spot market, and announced the "difference" on each of its seventeen grades "on" and "off" middling.

The New York Exchange, on the other hand, used the arbitrary procedure of "fixed difference." The New York difference committee simply announced, after deliberations, the "on" and "off" difference on grades to be used to fulfill its contracts. The system worked even more arbitrarily because the determination was made periodically, rather than daily. After 1888 the New York committee met monthly to decide the "fixed difference." Then from 1897 on, the committee met only twice annually, in September and November, to determine "on" and "off" prices. So "fixed difference" would not necessarily reflect the current prices on the spot market and, particularly when determined only in these two fall months, would bear no relationship to prices determined by the law of supply and demand in the remaining months of the year.

"Fixed differences," the Smith report concluded, "are an attempt substantially to render futures transactions a 'sure thing' for a limited class of speculative experts." This system, the report continued, "is uneconomical, in defiance of natural law, unfair, and . . . results in such complex and devious effects that the benefit of its transactions accrues only to a skilled few."[6] Criticism of the "fixed difference" method increased sharply because of developments in 1906. Following the Gulf area storm in that year,

_____

[6] Ibid., 912, pp. iii–ix.

the price on lower grades of cotton dropped rapidly on the spot markets because of the large supply caused by the bad weather. The decline on lower
grades of spot cotton ranged from one to two cents. Yet when the New York
committee met in November, they dropped the "fixed difference" on these
grades only .25 to .50 cents per pound. Some of the committee members sold
short and reaped a significant profit. Some of the cotton merchants who had
hedged, guesssed correctly, closed out their hedge, and hedged in other
markets. Many others, however, failed to take similar action and several
large firms, especially in Savannah, were forced out of business as a result.
Because of this development, the Smith report strongly urged legislation to
force the New York Exchange to adopt the more equitable system of "commercial difference."[7]

Following submission of this report, there was a flurry of legislative
activity to try to abolish or to rectify these practices. There then ensued a
congressional game of musical chairs and out of this confused activity
emerged a program in 1914 to control cotton futures dealings.

H.R. 24073, introduced in April 1910, was based on the power to con-
trol interstate commerce. This bill, reported by Republican Charles Scott of
Kansas, chairman of the Committee on Agriculture, sought to prevent the
use of interstate means of communications for handling cotton futures. The
House debated the measure and passed it on June 24 by a vote of 160 to 41.[8]
The bill was referred to the Senate Committee on Interstate Commerce, but
it was too late in the session for the proposal to be reported and debated.
Four similar bills were introduced in the next session of Congress but none
was reported in either house. In the second session of the Sixty-second
Congress one of these proposals, H.R. 56, was reported and debated. A
similar fate befell this bill. It was passed by the House and was referred to
the Senate in July 1912, again too late for consideration by the upper
chamber.[9]

In the meantime the Agricultural Appropriations Act of 1909 included
a provision for the secretary of agriculture to establish government standards for cotton grades.[10] The secretary subsequently standardized nine
grades, four above middling and four below, in hopes that the exchanges
would adopt these classifications. These grades, which became permanent,

[7] Ibid., pp. 16–18; 949, p. 141.
[8] *Congressional Record*, 61 Cong., 2 Sess., 1910, 45:4310, 8923–57.
[9] Ibid., 62 Cong., 2 Sess., 1912, 48:5381, 8997–9043, 9137–55.
[10] U.S., *Statutes at Large*, vol. 35.

were, from highest to lowest quality: middling fair, strict good middling, good middling, strict middling, middling, strict low middling, low middling, strict good ordinary, good ordinary.

Furthermore, the Democratic party by this time had officially reversed its previous unofficial opposition to control over such contracts. When the Democrats met in convention in 1912, the problem of futures and options and their supposed effect on farm prices had assumed such proportions that they alone, of the parties running candidates for the presidency, included the issue in their platform. A plank in the Democratic platform of 1912 read: "We believe in encouraging the development of a modern system of agriculture and a systematic effort to improve the conditions of trade in farm products so as to benefit both the consumer and producer. And as an efficient means to this end we favor the enactment by Congress of legislation that will suppress the pernicious practice of gambling in agricultural products by organized exchanges or others."[11]

With the Senate's failure to consider these bills in 1910 and again in 1912, the Democrats, after capturing the White House and Congress in the elections of 1912, made a determined effort in both houses to enact a cotton futures program. The lead was taken by two South Carolina Democrats, Asbury Lever in the House and Ellison Smith in the Senate.

When the House completed work on Woodrow Wilson's top priority revenue bill, the Underwood tariff, and sent it to the Senate, the committee of the upper house amended it to include a tax on cotton futures contracts. The Senate Committee on Finance added this amendment which was sponsored by Arkansas Democrat James P. Clarke. The committee estimated that 10 percent of cotton futures were for legitimate hedging and the remainder were for speculation and gambling. The latter category was "universally recognized as an evil," the committee stated, so it was necessary to eliminate this phase of futures. A tax of $\frac{1}{10}$ cent per pound was recommended on all cotton futures transactions if no actual delivery took place.[12]

In the following debate, Senator Clarke argued that while he had favored the House bills of 1910 and 1912, he had discovered subsequently that Congress would be unable to use the interstate commerce power to control futures. He then cited the Supreme Court case of *Ware and Leland* v.

[11] Kirk H. Porter and Donald Bruce Johnson, comps., *National Party Platforms, 1840–1964* (Urbana, Ill., 1966), p. 173.

[12] U.S., Congress, Senate, Report 80 (Serial 6510), 63 Cong., 1 Sess., 1913, pp. 27–28.

Mobile County, testing a state and local tax on futures contracts in Alabama. The Supreme Court validated the tax because these contracts were involved in intrastate commerce and subject to state control.[13] The use of the interstate commerce power to control futures contracts, therefore, would be invalid, Clarke noted, so the taxing power was "the only way to destroy this evil." "The taxing power," he added, "is one of the most comprehensive and flexible powers of the Government. It is the best means of regulation or suppression at its command."[14] When the tariff passed the Senate with this and other amendments which the House refused to accept, the bill went to conference.

Before Oscar Underwood attended the conference, he was given a different cotton futures tax proposal. This measure was drafted by officials in the Department of Agriculture, at the suggestion of Lever, embodying the provisions outlined by the Smith report of 1908. It was given to Wilson who, after careful consideration, approved it and handed it to Underwood personally to be submitted to the conference committee. This program would force the exchanges to use "commercial difference" and comply with government standards of grading; otherwise a tax would be levied on cotton futures contracts which ignored these restrictions. Underwood argued that the Clarke measure would destroy futures exchanges; his proposal instead would "wipe out the evils existing in them." The House conferees agreed to this approach, but the Senate managers refused to abandon the Clarke amendment. Thus Underwood asked the House to adopt his measure and it did, 171 to 161, which constituted a House amendment to a Senate amendment to a House bill.[15]

When the conference report was debated in the Senate, however, the upper house receded on the original Senate change, the Clarke amendment to the Underwood tariff. This presented an interesting parliamentary dilemma: did the Senate recession also wipe out the Underwood amendment accepted by the House? The question was delaying final passage of the tariff, a key part of the New Freedom program. Finally, in desperation

---

[13] 209 U.S. 405 (1908). This decision was based upon the opinion in *Paul* v. *Virginia*, 8 Wallace 168 (1869), in which the court held insurance contracts to be of an intrastate nature. The court held that futures contracts "are not therefore, the subjects of interstate commerce any more than in the insurance contracts." Three years previously the Supreme Court had held futures contracts to be legal in *Board of Trade of Chicago* v. *Christie*, 198 U.S. 236 (1905).

[14] *Congressional Record*, 63 Cong., 1 Sess., 1913, 50:4015–17.

[15] Ibid., pp. 5278, 5288.

Underwood presented a motion asking the House to recede from its amend-ment to the Clarke amendment and concur in the Senate action. His motion was accepted by the House in October and removed all doubt about the parliamentary status of the cotton futures tax by removing the clause en-tirely. The Underwood tariff then was accepted by both houses.[16]

Eight bills dealing with cotton futures were introduced in the next ses-sion of Congress—five to prohibit, two to tax, and one to prohibit the use of interstate communications. None of these was reported out of committee, however, except S. 110, sponsored by Senator Ellison Smith. His bill was designed to regulate through the interstate commerce power in the same manner as the House-passed measures of 1910 and 1912. Specifically, cotton brokers would be denied services for "the transmission of news" unless their futures contracts specified the grade of cotton and exact date of de-livery. The Senate Committee on Agriculture and Forestry recommended passage of S. 110. The committee report called attention to recent tests con-ducted by the Department of Agriculture on the spinnability of different grades of cotton. It was discovered that the difference in quality in terms of their use in spinning between good ordinary and middling fair, the two extremes of the nine grades established by the national government, was al-most negligible. The report further noted that in years of bad crops much low-grade cotton was attracted to New York City. Buyers then lowered their offering price on futures so that if they were forced to take good ordinary the "off" would not be so great. When news of the lower price of middling in New York was received in the Cotton Belt, the information "demoralized and practically ruined the cotton market."[17] S. 110, the Senate hoped, would help change this. Following a relatively short debate the bill passed the upper house without a roll call vote.[18]

The following June the House Committee on Agriculture, chaired by Asbury Lever, amended S. 110 and reported an entirely different bill. House committeemen determined to use the taxing power to regulate cotton ex-changes. Their report indicated they were well aware of actual operations of futures by stating that they were "not unmindful of the danger of tamper-ing with delicately adjusted machinery . . . and therefore . . . recommend legislation along regulatory rather than destructive lines." If properly

---

[16] Ibid., p. 5438.

[17] U.S., Congress, Senate, Report 289 (Serial 6552), 63 Cong., 2 Sess., 1914, pp. 1–4.

[18] *Congressional Record*, 63 Cong., 2 Sess., 1914, 51:5592.

regulated, exchanges could be useful in stabilizing prices, preventing violent price fluctuations, reducing the profit of middlemen, providing a ready market at all times, and maintaining a reasonable parity between spot and futures prices.

The amended bill provided for a tax of one cent per pound on all cotton futures transactions unless certain conditions were met. Contracts had to be settled on "commercial difference." No grades could be sold below good ordinary or, if tinged, below low middling or, if stained, below middling or of less than 7/8 inch staple. Five days prior to delivery the seller had to notify the buyer of the grade of each bale to be delivered. The "commercial difference" would be determined by the daily average prices of five or more spot markets, which were to be designated by the secretary of agriculture, and according to the prices listed on these markets six days prior to delivery. The contracts were to follow the nine government grades established in 1909 and all transactions had to be reported to the secretary of agriculture. There would be no tax on spot cotton sales or on foreign sales of futures if foreign exchanges complied with the provisions of this law in their contracts. "The undesirable or vicious contracts," the report declared, would be subject to a "prohibition tax of $100 per 100-bale contract" and thus "be legislated out of existence, together with the abuses made possible by them." The passage of this measure, the committee believed, would "enhance . . . the value of the cotton crop in the hands of the farmer of the South not less than $100,000,000 annually." [19]

The House, as well as the Senate, offered little debate on the measure, considering the importance of the proposition. Most of the opposition came from congressmen who favored the original Smith bill because, they believed, it would destroy cotton exchanges. Underwood, endorsing the tax approach, called upon the House to "wipe out the evils of the cotton exchange." "If you want to use the most effective power," he declared, "there is no greater power in the Government than the power to tax. [*applause*]" The House then approved a motion to suspend the rules and pass the Lever substitute, which required a two-thirds vote, 84 to 21.[20] The next day the Senate requested a conference. After discussion the conference committee raised the tax rate from one to two cents per pound.[21] The House then voted

[19] U.S., Congress, House, Report 765 (Serial 6559), 63 Cong., 2 Sess., 1914, pp. 1–24.

[20] *Congressional Record*, 63 Cong., 2 Sess., 1914, 51:11321, 11322.

[21] U.S., Congress, House, Report 1012 (Serial 6560), 63 Cong., 2 Sess., 1914, p. 1.

146 to 77 to accept the amended bill and the Senate approved it without a roll call vote.[22] President Wilson signed the Smith-Lever Act into law on August 18, 1914.[23]

Although the major features of the act were directed at activities on the New York Cotton Exchange, this market was able to adapt to the law with relative ease. During the consideration of futures bills in Congress from 1910 to 1913, the Exchange was having a debate within its own ranks. The conservative elements refused to change procedures, but the progressive brokers, fearing congressional action, argued that it would be best to reform themselves before change was forced upon them. The progressives finally won in 1913 when the New York Exchange accepted the national government's standards on grades and began to fix "difference" monthly rather than twice annually.[24]

The Department of Agriculture, charged with enforcing the act, praised it as "constructive and regulatory, not destructive or oppressive," and pledged every effort to "lay the foundations" for enforcement. After the first year of operation under the law the Agriculture Department reported general compliance "with negligible exceptions." At this point department officials were convinced the statute had already "accomplished the chief economic objectives anticipated by its framers." As a result of the law having been in effect only one year, the department noted, futures quotations "now represent spot values more accurately . . . , sharp and sudden fluctuations such as commonly occurred under the old practices have become much less frequent," and cotton prices were "increasingly stabilized."[25]

Despite threats voiced during the congressional debates on the act in 1914, that if the bill were enacted the exchanges and brokers would move their operations to Canada, nothing materialized along these lines. These warnings stemmed from the inclusion of Section 11 to the act which required foreign exchanges to comply with the law or United States citizens would be taxed for buying or selling these futures. But the attorney supervising the

[22] *Congressional Record*, 63 Cong., 2 Sess., 1914, 51:12851, 13661.

[23] U.S., *Statutes at Large*, vol. 38.

[24] I. Newton Hoffmann, "The Cotton Futures Act," *Journal of Political Economy* 23 (May 1915):480; see also Luther Conant, Jr., "The United States Cotton Futures Act," *American Economic Review* 5 (March 1915):1–11. Cedric B. Cowing, *Populists, Plungers, and Progressives* (Princeton, N.J., 1965), pp. 38–42, emphasizes the importance of the 1909 investigation sponsored by Governor Charles Hughes in bringing about self-reform.

[25] *Annual Reports of the Department of Agriculture, 1914* (Washington, D.C., 1914), p. 23; *1915*, pp. 31–32.

law in New York was able to report in 1916 that "a large majority [of brokers] . . . are in favor of every feature of the law, except that of Section 11." Because foreign exchanges refused to adopt United States standards, this section was detrimental to Americans hedging in foreign futures. Otherwise, the New York enforcement officer noted only three firms—Hubbard Brothers and Company, Stephen M. Weld and Company, and A. B. Gwatheny and Company—who refused to comply with the law. The Justice Department had not yet prosecuted these firms "pending . . . litigation to have the act declared unconstitutional."[26]

One of these firms, the Hubbard Company, brought suit in district court in New York charging the act to be unconstitutional. The plaintiff argued, in *Hubbard* v. *Lowe*, that the law, being a revenue measure, was invalid because it originated in the Senate rather than the House, in violation of Article I, Section 7. The district court judge reluctantly agreed that this made the law unconstitutional.[27] The House Committee on Agriculture immediately reported a bill to reenact the 1914 law "for the purpose of obviating the possible effect of Judge Hough's decision." The committee report observed that the results of the act had been "so patently and admittedly beneficial to the cotton producer, merchant and spinner, as to prove beyond question the wisdom of its . . . reenactment under the present circumstances." The report also recommended certain changes. It was suggested that the terms of the act be extended to futures orders placed in the United States by foreigners so that they would be subject to the same restrictions as United States citizens. To eliminate the question of constitutionality of this provision, the report asked for a declaration that the purpose of the tax, as applied to foreign futures, was not to levy an export duty on cotton. A new section also was to be added with "an express declaration" that if any part of the law was declared unconstitutional, such determination would not "affect the remaining parts of the act."[28]

This proposal had not yet been acted upon by the House when Lever introduced a measure to make the annual appropriation for the Department of Agriculture for the coming fiscal year. During the debate on this bill William Bennet, Republican of New York, questioned the propriety of the section appropriating money for the department to enforce the Cotton Fu-

[26] U.S., Congress, Senate, Document 648 (Serial 7125), 64 Cong., 2 Sess., 1916, pp. 23–24.

[27] 226 Fed 135 (1915).

[28] U.S., Congress, House, Report 229 (Serial 6903), 64 Cong., 1 Sess., 1915, pp. 1–3.

tures Act because of the district court's declaration that it was unconstitutional. Lever then proposed an amendment to the appropriation bill which would reenact the Cotton Futures Act of 1914 with the changes his committee had already recommended, and the House expressed its approval by vote of 101 to 23. The measure passed the Senate the following August,[29] and President Wilson signed the bill on August 11, 1916.[30] The case of *Hubbard* v. *Lowe*, on appeal to the Supreme Court by writ of error, was then dismissed on October 19, 1916.[31]

The Cotton Futures Act was amended in 1919 in regard to grades of cotton sold on futures. The grades currently used were limited to nine, but these were on white cotton. In addition, five grades of yellow-tinged, three yellow-stained, and three blue-stained were being bought and sold. This resulted in a considerable amount of low-grade cotton being marketed with "the effect of greatly depressing the value of the futures contract." The House Committee on Agriculture recommended eliminating several of these lower grades by establishing a maximum of ten grades—seven on white, two on yellow-tinged, and one on yellow-stained.[32]

This bill also was delayed in the House, so when the Senate debated the wheat bill in 1919, Senator Smith offered an amendment to the 1916 cotton act to provide for these ten grades as standards for cotton futures. The Senate accepted this change without roll call vote, as did the House.[33] It became law, under the Wheat Price Guaranty Act, on March 4, 1919.[34] After 1919, no grade of cotton below low middling could be offered for sale in futures.

There were various efforts to amend the law during the 1920s but to no avail.[35] The only significant change in cotton futures came in 1923. Using the commerce power, Congress enacted a law prohibiting the use in the United States of any cotton standards other than those of the United States

[29] *Congressional Record*, 64 Cong., 1 Sess., 1916, 53:6929, 7003, 12111.

[30] U.S., *Statutes at Large*, vol. 39.

[31] *Annual Reports of the Department of Agriculture, 1917* (Washington, D.C., 1918), p. 405.

[32] U.S., Congress, House, Report 1152 (Serial 7455), 65 Cong., 3 Sess., 1919, pp. 1–2.

[33] *Congressional Record*, 65 Cong., 3 Sess., 1919, 57:4445, 4965.

[34] U.S., *Statutes at Large*, vol. 40.

[35] In both the Sixty-ninth and Seventieth congresses bills were introduced to abolish both grain and cotton futures. In both cases the minority on the Committee on Agriculture and Forestry submitted a 108-page report praising the cotton futures tax and opposing any change. See U.S., Congress, Senate, Report 508 (Serial 8525), 69 Cong., 1 Sess., 1925; Report 497 (Serial 8829), 70 Cong., 1 Sess., 1927. The bills, however, never reached the point of debate in either house.

government for any foreign or interstate transactions in cotton. The act passed both houses of Congress without a roll call vote.[36] It was signed by President Warren Harding on March 3, 1923.[37] This law produced the desired result. A meeting was held in Washington, D.C., on June 11, 1923, with representatives of the "leading cotton exchanges of Europe."[38] These delegates agreed to United States standards of grades on cotton which meant, in effect, from 1923 on the world used these standards.

The Cotton Futures Act was never litigated in the Supreme Court although Section 4 was questioned. When Germany announced a policy of unrestricted submarine warfare in February 1917, the price of cotton in the United States dropped drastically. A cotton speculator wired his broker a "stop order" to sell 1,000 bales of his cotton at 17.20 cents and another 1,000 at 17.15 cents. The broker was able to sell for only 14 cents so suit was brought to recover the difference, reaching the Supreme Court in 1922. In *Brown* v. *Horne*,[39] plaintiff argued that while the tax on cotton futures was valid, Section 4 which regulated the contracts was unconstitutional because of the Supreme Court decision in *Hill* v. *Wallace* which struck down a grain futures tax on these contracts.[40] The high court decided in the Brown case, however, that Section 4 was a valid requirement for the purposes of that tax measure and that such "stop orders" to sell were understood to mean to sell at the highest possible price. Plaintiff, therefore, could not recover the difference he lost in the sale.

The lack of litigation over the statute can, perhaps, be accounted for by the relative ease with which the exchanges adapted to the requirements. The tax of $100 per 100-bale contract, which would be prohibitive, forced futures dealers to evade the tax by complying with the provisions. This revenue measure, designed to regulate, achieved the purpose of its authors by eliminating the worst features of cotton futures contracts and, because of the beneficial aspects, permitted the exchanges to continue to function. The regulation of cotton markets was far wiser, and of more benefit to cotton farmers, than the abolition of the exchanges as some congressmen wished. The next time Congress exercised the taxing power over an "evil" product, dangerous matches, it would be wielded with the intent to destroy.

[36] *Congressional Record*, 67 Cong., 4 Sess., 1923, 64:3662, 5264.

[37] U.S., *Statutes at Large*, vol. 42.

[38] *Annual Report of the Department of Agriculture, 1923* (Washington, D.C., 1924), p. 35.

[39] 260 U.S. 137 (1922).

[40] 259 U.S. 44 (1922). This case will be discussed at greater length in Chapter 9.

7   The Eradication
of Phossy Jaw

With the enactment of various taxes to control or to prohibit developments that seemed to affect prices of agricultural commodities, and the subsequent validation by the Supreme Court of most of the measures, the foundation was laid for the enactment of further prohibitory taxes when the need arose.[1] By 1900 the Progressive movement was gaining momentum and muckrakers turned their attention to the general problem of the lack of controls over food, drugs, and "evil" commodities or activities that threatened the welfare of American society.[2] This reform effort climaxed in the passage of the Pure Food Law of 1906 which established the principle of national inspection and regulation of foods and drugs in interstate commerce.[3] Congress enacted another law the same day the food act was passed providing for appropriations for the Department of Agriculture for the next fiscal year. Included in this measure was a provision for the Bureau of Animal Husbandry to inspect all meat in interstate commerce.[4]

Muckrakers and other reformers also became concerned at this time over another dangerous commodity, matches, and in this instance the taxing power was again used. Soon after the turn of the twentieth century public concern was aroused over the health menace created by the manufacture of matches from white phosphorus. As a result of this agitation, Congress eventually determined to tax them out of existence.

The health problem involved in the manufacture and use of white phosphorus matches existed from the beginning of this industry. The friction match was developed by an Englishman, John Walker, in 1827, and by 1835 there were several match factories in the United States.[5] The first patent in the United States for a friction match was taken out by Alonzo Phillips in October 1837.[6] The match industry quickly boomed in this country with the "strike-anywhere" parlor match dominating the market. It was soon discovered in Europe, however, that this wonderful device carried with it a horrible disease known as phosphorus necrosis, the first authentic case of industrial phosphorus poisoning being diagnosed in 1839 by a "Doctor Lorinser, of Vienna."[7] The suffering factory workers in France called this disease "mal chimique," and in the United States and England it was known as phossy jaw. Laborers contracted the malady in the match factories in those stages of the manufacturing process where the fumes of the white phosphorus—or yellow after it had been exposed to light—were present, such as in the mixing and dipping processes, or when the matches were physically handled, as in the sorting and packaging of the finished product.

A contemporary description of this loathsome affliction substantiates the dread with which phossy jaw was regarded by match workers:

Being readily volatile in the ordinary temperature of the air white phosphorus emits a bluish-white fume which affects the health of those who labor in match factories in three different ways: (1) By causing anemia; (2) by causing the bones of the body to become brittle and unable to withstand slight external violence without breaking; (3) by causing phosphorus necrosis of the upper and lower jawbones . . . .Phosphorus necrosis is caused by the absorption of the fumes or particles of white phosphorus through carious teeth and gums. The gums become swollen and purple and the teeth loosen and drop out. The organic or animal matter of the jawbones slowly rots away and passes off in the form of nauseating pus which breaks through the neck in the form of abscesses, or, if not almost continually washed out, oozes into the mouth where it mixes with the saliva and is swallowed, tending to produce a chronic toxaemia. The stench

[1] This chapter was published substantially in this form as "The Eradication of Phossy Jaw: A Unique Development of Federal Police Power," *Historian* 29 (November 1966) : 1–21. The author acknowledges with gratitude the permission given by this journal to reprint this material.

[2] For an account of this development, see especially Oscar E. Anderson, Jr., *The Health of a Nation* (Chicago, Ill., 1958).

[3] U.S., *Statutes at Large*, vol. 34.

[4] Ibid.

[5] Roger Burlingame, *The March of the Iron Men* (New York, 1938), p. 300; Herbert Manchester, *The Diamond Match Company: One Hundred Years of Progress* (New York, 1935), p. 14.

[6] Manchester, *The Diamond Match Company*, p. 17.

[7] T. E. Thorpe, Thomas Oliver, M.D., and George Cunningham, "Report to the Secretary of State for the Home Department on the Use of Phosphorus in the Manufacture of Lucifer Matches," London, 1899, quoted in John B. Andrews, "Phosphorus Poisoning in the Match Industry in the United States," *Bulletin of the Bureau of Labor* 20 (January 1910) : 59.

from the supperating bones is something that cannot be described in words, and is so nauseating that dentists and doctors alike avoid patients with advanced cases of necrosis.[8]

If a sufferer were lucky in this advanced stage, he could obtain a surgeon who would remove the jawbone. Such a man would then immediately grow a beard, "a refuge denied to the women sufferers who sometimes . . . went through the remaining years of life frightfully disfigured."[9]

With the spread of this dreadful disease among workers, efforts were made in Europe to prevent the affliction or to find a substitute material for match heads. The most successful replacement proved to be a "safety match," made from nonpoisonous red phosphorus, but it could be struck only upon the enclosing box which had a strip painted on the side for that purpose. Because the white phosphorus match would strike anywhere, it was so popular that production of the poisonous type continued unabated. The problem finally prompted European governments to take direct action.

The first restriction came in Finland in 1872, when that nation placed an absolute ban upon the manufacture, use, or sale of white phosphorus matches. Denmark took similar action in 1874.[10] A significant breakthrough was then achieved in France where the match industry was a government monopoly. The French government, with its system of state compensation for injuries incurred in employment, soon found its profits from the monopoly dissipated by disability payments to victims of phosphorus necrosis. Supported by government authorities, Henri Sevene and David Cahen of Paris developed a harmless substitute in 1897, called the sesquisulphide process, that was commercially practical.[11] That same year, therefore, France prohibited the use of white phosphorus in matches.

An investigation in Great Britain in 1899 revealed 102 cases of necrosis of which nineteen had been fatal. England immediately set up stringent regulation of match factories, including medical inspection of workers and sanitary and ventilation requirements to halt the spread of phossy jaw.

[8] U.S., Congress, House, "Memorandum Submitted by the Legislative Committee of the American Association for Labor Legislation to the Committee on Ways and Means," January 20, 1911, 62 Cong., 2 Sess., 1912, House Report 406 (Serial 6130), p. 3. Hereafter cited as House Report 406.

[9] Andrews, "Phosphorus Poisoning in the Match Industry in the United States," p. 90.

[10] A summary of the activities of the European governments is given in ibid., pp. 67–85.

[11] Earl Mayo, "The Work That Kills," *Outlook* 99 (September 23, 1911) :206.

These safety efforts failed to eliminate the disease, and in 1908 Britain prohibited the production of white phosphorus matches to be effective after January 1, 1910. The Diamond Match Company which had branches in several countries had purchased the patent rights to the French sesquisul-phide process in England, and when white phosphorus matches were banned in that country the firm allowed other match manufacturers to use the "safe" process on the same royalty basis that it enjoyed.

A major turning point in the elimination of phossy jaw in Europe oc-curred in 1906 when, under the stimulus of the International Association for Labor Legislation, an international conference met at Berne, Switzer-land, to discuss the problem. The members of this group agreed to a treaty prohibiting the manufacture, importation, or sale of white phosphorus matches. This agreement, signed by Finland, Denmark, France, Switzer-land, Luxemburg, Italy, Holland, and Germany, was the first international attempt to ban an industrial product.[12]

Meanwhile Sweden had concentrated on the production of safety matches, with only about one-tenth of the Swedish match workers producing the poisonous type. After 1870 production of the latter was allowed by the government only under strict regulations and solely for export purposes. Russia placed a heavy tax on white phosphorus matches in 1892, which was doubled in 1905, so that by 1906 only one match in every fifty produced in Russia was of the poisonous variety. These activities led labor groups in the United States to observe in 1911 that those countries which had first prohibited the use of white phosphorus in matches had not discovered any "case of phosphorus necrosis . . . in the last 35 years."[13]

The problem of phossy jaw was brought to public attention in the United States largely through the efforts of the American Association for Labor Legislation, a branch of the International Association. John B. Andrews, the secretary of the American organization, began an investigation of phossy jaw poisoning in 1909. Just prior to this, the Bureau of Labor had instituted a general investigation of the employment of women and children in fac-tories and several match companies were among those visited.[14] When it learned of Andrews's study, the Bureau determined to avoid duplication through cooperation between the two projects. Andrews consequently con-tinued his work under the auspices of the Bureau of Labor. The results were

[12] House Report 406.
[13] *Congressional Record*, 61 Cong., 3 Sess., 1911, 46:3628.
[14] The background for this study is presented in Chapter 9.

then published in the *Bulletin of the Bureau of Labor*.[15] This report covered rather thoroughly the process of manufacturing matches, the working conditions, wages, and health of the employees in the industry in the United States, as well as the European experience in eliminating phosphorus necrosis. But the highlight of the 115-page study was the presentation of case records of phossy jaw victims. These records were uncovered in an investigation of fifteen of the sixteen match factories in the United States which employed 3,591 people, among them 2,024 men, 1,253 women, and 314 children—121 boys and 193 girls—under sixteen years of age.

Andrews noted that he encountered unusual difficulties in securing the information he desired concerning the extent of phosphorus necrosis. The problems included the mobility of match workers, especially of girls who changed occupations and residence, or their names by marriage. He also discovered that older women, even when located, "often, for reasons of social pride, reluctantly admit[ted] that they ever worked in a match factory" or disclaimed "interest in the subject." Finally he noted that those employees currently at work in match factories expressed "the greatest alarm, even when at their homes, lest the giving of information cost them the loss of their positions."[16] Despite these obstacles, investigators inspected factories, consulted physicians, and interviewed necrosis victims. To counteract the claim of some match manufacturers that the problem had been eliminated years before, Andrews unearthed "within a very short time" the records of more than one hundred cases of the disease. He concluded that phosphorus poisoning not only existed in the United States but was present "in a form so serious as to warrant legislative action to eliminate the disease."[17]

The publication of this report stimulated a national effort to wipe out phosphorus necrosis. Muckraking magazines and newspapers seized upon the evils of the disease and publicized its effects. The *Independent*, for example, expressed doubt that the friction match would see its centenary celebration in 1927 because of increased competition from electricity, gas jets, cerium alloy of iron, and other rivals that eliminated "poisonous phosphorus . . . scratching on walls and trousers . . . blowing out in the wind . . . sulphurous odor . . . and danger of fire from matches thrown down."[18] To

15 Andrews, "Phosphorus Poisoning in the Match Industry," p. 31.
16 Ibid., pp. 33–34.
17 Ibid., pp. 32–33.
18 *Independent* 69 (December 1, 1910) : 1225–26.

achieve this goal, a campaign was begun to eliminate at least the white phosphorus, or dangerous, match in the United States, as had been done in Europe. On June 3, 1910, Republican John J. Esch of Wisconsin introduced a bill in the House of Representatives designed "to provide a tax on white phosphorus matches."[19] He readily admitted the proposal had been authored by the American Association for Labor Legislation which had persuaded him to introduce the measure in Congress.[20]

Esch explained to his colleagues that several approaches to the elimination of this health problem had been considered. The obvious and least questionable method would be for the state governments, through their police power, to set up regulations or prohibitions against the use of white phosphorus. But he pointed out that this would be ineffective because of the lack of uniformity in state laws which would permit the match factories to move to states without such legislation. Furthermore, Esch noted, there was an apparent lack of interest in the subject on this level of government. Not one state had as yet acted to curb the evil, although Ohio had prohibited the use of child labor in match factories. The reformers also considered the possibility of negotiating treaties between the United States and foreign nations which would provide for the mutual banning of the use of white phosphorus. But as Miles Dawson, counsel for the Labor Legislation organization, pointed out, to prohibit the use of poisonous phosphorus by a treaty would be "to invade the internal police power of the States . . . without any connection with international relations."[21] The Supreme Court decision in *Missouri* v. *Holland*, which validated the precedent for such a type of police regulation, was still a decade in the future.[22] Using the power to regulate interstate commerce had also been considered, but this, too, had been rejected because it would not affect intrastate commerce and thus the danger would continue on the state level.[23]

The rejection of these alternatives meant that "the only recourse, therefore . . . was the taxing power." Esch observed that the only constitutional restrictions on this power were the requirement of uniformity, apportion-

---

[19] *Congressional Record*, 61 Cong., 2 Sess., 1910, 45:7407.
[20] Ibid., 61 Cong., 3 Sess., 1911, 46:3629.
[21] Ibid., p. 3628.
[22] 252 U.S. 416 (1920).
[23] Dawson believed use of the interstate commerce power regulating these matches would be "a mistake and that no real protection of [*sic*] thorough-going prohibition would result therefrom." Miles M. Dawson to John J. Esch, June 21, 1910, John J. Esch Papers, State Historical Society of Wisconsin, Madison.

ment of direct taxes according to population, and the ban on taxing of exports. Esch then cited the Supreme Court decisions in *Hylton* v. *United States* (1796, validating a direct tax on carriages, 3 Dallas 171), *McCulloch* v. *Maryland*, *Veazie Bank* v. *Fenno*, and *McCray* v. *United States* to substantiate his argument that the use of the taxing power would be the best constitutional approach to the eradication of phossy jaw. A prohibitive tax on white phosphorus matches, he declared "would compel the use of an innocuous substitute."[24]

The key match business in the reform drive proved to be the Diamond Match Company which owned the process for "an innocuous substitute" match. The American branch of this firm had purchased on November 15, 1898, the United States patent rights to the Sevene-Cahen sesquisulphide process for $100,000.[25] The company had then attempted to produce the "safe" match in the United States, as it was doing in England, but was unsuccessful because of "humidity, temperature, and other climatic and physical conditions." Also, as a contemporary journalist noted, the sesquisulphide process increased production costs about 5 percent and this undoubtedly was an additional deterrent to its use.[26] In any case, the formula had been laid aside and forgotten until the tumult broke out during and after the Andrews investigation over the danger of white phosphorus. The general superintendent of the Diamond Match Company, William A. Fairburn, then "set to work doing research and experimentation" and soon succeeded in producing a sesquisulphide match in the United States.[27]

Because the Diamond Match Company's patent rights were valid until 1915, Fairburn's successful experiments were followed by an offer from his company to allow other match manufacturers to use its process "on equal terms" if the national government would prohibit the manufacture of dangerous matches.[28] In July 1910, soon after Esch introduced his measure, the Diamond Company defined what it meant by "equal terms" for other companies. Any other match manufacturer would be allowed to use the sesquisulphide process upon payment of a fair proportion of the $100,000 that was paid for the French formula and a royalty of four-tenths of a cent for every one thousand matches the licensee turned out in excess of the

[24] *Congressional Record*, 61 Cong., 3 Sess., 1911, 46:3628–29.

[25] *Scientific American* 104 (February 11, 1911) :143.

[26] Earl Mayo, "The Work That Kills," pp. 205–7.

[27] Manchester, *The Diamond Match Company*, p. 71.

[28] J. P. Heaton, "Making All Matches Safeties," *Survey* 25 (December 3, 1910) : 386; Andrews, "Phosphorus Poisoning in the Match Industry," p. 36.

quota it produced in the year ending June 31, 1910.[29] This offer, considered by Esch and others as reasonable, was apparently stimulated principally by the Diamond Match Company's fear that restrictive legislation by Congress or the several states was inevitable, and the company preferred a uniform national policy rather than a multitude of state regulations.[30]

In the meantime Esch's bill died in the House Ways and Means Committee, but the resulting publicity aroused national interest in the problem and even excited the interest of President William H. Taft. When Congress reconvened for a third session in December 1910, Taft, in his annual State of the Union Message, invited the attention of that body "to the very serious injury caused to all those who are engaged in the manufacture of phosphorus matches." He described phossy jaw as "frightful" and observed that inasmuch as a process for making safe matches was available, the dangerous matches "could be discouraged and ought to be discouraged by the imposition of a heavy federal tax."[31] Esch responded by introducing a new bill which added certain changes in his original measure advocated by "various departments of the Government . . . so as to make the law workable."[32] In the hearings by the Committee on Ways and Means, Fairburn again announced his success with the sesquisulphide process and repeated the Diamond Company's offer to license other manufacturers to use it. All but one manufacturer, a "very small operator in Brooklyn," accepted this offer, but this one dissent caused "Congress to hesitate."[33] The lone objector disliked both the idea of employing a new process and also of "using a patent owned by another company." He argued that the requirements in the Esch bill would prevent an increase in production, due to the royalty provision, and also would preclude the expansion of any new enterprise in the industry.[34]

To overcome this obstacle, the Diamond Company transferred the own-

[29] *Congressional Record*, 61 Cong., 3 Sess., 1911, 46:3629; *Survey* 25 (January 7, 1911) :523.

[30] *Congressional Record*, 61 Cong., 3 Sess., 1911, 46:3629.

[31] Ibid., p. 29; James D. Richardson, *Messages and Papers of the Presidents* (Washington, D.C., 1913), 10:7920. Miles Dawson was "gratified at the strong endorsement the President gave, not merely the purpose of the bill but the method we had selected for carrying out that purpose." Miles M. Dawson to John J. Esch, December 9, 1910, Esch Papers. John Andrews notified Esch that Taft's secretary had written the commissioner of Internal Revenue saying he wanted "the tax method used in this case." John B. Andrews to John J. Esch, December 17, 1910, Esch Papers.

[32] *Congressional Record*, 61 Cong., 3 Sess., 1911, 46:3629.

[33] Manchester, *The Diamond Match Company*, p. 73.

[34] *Congressional Record*, 61 Cong., 3 Sess., 1911, 46:3629.

ership of its patent to a board of trustees on January 6, 1911, thus assuring impartiality in licensing match manufacturers.[35] These trustees—Edwin Seligman, professor at Columbia University; Charles P. Neill, commissioner of labor; and Jack Ralston, an attorney for the American Federation of Labor—were eminent men whose names guaranteed fair treatment because no one would be "so suspicious as to charge them with being under the domination of the match trust."[36] Even Robert La Follette's magazine, the "most trustworthy of all progressive publications," endorsed these trustees as being "a strong guarantee of just dealing."[37] The *Survey* noted that, due to the exposure of the match industry by the Bureau of Labor and the American Association for Labor Legislation, this transfer of title was just the "latest concession to . . . public opinion." The first effect of the report had been the closure of a Diamond Match factory in Maine, "one of the worst match factories in the country," the journal added, and the second was the substitution of "a policy of publicity for one of suppression as to the facts of phosphorus necrosis."[38]

Despite the establishment of a trusteeship, or perhaps partially because of it, the suspicion grew that the Diamond Match Company was attempting to gain further control of the industry. This firm, producing about 65 percent of the more than $5.5 million worth of matches manufactured in the United States at the time, was known as the "Match Trust." At this point in the Progressive movement, the word trust was anathema and liberals opposed any activity that might promote monopoly. The *New York Times* editorialized that a lone New York match manufacturer told the Committee on Ways and Means that the Esch bill was a "device of the Match Trust to destroy its independent rivals." While the *Times* was uncertain whether the motives of the Diamond Company were good or bad in promoting this legislation, the editor concluded that Esch's proposal was "an excellent one."[39] But just the hint of suspicion in regard to the motives of the Diamond Match Company was sufficient to delay legislation. Instead of recommending Esch's second bill, the Committee on Ways and Means approved a substitute which requested the president to appoint "a competent person to investigate the manufacture of white phosphorus matches and report to the next ses-

35 Ibid.

36 *Survey* 25 (January 21, 1911) : 647.

37 *LaCrosse* (Wis.) *Tribune*, January 30, 1911, quoted in *Congressional Record*, 61 Cong., 3 Sess., 1911, 46:3631.

38 *Survey* 25 (January 21, 1911) : 648.

39 *New York Times*, January 23, 1911.

sion of Congress." One of the specific points to be investigated was the question of whether a trust was controlling the match industry and whether Esch's proposed prohibition would tend toward a monopoly "of what has become a necessity of life."[40] In defending this resolution on the floor of the House, Republican John Dalzell of Pennsylvania explained that the committee believed the Diamond Company's offer appeared unfair because "there still remained . . . a serious doubt as to whether the safe material . . . can be procured in sufficient quantities by outside companies to carry on their business."[41]

To counter this resolution and to promote his own measure, Esch had reprinted in the *Congressional Record* a series of editorials from leading newspapers endorsing his proposal. Many of these editorials described phossy jaw in detail and played up the deaths of little children that had resulted from sucking and swallowing the heads of white phosphorus matches. Most of the editorials agreed that the Diamond Match Company was a "good trust" and that the Esch bill would not promote monopoly. Esch also included letters from two Philadelphia insurance companies pleading for the elimination of these "fire-hazard" matches and extracts from insurance statistics reporting that between eight hundred and nine hundred people burned to death annually in the United States as a result of these matches.[42]

Despite the protests of Esch, the substitute resolution passed the House on February 11, 1911. The Senate then amended it to confine the investigation to the question of "whether or not white phosphorus matches were fit subjects for interstate commerce."[43] The House disagreed with this substitution because it would invoke the interstate commerce power instead of the taxing power. A conference of the two houses resulted in a deadlock which stymied the Esch proposal for that session of Congress.

Being aware of the distrust of the motives of the licensed companies, the three patent trustees wrote President Taft suggesting that he request the Diamond Company and its licensees to cancel the patent "in the interest of this humane legislation." If the companies took this action, they argued, it would remove "the already groundless suspicion of monopoly and, as a consequence, force the opponents of the measure to disclose the actual

[40] *Congressional Record*, 61 Cong., 3 Sess., 1911, 46:3102.
[41] Ibid., p. 3626.
[42] Ibid., pp. 3630–33.
[43] Ibid., pp. 3633, 4120.

grounds for their opposition." Taft replied with a letter to the company two days later, on January 26, 1911, describing his "great anxiety to see American labor protected from the ravages of a wholly unnecessary and loathsome disease" in the same manner that European countries had protected their workers. He was certain that everyone would be happy if the companies involved would "take the public-spirited action of canceling the patent" to free the sesquisulphide process for public use. This deed, the president observed, "ought to have the effect of dispelling any fear that the enactment of this legislation would result in a monopoly in the match industry." The Diamond Match Company responded two days later by filing a certification with the commissioner of patents to cancel its patent rights and grant the sesquisulphide process to the American public.[44]

This unique gift from a trust that could have yielded "hundreds of thousands of dollars," one magazine observed, was "an interesting spectacle."[45] Another periodical decided that even if the action were "dictated by enlightened self-interest," it was still "unselfish and to be praised cordially."[46] The *Rutland* (Vt.) *News* concluded that the Match Trust was "a trust that certainly has a soul."[47] The Diamond Company went even further. It revealed its formulas to its competitors, according to the company's historian, and even sent its employees to other factories to demonstrate its techniques.[48]

Esch reintroduced his measure in the next session of Congress on April 10, 1911, but again it died in committee.[49] Editorials and articles in periodicals continued to stress the need for legislation. *Outlook* described in September 1911 the process for making white phosphorus matches and the terrible results from contracting phossy jaw and concluded that, because the sesquisulphide process increased production cost about 5 percent over the cost of manufacturing the poisonous match, an act of Congress forbidding the use of poisonous phosphorus would "be required to do away completely with this serious occupational disease."[50] The following February the same journal noted that most foreign countries had forbidden the use of this "deadly form of phosphorus" by law and that of the great nations of

44 Ibid., pp. 3629–30.
45 *Scientific American* 104 (February 11, 1911) : 143.
46 *Outlook* 97 (February 11, 1911) : 293.
47 Reprinted in *Congressional Record*, 61 Cong., 3 Sess., 1911, 46 : 3632.
48 Manchester, *The Diamond Match Company*, p. 73.
49 *Congressional Record*, 62 Cong., 1 Sess., 1911, 47 : 144.
50 Earl Mayo, "The Work That Kills," pp. 205–7.

the world, only in the United States and Russia was "commercial greed permitted to expose men and women to this terrible danger."[51] *Everybody's* published a muckraking article in April 1912 describing phossy jaw as "the most terrible of occupational diseases" and narrated the European efforts to eliminate it. The author stated that the Diamond Company, which produced 67 percent of the nation's annual 250 billion matches, had "energetically" endorsed legislation banning white phosphorus and surrendered its patent for a safe match to the public but that the Esch bill had been stalled despite these generous activities.[52]

The Esch proposal was taken up by William Hughes, Democrat of New Jersey, when on February 16, 1912, he introduced legislation to place a prohibitory tax on white phosphorus matches.[53] The preceding month the Committee on Ways and Means had again held hearings on the problem of eliminating phossy jaw. A reporter described the committeemen as "a dozen gentlemen lolling back in their chairs, striking matches, chafing witnesses and each other." The hearings, he observed, "showed the members of the committee to be ignorant of the menace and nature of the disease, suspicious of the motives of the bill's friends, willing only after extended argument to believe it a matter of much consequence anyway."[54] John T. Huner, the Brooklyn match manufacturer, was the only match producer to oppose the measure. He declared again at these hearings, as he had previously, that "there never had been a case of phosphorus necrosis in his factory." The proponents of the bill, however, were ready for him this time. They produced a physician's certificate of the treatment of one of his workers; furthermore, they placed in evidence a letter from a former superintendent of Huner's factory stating that cases of phossy jaw had occurred in the factory "with the direct knowledge of Mr. Huner."[55]

John Andrews undoubtedly jarred the apathy of some of the committeemen in the course of these hearings. One of the questions asked of every witness was if he had ever actually seen a case of phossy jaw. When asked, Andrews testified that he had investigated about 150 cases and had "personally seen perhaps 50 cases of phossy jaw." He then produced a classic example in the person of B. Plaza of Passaic, New Jersey. Although this

[51] *Outlook* 100 (February 17, 1912) :349.
[52] Gordon Thayer, "Matches or Men?" *Everybody's* 26 (April 1912) :490–98.
[53] *Congressional Record*, 62 Cong., 2 Sess., 1912, 48:2489.
[54] Constance D. Lupp, "Playing with Matches," *Survey* 27 (January 27, 1912) : 1644.
[55] *Survey* 27 (January 27, 1912) :1636.

worker had spent fifty-nine days in a hospital and had his lower jawbone extracted so as to prevent certain death, he "was more fortunate than many." Following his operation he had offered "to do all he could in the interest of wiping out this terrible disease."[56]

In its report to the House on March 11, 1912, the Committee on Ways and Means summarized its findings over the preceding two years and recommended passage of the Hughes bill.[57] The report declared that the purpose of the bill was "to eliminate, through the exercise of the Federal taxing power, the use of white or yellow phosphorus in the manufacture of matches." It listed some of the statistics of the Andrews investigation to illustrate the need for the legislation and included additional information later supplied to the committee by Andrews on the menace of these white phosphorus matches to children. Andrews had gathered "as merely typical the data of 14 deaths of children from matches" which occurred in one calendar year. The report also summarized a memorandum from the American Association for Labor Legislation which declared the danger of phosphorus necrosis to be greater in the United States than elsewhere. It was pointed out that match manufacturers in foreign countries, prior to the bans on white phosphorus, had used from 6 to 7 percent poisonous phosphorus to make the match head but manufacturers in the United States used a solution of 14 to 20 percent. This increased percentage, plus "the peculiar conditions" in the United States, combined to make the poisonous vapor even more deadly than in European countries where lower humidity and temperatures generated less poisonous fumes. In regard to the constitutionality of this use of the taxing power, the report listed the testimony of Miles Dawson and P. Tecumseh Sherman, well-known New York lawyers, and Professor Ernst Freund of the University of Chicago Law School. These eminent authorities agreed that, particularly in the light of the McCray decision on the oleomargarine tax, this would not be an unconstitutional abuse of the taxing power. The committee report concluded with the observation that a serious barrier to the elimination of poisonous phosphorus match production was finally removed when the Diamond Company relinquished its patent.[58]

During the floor debate on the measure, which was rather brief, Democrat Charles Bartlett of Georgia voiced his objections to it as being "an

[56] House Report 406, p. 2.
[57] *Congressional Record*, 62 Cong., 2 Sess., 1912, 48:3148.
[58] House Report 406.

improper exercise of the power of Congress and a false pretense of the use of the taxing power." But Virginia Democrat Edward Saunders observed that the opposition was mistaken in thus seeking "refuge behind the doctrine of State rights," because the taxing power "is in no sense the police power." E. R. Bathrick, Democrat of Ohio, surmised that if the national government had the power to halt the poisoning of food, as in the Pure Food Act, it would be "as thoroughly proper and constitutional to prevent the putting of poisoning into a match." Henry Rainey, Democrat of Illinois, charged that the members of the House, himself included, would vote for the measure because they had been intimidated by "letters from college professors, women's clubs, and uplift organizations of various kinds" and press agents were "at work promoting this legislation to an extent unheard of before in this country." As Rainey predicted, the House passed the bill, with the inclusion of a few minor amendments, on March 28 by vote of 162 to 31, with 192 not voting and eight answering "present."[59]

When the proposal reached the Senate floor, some senators raised the same arguments against the use of the taxing power. Texas Democrat Joseph Bailey declared that each time the national government exercised such a power "under the guise of taxation, it practices a miserable and a false pretense." Once this industry was taxed out of existence, he warned, Congress could "select for destruction . . . any industry which a majority of the two houses of Congress may condemn." Republican Henry Cabot Lodge of Massachusetts, sponsor of the bill in the Senate, replied with the observation that the problem had "all been passed on in the oleomargarine case," not a particularly profound counterargument. Senator Bailey returned to the fray complaining that because the matches retailed at five cents per thousand this tax would quadruple the selling price, and he would rather close all match factories and "go back to the time when our fathers struck fire from flint" than "practice this kind of a fraud upon the Constitution." Despite Bailey's protests, the bill passed the Senate on April 3 without a roll call vote. President Taft signed the measure into law on April 9, 1912.[60]

The White Phosphorus Match Act of 1912 required match manufacturers who used poisonous phosphorus to register with district collectors of internal revenue and file periodic notices, inventories, and returns. It levied a tax of two cents per hundred matches, if of white phosphorus, and required the manufacturer to affix such revenue stamps to the match boxes.

[59] *Congressional Record*, 62 Cong., 2 Sess., 1912, 48:3968, 3969, 3975, 3976, 3979.
[60] Ibid., pp. 4235, 4238, 4241, 4679.

The penalty for violation was a one-thousand-dollar fine for each offense and/or a two-year prison term. The provisions of the law were to go into effect as of July 1, 1913, with the importation of such matches being forbidden after January 1, 1913, and a ban was placed upon their exportation beginning January 1, 1914.[61]

The enactment of the White Phosphorus Match Act is a prime example of the Progressive movement at its best in the endeavor to alleviate a social malady. The efforts to eradicate phossy jaw in the United States marked the real beginning in this country of attempts to control and to eliminate industrial diseases. A study of the struggle to destroy this terrible poisoning in the world also illustrates how far the United States lagged behind Europe, despite the tremendous efforts of the Progressive movement, in bringing about social justice to the laboring class.

The White Phosphorus Match Act was never litigated in the national courts[62] and thus became the only law which validly taxed out of existence a commodity considered evil by Congress.[63] A writer in the *Journal of Political Economy* described the passage of this act as "an interesting step in the direction of federal industrial legislation which may have far-reaching results."[64] But despite the fears of Senator Bailey and the perhaps hopeful supposition of the *Journal of Political Economy* writer, Congress did not proceed to tax out of existence any industry. In fact, the taxing power was never again used to destroy completely a product as in the case of dangerous matches. But this tax built further on the foundation of the existing national police power and the taxing power was used again in this manner two years later. When next used, however, on narcotics, it was based on a reversion to the control principle; the next such revenue measure was designed primarily to force registration of dealers rather than to destroy the "evil" traffic in narcotics.

[61] U.S., *Statutes at Large*, vol. 37.

[62] Robert Cushman, "Social and Economic Control Through Federal Taxation," in Association of American Law Schools, *Selected Essays on Constitutional Law* (Chicago, 1938), 3:557; see also *United States Code Annotated*, 26 ss 4801–6.

[63] The Match Act was revised and extended as late as August 1954; *United States Code Annotated*, 26 ss 4801–6.

[64] *Journal of Political Economy* 20 (May 1912) :514.

8 *The Crusade against Narcotics*

The use of opium and other narcotics to satisfy addictions became a major issue during the Progressive movement and, as a result of United States agitation, an international crusade emerged to eliminate the use of drugs for that purpose. The question first arose in regard to smoking opium; later, however, its derivatives, morphine and heroin, were used by drug addicts. The addictive drug cocaine, derived from coca leaves, and marijuana, made from hemp, were also in use. The reform movement eventually enveloped all types of illicit drugs. Enactment of a comprehensive program of regulation, rooted in the taxing power, resulted.

Opium, obtained from the seeds of the opium poppy, has been known to man for thousands of years; the earliest references are from Assyria and Sumeria, ca. 4000 B.C., where it was used for medicinal purposes.[1] But the preparation on a large scale of opium for smoking to satisfy addiction did not come about until the European penetration of the Far East in the seventeenth century. One source maintains that the Dutch first smoked opium in Formosa and from thence it was taken into China proper; another source states that the Portuguese introduced the habit to the Chinese.[2] Whatever the original contact, Chinese addiction to the drug, fostered by European countries through their Far East colonies, was so widespread that by the nineteenth century Westerners believed that the opium habit was native to the Orient.[3] Opium addiction in China became such a problem that as early as 1729 the emperor issued an edict prohibiting the manufacture and sale of smoking opium. Punishments for violations were extreme according to Western standards. Dealers in illicit opium were to be "exposed with the wooden collar about their necks one month and then sent to the army on the frontier"; accomplices were given "a hundred blows and then transported three years."[4]

This harsh suppression of the vice seemed necessary because of the debilitating effect of smoking opium on the user. A nineteenth-century English doctor, from contact with addicts, described its effects which included "stupor, forgetfulness, general deterioration of all the mental faculties, emaciation, debility, sallow complexion, lividness of lips and eyelids, languor and lack-lustre eye." If the dosage was not repeated at the usual time, the addict suffered "a great prostration, vertigo, torpor and discharge of water from the eye." Continued deprivation caused "coldness . . . aching pains . . . diarrhoea and the most horrid feelings of wretchedness." Complete denial of the drug, he said, resulted in death.[5]

The opium poppy grew chiefly in India, Oriental countries, and the Middle East. Turkish and Persian opium contained a high percentage of morphine and was most sought-after for medicinal purposes. Indian opium, by contrast, contained only 9 percent or less of morphine, so it was used principally to supply the smoking opium traffic. Chinese governmental opposition to this trade resulted in the so-called Opium War of 1839. Americans sympathized with the Chinese in this struggle, particularly in the aftermath by which, it was widely believed, the British forced the Chinese to legitimize the opium trade in the Treaty of Nanking. American opposition to the opium traffic was indicated in the Treaty of Wanghai in 1844 which waived extraterritorial rights for United States citizens brought to trial in China for engaging in the illicit trade.

American sympathy with Chinese efforts to eliminate their opium problem was further demonstrated in 1880 when the two countries negotiated a commercial agreement. This treaty forbade participation by United States

[1] "Drug Addiction," *Encyclopedia of the Social Sciences*, 5:243.

[2] Ibid., 11:471.

[3] Arnold H. Taylor, "American Confrontation with Opium Traffic in the Philippines," *Pacific Historical Review* 36 (August 1967) :307. The international aspect of this twentieth-century problem is detailed by the same author in "The United States and the International Movement to Control the Traffic in Narcotic Drugs, 1900–1939" (Ph.D. diss., Catholic University of America, 1963). This is the most thorough account of the international, diplomatic crusade against narcotics from its beginning to 1939. Taylor made good use of the Department of State and Bishop Charles Brent papers in this study. I have relied heavily upon this source for background material for this chapter.

[4] "The Opium Trade," *Living Age* 35 (December 1852) :547.

[5] Ibid., p. 549.

citizens in any aspect of the opium traffic with China or any Chinese nationals under United States jurisdiction to engage in the trade. The latter would include, of course, all Chinese residing in the United States except the native-born. The Chinese were considered to be the principal, if not the only, consumers of smoking opium in America. This agreement, therefore, would facilitate curtailment of the domestic opium problem in the United States.

Although the Senate passed a bill to implement this provision on June 2, 1884, the House of Representatives failed to consider the proposal.[6] On May 21, 1886, President Grover Cleveland called the attention of Congress to this oversight. He pointed out that Charles Denby, the United States minister to Peking, had been confronted with the situation of an American citizen in China leasing part of his dwelling to a British subject for use as an opium den in violation of the treaty. Thus, Cleveland noted, enforcing legislation was needed "without further delay."[7] Congress responded to his request in the next session. A Senate report observed that the opium trade was one of the greatest social evils China faced and the United States should assist in the struggle to eliminate it. In addition, American help here would foster friendlier relations which, it was intimated, would stimulate growing commercial relations with China.[8]

As a result, a bill was introduced in the Senate in December 1886 and passed the next month. It was reported and approved in the House in February 1887.[9] The measure prohibited any Chinese subject from importing opium into an American port and forbade United States citizens from importing opium into "any of the open ports in China" or engaging in the Chinese opium traffic.[10] With this legislation the United States laid the foundation for "pretensions to a superior moral position" that was to be followed during the twentieth century in regard to narcotics.[11] For the next decade Americans made no further effort to suppress the drug traffic except through revisions of tariff laws.

[6] *Congressional Record*, 48 Cong., 1 Sess., 1884, 15:4742.

[7] U.S., Congress, Senate, Executive Document 148 (Serial 2340), 49 Cong., 1 Sess., 1885, pp. 1–3; James D. Richardson, *Messages and Papers of the Presidents* (Washington, D.C., 1913), 7:4986, 5083.

[8] U.S., Congress, Senate, Committee on Foreign Relations, Senate Report 1621 (Serial 2456), 49 Cong., 2 Sess., 1887, pp. 1–3.

[9] *Congressional Record*, 49 Cong., 2 Sess., 1886, 18:326, 392, 1512–13.

[10] U.S., *Statutes at Large*, vol. 24.

[11] Taylor, "The United States and the International Movement," p. 19.

Opium was mentioned in the tariff of 1832 but was admitted free; it was not until the tariff of 1842 that a duty was levied. During the next few decades the duty on imported opium varied from nothing to $2.50 per pound. Then the "Mongrel" tariff of 1883 raised the rate to $10 per pound, and opium with less than 9 percent morphine content, or smoking opium, was banned. The law created problems for the Treasury Department. Opium for smoking was smuggled into the United States and then exported, legally, so the treasury secretary asked Congress in 1888 to prohibit also the exportation of opium with less than 9 percent morphine in order to help suppress smuggling.[12]

Congress, however, merely adjusted the tariff rates on opium. The McKinley tariff of 1890 taxed morphine fifty cents per ounce, opium at 40 percent ad valorem, and all smoking opium at $12 per pound.[13] The Treasury Department, though, discovered further problems arising from this law, for it also included an internal tax of $10 per pound on all smoking opium manufactured in the United States and restricted such production to American citizens. With these provisions, smoking opium manufactured in the United States would cost at least $40 per pound, counting the bulk loss in reducing it to a smokable form, and yet opium smuggled in was sold for less than half that price.[14] If detected and seized, Treasury agents, under existing laws, could not sell confiscated opium for more than half the tariff rate or about $6 per pound. In other words, the seized opium could be purchased and manufactured into smoking opium, legally, for a total cost of $16, or less than half the cost of domestically produced smoking opium. With this development, the secretary of the treasury asked for authority to sell seized opium to the highest bidder.[15] The House passed a bill to allow this, but the Senate amended it to provide that confiscated opium "shall be destroyed."[16] The House remained adamant and the final bill fulfilled the Treasury Department's request.[17] With these statutes the nation's conscience was salved. America had done everything considered possible to restrict the

[12] U.S., Congress, House, C.S. Fairchild to the Speaker of the House John G. Carlisle, January 12, 1888, House Executive Document 79 (Serial 2557), 50 Cong., 1 Sess., 1887, pp. 1–2.

[13] U.S., *Statutes at Large*, vol. 26.

[14] *Scientific American* 78 (March 5, 1898) : 147.

[15] U.S., Congress, House, Secretary of the Treasury to Nelson Dingley, Chairman of House Ways and Means Committee, January 21, 1897, House Report 2785 (Serial 3556), pp. 1–2.

[16] *Congressional Record*, 54 Cong., 2 Sess., 1897, 29:1631, 2525.

[17] U.S., *Statutes at Large*, vol. 29.

illicit drug traffic; from then on the opium problem was "strictly an Anglo-Chinese affair."[18]

Almost immediately, however, the United States faced an opium crisis resulting from the current developments of imperialism and the Progressive reform movement. With the acquisition of the Philippine Islands in 1898, America became directly involved in Far Eastern affairs and quickly discovered an opium problem in its new possession. American missionaries in the Orient had long insisted the United States use its influence to help the Chinese combat their opium traffic. They now added their influential voices to the demand that America assume the lead in suppressing the vice entirely and by doing so comply with the requirements of the white man's burden in bringing a "superior civilization to underdeveloped peoples." The United States, they believed, should use its new colonialism for altruistic purposes. Also, the various reform efforts of the Progressive era added weight to the momentum of this drive. Finally, such efforts dovetailed with the benevolent objectives of the open-door policy in China.[19]

The opium-smoking habit prevailed in the Philippines chiefly among the Chinese inhabitants which was proportionately a rather large population. Spain, beginning in 1843, instituted a "farming" program to control the vice. This involved the sale to the highest bidder of a monopoly on all transactions of the drug in the islands. Use of opium under this system was confined to Chinese adults with sale being forbidden to any Filipino. The Spanish system had the merits of raising revenue, placing the prevention of smuggling in the hands of the monopolist, which cut government expenses, and curtailing the spread of drug addiction to the native population. But the United States immediately ended this governmental sale of a monopoly and for the next few years taxed only the importation of opium into the Philippines. The results of this policy were immediate.

In 1899 opium imports into the Philippines were valued at $328,713. By 1901 this figure had tripled and there was an alarming spread of the opium habit to the Filipinos.[20] Because certain features of the opium traffic were peculiar to the islands, the Philippine Commission, the governing body, determined to solve the problem in 1903 by reinstituting the Spanish "farming" system. This decision precipitated a storm of protest, particularly from missionaries and their societies, and as the Commission ap-

[18] Taylor, "American Confrontation with Opium Traffic," p. 308.
[19] Ibid., p. 309.
[20] "The Philippine Opium Trade," *Nation* 77 (October 1903) : 261.

proached final approval of the "farming" proposal, appeals were made to Washington to halt passage of the measure. The president of the International Reform Bureau, the Reverend Wilbur F. Crafts, communicated with President Theodore Roosevelt and, simultaneously, sent 2,000 petitions on telegraphic blanks to prominent people throughout the nation for their signature and submission to the president.[21] Secretary of War Elihu Root consequently ordered suspension on final passage of the measure until a special committee could study the problem thoroughly.[22]

By this time the reform movement had achieved success in another area. Congress enacted a law which forbade anyone subject to the jurisdiction of the United States to supply firearms, intoxicating liquors, or opium to "any aboriginal native" of the New Hebrides Islands not under the jurisdiction of any "civilized" power.[23] This achievement further encouraged missionaries and reformers to attack the Chinese opium problem. Many of these persons began petitioning the president to help China end the opium traffic with British India.

With the current Russo-Japanese War, the International Reform Bureau believed the president might be able to use his influence to include other Far Eastern problems, especially China's opium traffic, in the negotiations terminating that struggle. To climax and to dramatize its position, the bureau requested and received an interview with Secretary of State John Hay. The reformers praised Hay for his "Golden Rule Diplomacy" and urged him to extend his diplomatic principles by helping China with its opium problem. In addition, the interviewers emphasized the material motive that this assistance to China would also undoubtedly increase American trade and commercial relations with that country. A summary of the recent investigation of the opium problem in the Orient made by the committee appointed by the Philippine Commission in 1903 was included in this hearing.[24]

The Philippine Commission chose well in selecting the investigating

[21] Taylor, "American Confrontation with Opium Traffic," pp. 313–14. This article details the provisions of the proposed system and also the pressure from reformers who opposed it, pp. 311–18.

[22] "Opium in the Philippines," *Independent* 55 (July 16, 1903) :1651–52.

[23] U.S., *Statutes at Large*, vol. 32.

[24] U.S., Congress, Senate, *Report of the Hearing at the American State Department on Petitions to the President to Use His Good Offices for the Release of China from Treaty Compulsion to Tolerate the Opium Traffic, with Additional Papers*, Senate Document 145 (Serial 4765), pp. 1–3.

team. Major Edward C. Carter, chief health officer in the Philippine Islands, and Jose Albert, a native physician, were appointed although, due to family illness, Albert did not make the tour of the Orient but confined his investigations to the opium problem in the Philippines. Charles H. Brent, the Episcopal bishop of the Philippines, was the most prominent member of the group and was the one who, along with Hamilton Wright, did more than anyone else to further the international effort to suppress the illicit opium trade.[25]

The unique results of the committee investigation came from the instructions given the members to collect information on the total Oriental opium problem. The group accordingly approached the issue from the social and moral aspects as well as its economic features.[26] The committee spent five months visiting Japan, Formosa, Shanghai, Singapore, Burma, and Java and submitted a 283-page summation of their findings. The report noted that any feasible solution to the problem was complicated by the fact that opium constituted a major source of income for many of the governments involved. The committee had high praise for the Japanese who viewed opium as a moral problem and followed a program of absolute prohibition except for medicinal purposes. Especially noteworthy, the members believed, was the system Japan had instituted when it acquired Formosa in 1895. Formosa, being almost completely Chinese in population, had an acute opium problem so the Japanese undertook to eliminate it by imposing a government monopoly with strict control "looking to the gradual suppression" of the habit.[27] The investigating committee strongly recommended that a similar regulatory system be established in the Philippines. They proposed: 1) a government monopoly on the importation, wholesale, and retail activities of handling opium; 2) registration and licensing for chronic opium smokers, limited to Chinese over twenty-one years of age; 3) free treatment for addicts who wished to break the habit; and 4) after three years, a ban on importation of opium except for medic-

[25] Taylor, "American Confrontation with Opium Traffic," p. 316; Taylor, "The United States and the International Movement," p. 69; "Persistence in Reform," *Outlook* 115 (January 17, 1917) : 94.

[26] See, e.g., William J. Collins, "The Work of the International Opium Conference at the Hague," *Contemporary Review* 101 (March 1912) : 317–18.

[27] U.S., Congress, Senate, *Message from the President Transmitting the Report of the Committee Appointed by the Philippine Commission to Investigate the Use of Opium and the Traffic Therein*, Senate Document 265 (Serial 4914), 59 Cong., 1 Sess., 1905, pp. 21–25.

inal purposes. The members acknowledged that these recommendations would "encounter opposition and disapprobation, but they are at least honest."[28]

Based upon this report, Congress in early 1905 amended the tariff law applying to the Philippine Islands by incorporating these proposals into the new law. There was no congressional opposition to this measure; the only protest came from congressmen who wanted to close the traffic at once. The original House version contained a provision for an immediate ban, but the current secretary of war, William H. Taft, persuaded the Senate committee to allow for a three-year transition period which the Senate, and later the House, accepted.[29]

The law provided for absolute prohibition of importation of opium into the Philippines except for medicinal purposes after March 1, 1908. In the meantime the Philippine Commission could impose any system deemed feasible as long as no opium was sold to native Filipinos except for medicine.[30] During the interim the Commission instituted the High (fee) License program rather than the government monopoly system. But even after the 1908 ban, opium addiction was not eliminated in the Philippines. The traffic merely went underground with increased smuggling and illicit operations.[31] Reformers and regulatory agencies would repeatedly discover that suppression of the narcotics vice was difficult if not impossible.

Reformers next sought to attack the problem on a world basis. Due, in part, to the force of world public opinion, Great Britain signed an agreement with China in 1906 which provided for Britain's decreasing the exportation of Indian opium into China by 10 percent a year if China would cut its domestic production of opium correspondingly. This *pari passu* arrangement worked so well that this aspect of the opium trade, considered to be the worst phase of the world traffic, was nearly eliminated and in 1914 Britain halted further exports of the drug to China.

The 1906 treaty stimulated optimism that through concerted effort the governments of the world might be successful in abolishing the traffic. President Roosevelt, therefore, directed Secretary of State Root to correspond with nations concerned with the Oriental opium trade in order to ascertain the feasibility of an international conference. A favorable reaction

[28] Ibid., pp. 49–55.
[29] *Congressional Record*, 58 Cong., 3 Sess., 1905, 39:3066, 3714, 3786.
[30] U.S., *Statutes at Large*, vol. 33.
[31] Taylor, "American Confrontation with Opium Traffic," pp. 322–23.

was forthcoming so an invitation was sent to the nations involved–Great Britain, France, Germany, Russia, Portugal, Persia, Japan, China, Siam, and the United States–to send delegates to a meeting in Shanghai in early 1909.[32] To prepare for participation in this meeting government officials decided the United States should begin an investigation and determine the extent of its domestic opium problem. Hamilton Wright, a New England physician who was an expert on tropical diseases and subsequently became involved in the problem of opium addiction, was placed in charge of the probe. To the surprise and dismay of most Americans, Wright discovered the United States faced a far greater problem of drug addiction than had been realized.

By surveying those involved in the drug industry, including importers, physicians, and hospitals, Wright found that the United States annually imported 500,000 pounds of opium or its derivatives while about one-tenth of that amount would supply current medical and scientific needs. In addition, the nation was annually consuming 200,000 ounces of coca leaves, or derivatives, from South America while experts estimated that some 15,000 ounces would suffice for legitimate needs.[33] These revelations of a serious domestic drug problem were, to say the least, embarrassing, especially when announced on the eve of the international conference called by the United States. A bill was immediately introduced in Congress designed to meet the crisis. A letter from Root to the House of Representatives informed congressmen that passage of the measure was imperative "in time to save our face in the conference at Shanghai."[34]

Because haste was of utmost importance, the sponsors decided to keep the bill simple by restricting its provisions to smoking opium; a bill with broader coverage, dealing with the entire drug traffic, would be "too complicated and controversial for hurried consideration by Congress."[35] When Senator Lodge introduced S. 8021 he asked for unanimous consent of the Senate to consider it immediately. To justify this unusual procedure, he quoted a letter Root had received from the United States delegation to Shanghai. The delegates, then in session, believed the prospects were favor-

[32] U.S., Congress, House, *Message from the President*, House Document 926 (Serial 5377), 60 Cong., 1 Sess., 1907, pp. 1–3.

[33] Elbert Francis Baldwin, "The Background of the Opium Conference at the Hague," *Review of Reviews* 45 (February 1912) :218.

[34] U.S., Congress, House, E. Root to James E. Sherman, December 26, 1908, House Report 1878 (Serial 5384), 60 Cong., 2 Sess., 1908, p. 2.

[35] Arnold, "The United States and the International Movement," p. 76.

able for a successful convention but that "pasage of the opium bill before February 1 [was] of utmost importance" to assure desired action.[36] If the United States were to ask other nations to suppress the opium traffic, it would have to appear before them with its record as clean as possible.

Despite the urgency, Senator Joseph Bailey, Democrat of Texas, expressed concern over the trend of Congress toward prohibition of products. "Clearly," he said, "the Federal Government has no general police powers," but if Congress were to act on child labor laws "and other enactments of that kind," the result would be the establishment of such powers. Senator Weldon Heyburn, Republican of Idaho, agreed the national government had no police power, but observed that because Congress could determine which commodities were "merchantible," it could exclude smoking opium if desired. Fortified by this reasoning, the Senate passed the bill without a roll call vote.[37]

Because the bill provided for an amendment to the tariff law, and bills of revenue must originate in the House of Representatives, the lower house regarded S. 8021 as an invasion of its prerogative and substituted a similar measure, H.R. 27427, for it. The House immediately approved its proposal without roll call vote and sent it, along with an indignant resolution explaining the action, to the upper house. The Senate meekly acquiesced in H.R. 27427 and sent it to the president for signature.[38] This law forbade importation of opium into the United States for any purpose other than medicinal and provided that possession of illegal opium after April 1, 1909, would be deemed sufficient for conviction unless the defendant could legally justify possessing it.[39]

The Shanghai conference, meanwhile, was a great success from the American viewpoint. Bishop Brent was chosen to preside and in his opening remarks reminded the delegates the meeting was an investigatory one without powers of commitment binding on the governments involved.[40] The major result of the convention was adoption of a series of resolutions to be recommended to the governments concerned. These included the suggestion that every country examine its regulations on opium and try to suppress its

[36] *Congressional Record*, 60 Cong., 2 Sess., 1909, 43:1398. See also "The War against Opium Smoking in America," *Outlook* 91 (February 6, 1909) :275.

[37] Ibid., pp. 1397–99, 1400.

[38] Ibid., pp. 1649, 1684, 1716.

[39] U.S., *Statutes at Large*, vol. 35.

[40] "The Fight against Opium," *Nation* 89 (July 29, 1909) :92.

illicit use; they were requested also to assist China in her fight against the traffic by enacting laws prohibiting shipment of smoking opium to countries forbidding importation of it. Most important, the nations were asked to join in an international investigation of the opium trade in order that all might take strong measures to suppress the "ominously spreading morphine habit."[41] When the Netherlands government subsequently offered to serve as host, the United States Department of State in September 1909 asked all countries directly involved in the opium problem to send delegates to The Hague to discuss and take steps to abolish the traffic.[42]

To comply with the Shanghai recommendations and to prepare for conference at The Hague the State Department directed Hamilton Wright to continue his study of the opium problem, both in the United States and abroad. Wright reviewed the history of United States tariff laws on opium and concluded that the low duty on raw opium had encouraged, rather than discouraged, the importation and manufacture of smoking opium, which had led to the steady growth of its misuse. He also disclosed that during the past twenty years a new and "almost strictly American vice" had developed in the use of cocaine for drug addiction. Wright discovered that during the decade of 1900–1909 the importation into the United States of opium had increased 59.1 percent over the previous decade, with a concurrent increase of only 15.9 percent in population, thus suggesting an acceleration in illicit drug traffic.[43]

He learned from importers and manufacturers of opium that 70 to 80 percent of all imported crude opium was manufactured into morphine and 75 percent of this amount was consumed by addicts. Current opinion, Wright noted, held that this use of opium and cocaine increased criminal activity, particularly cocaine because its effects were "more appalling than any other habit-forming drug." Wright found that drug addiction was a problem especially among "the lower order of working Negroes" in the South. Part of this could be attributed to the practice of some Southern labor contractors who forced cocaine upon their laborers "under the impression that they can get more and better work" from them. But he ob-

[41] All these resolutions are listed in "The International Anti-Opium Conference," *Outlook* 91 (March 20, 1909) : 611.

[42] U.S., Congress, Senate, *Message from the President*, Senate Document 736 (Serial 5943), 61 Cong., 3 Sess., 1910, p. 4.

[43] U.S., Congress, Senate, *Message from the President*, Senate Document 377 (Serial 5657), 61 Cong., 2 Sess., 1910, p. 34.

served, however, that drug habits were also spreading "to the higher ranks of society" in America.[44]

The State Department asked Wright to draft a proposed law based upon this report. The basic weakness in the 1909 law, Wright believed, lay in the lack of control over the destination of imported opium. Despite the restriction against smoking opium, a loophole resulted from the provision to import opium for medicinal purposes and then manufacture it for illicit uses. Wright's proposal, then, would tax prohibitively the production of smoking opium by raising the current processing tax of $10 per pound to $1,000. His approach received the endorsement of the Committee of One Hundred of the American Association for the Advancement of Science on National Health.[45] Wright also recommended, and drafted a bill to provide for, a comprehensive program of drug control. Congress enacted the basic features of this proposal in 1914 with the passage of the Harrison Act.

President Taft endorsed the idea of a prohibitive tax on smoking opium as did Philander Knox, his secretary of state. Knox particularly emphasized the importance of the coming Hague conference, calling the attention of Congress to the responsibility of the United States "to see that its own house is in order" before the convention met. The secretary noted that although forty-five (of the current forty-six) states prohibited the illicit use of cocaine and twenty-four regulated the sale of opium, these efforts were generally ineffective because of the problem of interstate commerce. He also recommended Wright's proposal for more comprehensive control which had been introduced in Congress, known as the Foster bill from the name of its original sponsor.[46]

From December 1911 through January 1912 delegates from the twelve countries that had participated in the Shanghai conference met at The Hague. This meeting also unanimously chose Bishop Brent to preside over the deliberations. Basically the delegates discussed and recommended the same resolutions proposed at the Shanghai conference in 1909.[47] But the delegates also perceived that it would be useless to implement these proposals without the cooperation of all the nations not represented. It was

[44] Ibid., pp. 46–51.

[45] Ibid., pp. 56–59.

[46] U.S., Congress, Senate, *Message from the President*, Senate Document 736 (Serial 5943), 61 Cong., 3 Sess., 1910, pp. 1–7; Richardson, *Messages and Papers of the Presidents*, 10:7849–50, 7976–78.

[47] These recommendations are listed in U.S., Congress, Senate, *Message from the President*, Senate Document 733 (Serial 6178), 62 Cong., 2 Sess., 1911, pp. 17–21.

agreed, therefore, that the thirty-four other major governments of the world would be invited, and urged, to participate in the crusade by adopting their recommendations and a second conference would be held later in 1912 for all participating nations to deposit ratifications of The Hague Convention.[48]

The United States assumption of world leadership of the crusade against the opium evil pressured Congress to establish a comprehensive regulatory system and thus set an example for other nations. Congressman David Foster, Republican of Vermont, took the congressional initiative in sponsoring legislation to control the domestic traffic in drugs through bills drafted by Hamilton Wright for the State Department. In the second and third sessions of the Sixty-first Congress, following the Shanghai meeting, Foster introduced several measures to achieve this purpose. When Foster died in 1912 the Department of State asked Francis Harrison, Democrat of New York and the new chairman of the House Ways and Means Committee, to sponsor the legislation.[49] Although Harrison resigned from Congress in late 1913 to become governor general of the Philippines, he had performed so well in promoting drug legislation that the major law, passed in 1914, was given his name.

The 1909 prohibitory law brought an increase in smuggling. Opium would be brought into San Francisco Bay, transshipped to Mexico, and then smuggled into the United States by land. Smugglers packaged the opium in old containers with the necessary revenue stamps and, if discovered, defended their possession on the grounds that the drug had been imported prior to 1909, which was legal.[50] H.R. 1966, introduced in 1913, provided for closure of this outlet by making mere possession of illicit opium presumptive of guilt. The burden of proof of innocence was placed upon the defendant. The bill also banned exportation of opium, cocaine, or their derivatives, except for medicinal purposes, and then only under the regulatory provisions of the country to which it was shipped, fulfilling the United States' obligation accepted at the first Hague meeting. The bill easily passed the House on June 16 and was sent to the Senate where it was accepted without debate and with minor amendments in wording the following December.

---

[48] Ibid., p. 25; "The International Opium Conference," *Outlook* 104 (July 12, 1913) : 547–48.

[49] *Congressional Record*, 63 Cong., 1 Sess., 1913, 50:2201.

[50] See U.S., Congress, House, Report 24 (Serial 6513), 63 Cong., 1 Sess., 1913, pp. 2–3.

The House agreed to these changes and forwarded it to President Woodrow Wilson in January 1914.[51]

The companion to H.R. 1966, H.R. 1967, was introduced, debated, and passed by both houses on the same days, without opposition. H.R. 1967 was also designed to bring the United States into line with The Hague agreement. This bill sought to curtail domestic production of smoking opium by raising the manufacturing tax to a prohibitive level. The tax of 1890 imposed a levy of $10 per pound on all smoking opium produced domestically and restricted its production to American citizens who had to post a $5,000 bond to engage in manufacturing it. A Senate report noted that opium poppies were grown on the Pacific slope of the United States and the current low manufacturing tax, without the additional tariff, stimulated a very profitable domestic production of smoking opium.[52] H.R. 1967 retained the restriction limiting this business to American citizens and increased the bond to $100,000 and the tax per pound on smoking opium to $200. Following House passage of this measure, the Senate amended the levy to raise it to $300 per pound, which the House agreed to, and sent it to the White House where President Wilson signed it in January 1914.[53]

The most important of these bills, H.R. 6282, provided for a comprehensive system of control of narcotics in the United States. This proposal resulted from a long series of conferences among members of the House Ways and Means Committee, the departments of State and Treasury, and representatives of the various organizations of the legitimate drug industry. All agreed upon the main provisions of the Harrison bill. The House easily accepted the bill on June 26, 1913.[54]

The most important alteration made to the bill in the Senate included a required registration of all who used hypodermic needles or syringes in any way, with the exception of veterinarians; this committee amendment was eventually deleted.[55] The House requirement that all doctors had to report, and keep records of, all opiates they administered was deleted by the Senate.

51 *Congresional Record*, 63 Cong., 2 Sess., 1913, 51:1288, 1543, 2201; U.S., *Statutes at Large*, vol. 38.
52 U.S., Congress, Senate, *Manufacture of Smoking Opium*, Senate Report 130 (Serial 6510), 63 Cong., 1 Sess., 1913, p. 6.
53 *Congressional Record*, 63 Cong., 2 Sess., 1913, 51:1288; U.S., *Statutes at Large*, vol. 38.
54 *Congressional Record*, 63 Cong., 1 Sess., 1913, 50:2201–22.
55 For the pressure of the State and Treasury departments to eliminate this amendment, see U.S., Congress, Senate, Document 473 (Serial 6594), 63 Cong., 2 Sess., 1914, pp. 3–4.

The upper house then accepted the bill on August 15, 1914.[56] Physicians throughout the nation, especially country doctors, objected to the records requirement, but the House refused to accept the Senate change and a conference committee was appointed to discuss the conflict. The resulting compromise exempted all doctors, dentists, and veterinarians from making reports of administrations of opiates if they were in personal attendance upon the patient. The Senate accepted this version on October 17, 1914, and the House gave final approval to the act on December 10, 1914.[57]

The Harrison Anti-Narcotic Act required, after March 1, 1915, that anyone who dealt in any way with opium or coca leaves, or their derivatives, must register with the district collector of Internal Revenue and pay a one dollar annual fee for a license. Any sale of narcotics must be recorded on special order blanks provided by the Bureau of Internal Revenue except if the physician prescribed through a personal attendance upon the patient. Also exempted were dealers in drugs who filled orders upon a written prescription from a registered doctor. All records of sales must be filed and kept for a two-year period. These provisions applied to all exchanges of narcotic drugs if the preparations were in excess of two grains of opium, one grain of codeine, one-fourth grain of morphine, and one-eighth grain of heroin.[58] Amounts of this size or less were not considered sufficient dosages for drug addiction.

The drug laws were challenged in the Supreme Court and the Harrison Act barely gained the approval of the High Tribunal. The Court that heard these cases was composed primarily of Taft appointees. In four years Taft was able to name as many justices as Theodore Roosevelt and Woodrow Wilson did in almost sixteen years. Roosevelt and Wilson advocated extensive governmental activity and appointed men they believed agreed with this constitutional philosophy; Taft was of a more conservative bent and his nominees reflected this approach to constitutional problems. With the Progressive movement at its peak during his presidency, Taft looked to the Court to protect the status quo against assaults of reformers.[59]

Edward White became chief justice after Fuller's death. Taft was willing to break precedent and elevate a justice from the opposing party because

[56] *Congressional Record*, 63 Cong., 2 Sess., 1914, 51:9938.

[57] Ibid., p. 16807; 63 Cong., 3 Sess., 1914, 52:99.

[58] U.S., *Statutes at Large*, vol. 38. These fees were raised in the Revenue Act of 1918; ibid., vol. 40.

[59] Daniel S. McHargue, "President Taft's Appointments to the Supreme Court," *Journal of Politics* 12 (August 1950) :478–510.

White's views coincided with his own. Taft also appointed Horace Lurton, his former circuit court colleague, and Joseph Lamar who was relatively unknown but proved to be ultraconservative. Willis VanDevanter, a Union Pacific Railroad lawyer, and Mahlon Pitney, another conservative, were appointed by Taft as well as Charles E. Hughes who resigned in 1916 to run for the presidency.

Joseph McKenna was the only nineteenth-century appointee still on the Court. William Day and Oliver Wendell Holmes, the great dissenter, remained on the bench. Holmes was joined in his dissents in 1916 by two Wilson appointees, Louis Brandeis and John Clarke. Brandeis was one of the leading liberal reformers of his time; his views, in fact, touched off a vigorous fight over confirming his nomination. Clarke was also a well-known liberal and he and Brandeis, even more than Holmes, were deeply committed to broad governmental intervention in economic affairs.

Wilson's first nominee, James McReynolds, proved to be one of that president's worst disappointments in domestic affairs. As Wilson's attorney general, McReynolds was an ardent trustbuster. But after elevation to the Supreme Court he became one of the most illiberal men ever to sit on the bench.

The first major test of the Harrison Act involved a district court quashing an indictment for a conspiracy to sell a dram of morphine, not for medicine but to supply an addict, by a nonregistered person. The United States appealed the decision to the Supreme Court partially on the grounds that the law was designed to carry out a treaty, The Hague Convention, and to do so Congress "gave it the appearance of a taxing measure in order to give it a coat of constitutionality." Thus, although the law invaded the states' police power by controlling a commodity beyond the reach of the national government's power, it should be sustained because a treaty, or a law fulfilling a treaty obligation, should be the supreme law of the land.[60] The Supreme Court disagreed with this argument, declaring the required registration could not be applied to everyone in the nation. Although the statute also had a "moral end," it was fundamentally a revenue measure and must be interpreted as such in all its provisions. The section requiring presumption of guilt for "any person not registered" and possessing illegal drugs, the Court held, must apply only to "the class the law deals with"—those

---

[60] *Transcripts of Records and File Copies of Briefs*, Case #525, 1915 Term, vol. 77, U.S. Supreme Court Library.

engaged in the vocation of handling drugs—and could not be interpreted to apply to "any person in the United States." A blanket application of the presumption-of-guilt clause, therefore, could not be sustained.[61]

In the Revenue Act of 1918, which raised the tax rate on drugs, Congress inserted a clause prohibiting "any person to sell, dispense or distribute" drugs except under provisions of the Harrison Act. This permitted the Supreme Court to clarify the confusion caused by the Jin Fuey Moy case. In 1922 a Wong Sing appealed his conviction for purchasing drugs for the purpose of reselling them. He argued that because of the Jin Fuey Moy decision he could not be prosecuted because purchasers were not required to register under the Harrison Act. The Supreme Court, however, sustained his conviction because of the phrase *any person* in the 1918 law which therefore did not require registration of purchasers. The term *any person* was broad enough to cover everyone in the United States so anyone could be held liable to the restrictions of the Harrison Act.[62]

The Harrison Act received its most important test in 1919 in *United States* v. *Doremus*.[63] This case involved a physician who was registered and had complied with all the drug requirements but had been prosecuted for selling five hundred $\frac{1}{6}$ grain tablets to Alexander Ameris to satisfy his habit. The district court of West Texas refused to convict the doctor because the law was an unconstitutional invasion of the states' reserved police power.[64] By the narrowest of margins—five to four—the Supreme Court reversed this decision. The majority opinion cited the precedents of the *License* Cases and the *Veazie* decision to illustrate that there were but few limitations to the congressional power to tax. In this instance Congress had "full power . . . short of arbitrary and unreasonable action." The Harrison Act specifically provided for the raising of revenue which was quite valid so it also had the power to make provisions for collecting the taxes. In a very brief dissent, Chief Justice Edward White, joined by Justices Joseph McKenna, Willis VanDevanter, and James McReynolds, held that Congress had exerted "a power not delegated" by controlling narcotics and thus had invaded the "reserved police power of the states."

That same day in the Webb case the Court also upheld the act's prohibi-

[61] *United States* v. *Jin Fuey Moy*, 241 U.S. 394 (1916).

[62] *United States* v. *Wong Sing*, 260 U.S. 18 (1922).

[63] 249 U.S. 86.

[64] *Transcripts of Records and File Copies of Briefs*, Case #367, 1918 Term, vol. 83, U.S. Supreme Court Library.

tion of selling drugs without the prescribed order form as being a constitutional condition for assisting in the collection of the revenue.[65] W. S. Webb, a physician, and Jacob Goldbaum, a retail druggist, were both registered but were convicted for prescribing and selling narcotics not to cure but to keep the addicts comfortable. They appealed their conviction on the grounds that if the Harrison Act was a revenue measure then Congress could not stipulate to whom the drugs could not be sold.[66] This decision resulted in doctors refusing to prescribe for drug addicts.

Justice McReynolds ,who consistently questioned the constitutionality of the Harrison Act, was able to qualify the Webb decision six years later. During his twenty-seven years on the Supreme Court, this justice proved to be one of the most consistent and most determined advocates of laissez-faire of any of the Supreme Court justices of the twentieth century. In the Linder case he was able to strike a blow for freedom in medical practice. Dr. Charles Linder was convicted for selling morphine and cocaine to an addict, Ida Casey, who could not legally obtain an order form to continue her habit. He prescribed and sold these drugs for the purpose of relieving her suffering. Cross-examination during the trial revealed that Mrs. Casey was used by the local narcotics agent to trap Dr. Linder by paying him with a marked five-dollar bill. Linder defended his action by claiming he did not know the patient was an addict and that she had displayed symptoms of a stomach ulcer which required narcotic treatment for relief.[67]

McReynolds, speaking for the Court, reversed Linder's conviction. Congress cannot, "under the pretext of executing delegated power, pass laws for the accomplishment of objects not entrusted to the Federal Government," McReynolds insisted. The drugs in this case were medically prescribed, he said, and the enforcing provisions of the Harrison Act could not extend to "direct control of medical practice in the states." Such a broad interpretation of the order forms in order to collect taxes from this revenue measure would be "plainly inappropriate and unnecessary" for a "reasonable enforcement." "The Narcotic Law," he declared, "is essentially a revenue measure, and its provisions must be reasonably applied with the primary view of enforcing the special tax."[68] Despite this interpretation, narcotics

[65] *Webb* v. *United States*, 249 U.S. 96 (1919).

[66] *Transcripts of Records and File Copies of Briefs*, Case #370, 1918 Term, vol. 84, U.S. Supreme Court Library.

[67] Ibid., Case #183, 1924 Term, vol. 36.

[68] *Linder* v. *United States*, 268 U.S. 5 (1925). For McReynolds's conservative con-

officials continued to paraphrase the *Webb* decision in their regulations issued to medical people and doctors continued to abstain from prescribing for addicts.[69] This drove drug addicts into the arms of illicit drug peddlers.

The next year another case presented McReynolds a further opportunity to call attention to the question of the constitutionality of the Harrison Act. A person had received the maximum sentence of five years imprisonment on each of three separate counts for violating the law. The Supreme Court denied his appeal which had asked that these sentences be run concurrently, not consecutively, because they were for the same offense. But in a procedure rarely employed by justices, McReynolds used this case as an opportunity to invite litigation which would permit the Supreme Court to review its five-to-four decision on the constitutionality of the Harrison Act. Because the court was "so sharply divided" in the Doremus case, he observed, and because of the doctrine announced in the *Hammer* v. *Dagenhart, Hill* v. *Wallace*, and *United States* v. *Linder* cases, this might "necessitate a review of that question if hereafter properly presented."[70]

The following year the Supreme Court accepted such a case. A conviction based on violation of the provision that a person could buy drugs only in, or from, the properly taxed, stamped containers was appealed on the basis that the Harrison Act thus regulated a state matter. The Eighth Circuit Court, in certifying questions to the Supreme Court, noted the language McReynolds used in the *Daugherty* case was *obiter dictum*, but understood it to be "an invitation and permission" to ask the Court to reexamine its *Doremus* decision.[71] Justice McReynolds, announcing the decision, surprisingly rejected this argument. He noted that the provisions did not "absolutely prohibit buying or selling" drugs; the act had "produced substantial revenue" and contained "nothing to indicate that by colorable use of taxation" Congress had attempted to invade the realm of state-reserved powers. Because the "impositions" were not "penalities," he said, this was a valid exercise of the revenue power of Congress.[72]

---

stitutional philosophy see William F. Swindler, *Court and Constitution in the Twentieth Century* (Indianapolis, Ind., 1970) 1:216–18; 2:28, 36–37.

[69] Rufus King, "Narcotic Drug Laws and Enforcement Policies," *Law and Contemporary Problems* 22 (Winter 1957) : 120–23.

[70] *United States* v. *Daugherty*, 269 U.S. 360 (1926). The Hammer and Hill cases will be discussed in the next chapter.

[71] *Transcripts of Records and File Copies of Briefs*, Case #898, 1926 Term, vol. 136, U.S. Supreme Court Library.

[72] *Alston* v. *United States*, 274 U.S. 289 (1927).

The next year the Supreme Court again held the act to be valid. Mc-
Reynolds, however, with Sutherland and Butler, inexplicibly dissented
from this opinion. "Although disguised," this dissent argued, "the real and
primary purpose is not difficult to discover and it is strict limitation of the
traffic." McReynolds pointed out that the effects of tobacco, diamonds, and
even silks, as well as opium, were "often deleterious"; the desire for these
luxuries sometimes led "to extravagance and frequently to crime" to obtain them. Yet Congress merely taxed these items, except for opium, and
did not attempt an "elaborate regulation" of them as in the case of drugs.
"Whether, or how far," these commodities could be sold within a state "is
primarily for the States to decide," he declared, and not Congress.[73]

As a result of these decisions, doctors carefully remained within the
limits of the Linder loophole and addicts could legally obtain drugs only in
small amounts.[74] These opinions also provided the public policy framework
for the drug laws that followed the Harrison Act, such as the tax on marijuana in 1937.

Significantly, the Harrison Act came closer to being nullified by the
Supreme Court than any regulatory tax to that time. For the first time, in
1919 four justices agreed that a regulatory tax invaded the states' reserved
police powers. The next two regulatory taxes to come before the High
Tribunal were declared to be an unconstitutional invasion of state police
powers. Regulatory taxes on child labor and grain futures were struck down
as violating the Tenth Amendment.

[73] *Nigro* v. *United States*, 276 U.S. 332 (1928).
[74] Harold Gill Reuschlein and Albert B. Spector, "Taxing and Spending," *Cornell
Law Review* 23 (December 1937) : 21.

9 Two Setbacks for the Taxing Power

On May 15, 1922, the Supreme Court declared unconstitutional the taxes on both the employment of child labor and grain futures contracts. These twin opinions presaged a rising judicial conservatism and an increasing reliance on the concept of Dual Federalism that characterized the Supreme Court's interpretations until the "Roosevelt Revolution" of the New Deal. In the immediate sense, the decisions cast an aura of doubt over the feasibility of the further use of the taxing power to achieve social and economic reforms.

The elimination of child labor in mines and factories became one of the chief objectives of the Progressive movement. The early years of the Industrial Revolution in the United States engendered, as it did in other countries, the exploitation of child labor. Children had commonly worked in agriculture under parental supervision but their use in mines and factories, under the care of not-always-gentle strangers, led to terrible abuses in hours and working conditions. Even before 1900, reformers had made significant gains in the North in restricting these practices. The emergence of the New South, however, with its emphasis on industrialization, permitted the domination of laissez-faire thought in this area longer than in the North which had industrialized decades earlier. The South as a region vigorously opposed regulation of industry, including use of child labor which was an "entrenched interest," long after correctives had been made in the North.[1]

Progressive reformers formed a National Child Labor Committee in 1904 for the purpose of promoting child labor legislation in the states that had not yet enacted such. The committee efforts resulted in focusing national attention on the South where the use of child labor in textile mills constituted the worst child labor problem in United States industry.[2] Southern mill owners resisted these reform efforts, arguing that child labor was necessary so that their products could compete with New England textiles. Promoting the argument that this reform movement was a plot undertaken by New England textile millers, they were able to play succesfully upon resentment to Northern interference with the Southern way of life, and child labor laws came haltingly to Dixie.[3]

A governmental investigation of child labor conditions, conducted in 1908 and 1909, revealed that use of child labor in textile mills was more prevalent in the South than elsewhere in the nation. More important, the statistics of this study showed that the abuse was steadily increasing rather than decreasing. In 1880, of the 28,320 children working in textiles in the United States, 4,097 were in the South; by 1890 this number had increased to 8,815 of the total 23,432 (the smaller total figure represents the results of the reform movement in the North); by 1900 the number had risen to 24,438 of a total of 39,866 children and in 1905 the numbers were 27,571 Southern children of a total of 40,029.[4] Employing children under fourteen years of age, working them long hours, and especially making them work night shifts were practices that reformers focused upon in efforts to eliminate the worst features of the problem.

As a result of agitation, Southern states legislated against these practices and by 1912 all Southern states had laws governing child labor in terms of hours and ages.[5] These limitations, however, were usually twelve years of age and the hours ranged from sixty-six to sixty hours per week, standards far below those sought by the National Child Labor Committee. More important was the absence of enforcement provisions in most of these states. It was found that 107 of the 143 mills inspected in five Southern states in 1908–1909 employed children under the legal ages; South Car-

[1] C. Vann Woodward, *Origins of the New South, 1877–1913* (Baton Rouge, La., 1967), pp. 416–20.

[2] Stephen B. Wood, *Constitutional Politics in the Progressive Era: Child Labor and the Law* (Chicago, Ill., 1968), pp. 6–13. I have relied heavily on this study for background to the tax on child labor.

[3] The fact that they were probably correct in assuming a Northern plot is suggested by Northern efforts to promote, unsuccessfully, a national labor legislation amendment as early as 1898. See Patrick J. Hearden, "The New South's Quest for Empire" (Ph.D. diss., University of Wisconsin, 1971), chapt. 7.

[4] U.S., Bureau of Labor, *Report on Conditions of Woman and Child Wage Earners in the United States*, Senate Document 645 (Serial 5685), 61 Cong., 2 Sess., 1910, p. 28. Hereafter cited as Document 645.

[5] Woodward, *Origins of the New South*, p. 419.

olina was the worst offender where 91.7 percent of the mills in that state ignored the child labor law. Investigators discovered a collusion between mill owners and parents in regard to the law. The operators wanted the cheap labor and the parents wanted additional family income, so the laws were virtually ignored in many areas until the inspectors approached; the owners accepted without proof parental untruths of the ages of their children. The Bureau of Labor of the Department of Commerce and Labor concluded that, as a result, "child labor laws without provision for enforcement are in most cases farcical." [6]

When the Supreme Court validated congressional use of the commerce power to ban lottery tickets from interstate commerce in *Champion* v. *Ames*,[7] reformers decided this prohibition should be applied to child labor inasmuch as some states were failing to take corrective action. A leading Progressive senator, Albert J. Beveridge, Republican of Indiana, delivered a moving speech in January 1907 calling on Congress to ban child labor products from interstate commerce. The previous December, President Theodore Roosevelt had urged Congress to "provide for a thoro [*sic*] investigation of the conditions of child labor and of the labor of women in the United States."[8] A month following Beveridge's speech, Congress authorized the Department of Commerce and Labor to conduct such an examination. The result was a nineteen-volume study which provided child labor reformers with statistical ammunition for a national effort to abolish the abuse.[9]

Opponents of child labor reform argued that the power to regulate commerce did not extend to the power to prohibit. *Champion* v. *Ames*, however, weakened this argument and it was completely negated in 1913 when the Supreme Court upheld the Mann Act which forabade the transportation of women in interstate commerce for immoral purposes. In *Hoke* v. *United States*, the Supreme Court determined that the power of Congress in this field was complete even to the point where the means of regulation "may have the quality of police regulations."[10] Insisting that child labor was immoral, reformers were now constitutionally buttressed in their demands

[6] See Document 645, pp. 170–71, 210.

[7] 188 U.S. 321 (1903).

[8] James D. Richardson, *Messages and Papers of the Presidents* (Washington, D.C., 1913), 10:7415.

[9] Document 645.

[10] 227 U.S. 308 (1913).

that Congress could, and should, ban products made by this "evil" practice.

From 1907, when Beveridge first sought to prohibit child labor products, to Woodrow Wilson's presidency, proposals to do this were introduced in every session of Congress. But it was not until after tthe high priorities of Wilson's New Freedom program were enacted in 1914 that congressional attention was concentrated on child labor. After deliberation over whether to use the taxing power or the commerce power, the National Child Labor Committee determined the commerce power to be the best approach. Accordingly, a bill was prepared and introduced in the House of Representatives by Democrat Edward Keating of Colorado and in the Senate by Oklahoma Democrat Robert Owen in the first session of the Sixty-fourth Congress.

Southern opposition to the proposal was engineered by David Clark, editor of the *Southern Textile Bulletin*, who formed the Executive Committee of Southern Cotton Manufacturers to gather contributions and to rally support for the Southern cause.[11] Representatives of the Executive Committee made the plea to Congress that enactment of a national child labor law would force the closing of Southern textile mills because they could not compete without this cheap labor; furthermore, they argued, such a prohibition would violate the Tenth Amendment by invading state control over the conditions of manufacturing.[12] Despite this opposition, Progressive antipathy toward the evil of child labor was so great that both houses of Congress passed the Keating-Owen Act by large majorities. The House vote was 337 to 46 and the Senate was 52 to 12.[13] The law closed the channels of interstate commerce to goods if child labor were employed in their manufacture. Child labor was defined as anyone under the age of sixteen working in mines, fourteen years of age in other types of industry, or if children fourteen to sixteen were worked over eight hours per day, six days per week, or between the hours of 7:00 P.M. and 6:00 A.M. The provisions of the law were to take effect one year after its enactment.[14]

David Clark and his executive committee immediately turned to the courts for relief. It was necessary, to him, to prevent the law from going into

---

[11] Wood, *Constitutional Politics*, pp. 42–46, passim.

[12] They cited the case of *United States* v. *E. C. Knight*, 156 U.S. 1 (1895), in which the Supreme Court drew a sharp distinction between manufacturing (controlled by states) and goods actually in the stream of interstate commerce (under national control).

[13] *Congressional Record*, 64 Cong., 1 Sess., 1916, 53:2035, 12313.

[14] U.S., *Statutes at Large*, vol. 39.

effect, which necessitated injunctive proceedings at once. He found a district court judge, James Edmund Boyd of the Western District of North Carolina, who was sympathetic to the cause of state sovereignty. Judge Boyd issued an injunction ordering the Fidelity Manufacturing Company not to discharge the two underage children of Roland Dagenhart who were employed in the company textile mill. In the following litigation of *Hammer* v. *Dagenhart* Judge Boyd declared the child labor law an unconstitutional regulation of local conditions that were under state jurisdiction.[15] The case was appealed to the Supreme Court which handed down a decision in June 1918.[16]

By the narrowest of votes—five to four—the same Supreme Court that almost struck down the Harrison Act agreed with Judge Boyd. Justice Day, speaking for the majority, insisted that the grant of power to Congress to regulate interstate commerce was not intended to extend to control over states "in their exercise of the police power over local trade and commerce." It was to control the *means* by which commerce was conducted. "The making of goods and the mining of coal are not commerce," Day declared in a phrase reminiscent of the *E. C. Knight* case, and the "production of articles intended for interstate commerce is a matter of local regulation."

Day conceded the Supreme Court had sustained prohibitions of lottery tickets, impure foods, white slavery, and liquor in interstate commerce. But in each of these instances "the use of transportation was necessary to the accomplishment of harmful results." This element, he said, was wanting in the present case. "The goods shipped are of themselves harmless," the majority observed, and Congress had no power to do indirectly what it could not do directly. The intent of the child labor law was to regulate local labor conditions by an indirect means by an exclusion of goods from interstate commerce, a purpose, however beneficial, that the national government lacked the authority to achieve. If such a power were sustained, Day warned, "all freedom of commerce will be at an end, and the power of the States over local matters may be eliminated, and thus our system of government be practically destroyed."[17]

Justice Holmes remonstrated against this emphasis on Dual Federalism

[15] These developments are detailed in Wood, *Constitutional Politics*, chapt. 4.

[16] *Hammer* v. *Dagenhart*, 247 U.S. 251 (1918).

[17] Robert Dahl, "Decision-Making in a Democracy: The Supreme Court as National Policy-Maker," *Journal of Public Law* 6 (Fall 1957) :290. Dahl also notes that "the two child labor cases represent the most effective battle ever waged by the Court against legislative policy-makers."

for the minority, composed of himself, Brandeis, Clarke, and McKenna. He perceptively noted that it mattered not if the evil which Congress sought to eliminate preceded or followed the transportation of goods; the important point, Holmes said, was that Congress believed "transportation encouraged the evil" and this was sufficient for action on the national level. The majority of the Court, however, caught in the dilemma of wanting "to preclude further congressional interference in the realm of industrial relations," and yet "unwilling to overturn the earlier police power cases," found their answer in the *E. C. Knight* principle.[18] Lottery tickets and white slavery were evils that could be excluded from interstate commerce; the products of child labor were not, in themselves, inherently evil, but rather the local conditions of their manufacture, which was beyond congressional authority, constituted the moral issue. Yet, of course, one could be certain that Holmes's reply would be that white slavery conditions were identical in constitutional principle; the prostitution would actually take place on the local level.

The *Hammer* v. *Dagenhart* decision stimulated much adverse criticism from legal scholars. One critic particularly castigated the majority doctrine that prohibiting harmful commodities is a just exercise of the commerce power while prohibiting harmless goods made by children is not by noting the previous decisions upholding the commerce power which had to be overlooked to arrive at this conclusion. The case of *United States* v. *American Tobacco Company* in 1911 sustained the clause in the Sherman Act which forbade shipment of "trust-made" products in interstate commerce; the Pure Food and Drug Act which forbade shipment of mislabeled goods was upheld by the Court in *Hipolite Egg Company* v. *United States* in the same year; and in 1918 the Court held valid the commodities clause in the Hepburn Act by refusing to allow a railroad to haul coal worked in its own mines in *Delaware and Hudson* v. *United States*. All these products, the writer pointed out, were no more harmful in themselves than child-made goods or convict-made products that were excluded from interstate commerce in 1894 (the latter had not been tested yet in the courts).[19]

Thomas Reed Powell, one of the leading legal scholars of that period,

---

[18] Wood, *Constitutional Politics*, p. 158.

[19] Thurlow M. Gordon, "The Child Labor Law Case," *Harvard Law Review* 32 (November 1918) :49. The prohibition against convict-made goods was sustained in 1937 in *Kentucky Whip and Collar Company* v. *Illinois Central Railroad Company* (299 U.S. 334).

was particularly critical. In denouncing the opinion, Powell premised his objections in the concept that "no state may dictate legal events beyond its dominions." Prior to the adoption of the Constitution, states had full authority over commerce but only over events within their own borders. The Constitution left this unchanged, he declared; it took some powers from states but it certainly did not add any powers to states. The idea that denial of markets for North Carolina goods in other states would violate North Carolina's reserved powers seemed ludicrous to Powell. "If the matter is local in any sense," he emphasized, "it is much more local" to states receiving child-made goods than to the state sending them.[20]

Powell agreed that only states could outlaw child labor but noted that Congress had not prohibited the practice. Congress had only made the practice less profitable by denying markets for these goods in other states. He made the obvious point that individuals and groups could legally do the same thing. Labels of the National Consumers League regulated sale of goods in interstate commerce, for example, or Louisiana church officials could refuse to buy bricks made on Sunday for their buildings which would force the North Carolina brickmaker to stop work on the Sabbath or lose this market. These activities did not violate the Tenth Amendment. The decision, Powell insisted, "neglects history, logic and judicial precedents." He thought it "unfortunate . . . that the narrow margin by which the decision was reached invited the inference that the . . . majority were influenced by their personal predilections on a question of policy."

The Hammer decision, however, provided only a temporary setback to reform efforts to end child labor. If the power over interstate commerce was not broad enough, Progressives reasoned, then the taxing power, which the Supreme Court had interpreted as being almost without limitation, could be used. United States participation in World War I, and the increased need for industrial production in conjunction with a labor shortage, had brought an increase in the use of child labor at the very time the Dagenhart decision was announced. As a result, within a few days after the Dagenhart opinion, congressional reformers introduced several bills to strike at child labor again. Senator Atlee Pomerene, Democrat of Ohio, introduced a rewritten Keating-Owen proposal to achieve identical objectives through a tax.

[20] Thomas Reed Powell, "The Child Labor Law, the Tenth Amendment, and the Commerce Clause," *Southern Law Quarterly* 3 (1918), reprinted in Association of American Law Schools, *Selected Essays in Constitutional Law*, 4 vols. (Chicago, 1938), 3:314–16.

Democratic Senator Furnifold Simmons of North Carolina objected to referral of the tax bill to the Senate Committee on Interstate Commerce, observing that such proposals belonged to the Finance Committee. Pomerene, however, called attention to the extensive hearings the Interstate Commerce committee had already conducted on child labor abuses in order to present the Keating-Owen bill and noted that it would be wasted effort for the Finance Committee to duplicate this work. By vote of 41 to 42, Simmons's motion was rejected and the bill was sent to the Committee on Interstate Commerce.[21] After a favorable committee report it was attached to a revenue act as an amendment.

Child labor advocates were certain the taxing power would be sustained in carrying out their reform. Chief Justice White, although voting with the majority on the Dagenhart decision, had authored the Supreme Court opinion in *McCray* v. *United States*, in which he declared in sweeping language that the motives of Congress in taxation could not be considered.[22] Surely, proponents reasoned, White's Court would not overturn its precedent by which the discriminatory colored oleomargarine tax was sustained.

Thomas Hardwick, Democrat of Georgia, led the opposition to the child labor tax, just as he had spearheaded the fight against the Keating-Owen bill two years earlier. Hardwick denied the proponents' argument that this tax was similar in principle to the oleomargarine and state bank note taxes, insisting that, unlike these earlier taxes, Congress was here attempting to use the taxing power on child labor to achieve indirectly what could not be done directly. "The confessed purpose, the real objective" of the oleomargarine tax, he said, was to destroy that product "in the interests of the dairymen" which Congress could have done in other ways. He warned, though, the Supreme Court had decided that Congress could not control child labor and it could be expected the Court would decide on this tax in a similar manner as in the first child labor case "when the question is presented there for settlement again, as it probably will be if we take this action."[23]

Senator Irvine Lenroot, Republican of Wisconsin, interrupted at this point with the observation that the match tax had a moral purpose, to abolish a dangerous product, and yet Congress also struck at oleomargarine

---

[21] *Congressional Record*, 65 Cong., 2 Sess., 1918, 56:8341.

[22] 195 U.S. 27 (1904). Robert Cushman "Social and Economic Control Through Federal Taxation," in *Selected Essays*, 3:563, says that, based on the 1904 decision, White's "objective constitutionality" doctrine would result in validation of both the child labor tax and grain futures tax.

[23] *Congressional Record*, 65 Cong., 3 Sess., 1918, 57:609.

where no danger was involved. The Supreme Court had sustained the exercise of the taxing power as long as no fundamental right was destroyed. Hardwick agreed the McCray decision was good law but in the case of child labor, he responded, a tax on such employment would collide with the fundamental right of the states to control local labor conditions The opinion of the Supreme Court, that child labor was a state concern, Senator Kenyon noted, was by a five-to-four vote. Hardwick denied the validity of this argument, saying "the same statement could be made about almost every important decision that has been made recently by the Supreme Court of the United States." The Georgia senator had no doubt the Supreme Court would rule on this use of the taxing power as it had in connection with the interstate commerce power in the *Dagenhart* decision; otherwise the taxing power "may become the Frankenstein which will utterly destroy all other constitutional powers and limitations, and will finally change both the form and substance of the government, after devouring the Constitution itself."[24]

Henry Cabot Lodge, for two decades one of the dominant spokesmen for the congressional wing of the Republican party, agreed that using the taxing power in this way, while constitutional, was an "extreme method." Lodge declared himself to be "no fonder of resorting to that power for this purpose than anyone else," but it seemed to be the only resort left to Congress. The fault, he lamented, lay in state governments having neglected to control the "evil" sufficiently. "The States had ample and abundant opportunity" to act, and most of them had done so, he said. But "some have not," with the result that certain states had "failed to regulate it as it should be regulated," so it was up to Congress to do so. Ellison Smith of South Carolina admonished Lodge that such thinking would result in the United States becoming "a great centralized socialist body without the power of self-determination in any local form whatever."[25]

Southern senators, filling pages of the *Congressional Record* for the benefit of the Supreme Court as well as their constituents, emphasized that the purpose of the tax was to nullify a Supreme Court decision and not to raise revenue. Democrat Lee Overman of North Carolina observed that when it became obvious from the debates in the *Congressional Record* that the tax was a subterfuge, "and I suppose the Supreme Court will read this *Record* . . ., that court is not going to uphold this section [of the revenue

[24] Ibid., pp. 610–11.
[25] Ibid., pp. 611–12.

act]." When he continued to stress this as the congressional motive, Pomerene remonstrated there was no "Senator here who can admit to a motive
of Congress," and the purpose of the bill was to raise revenue "and at the
same time to meet the child labor problem." When Overman asked if he
really believed it would result in raising revenue, Pomerene assented, observing that "even if it does not, then you will have nothing to complain of."
Lenroot noted that if the Court invalidated the tax, this would necessitate
"overruling . . . a hundred cases . . . one long unbroken line of doctrine,"
including the decision in the oleomargarine case." Reformers won by a
large margin when the Senate accepted the child labor tax 50 to 12, with 34
not voting.[26]

When the amended bill was discussed in the House, Democrat W.W.
Venable of Mississippi voiced opposition toward such use of the taxing
power. He declared there were "a thousand decisions" holding that the
states had never surrendered their police powers. When asked to distinguish
in principle the difference between the proposed child labor tax and the
cotton futures tax, he replied that the latter was a tax on a specific product.
This new tax, he said, constitutes "the first time where you have undertaken
to tax not an article, but an act." This, of course, overlooked the discriminatory tax placed on the action of coloring oleomargarine. But Venable
warned that if Congress began "taking the police powers away from the
States under the guise of taxation, there is nothing in the world you can not
regulate in that way. You can completely socialize the entire Government in
a year." Despite this dire warning, the House accepted the child labor tax
section 312 to 11 and President Wilson signed the revenue act on February
24, 1919.[27]

The child labor tax, effective one year after its enactment, levied a 10
percent tax on the net profits of any company that worked children under
sixteen years of age in mines or fourteen years in other types of industry, or
over eight hours per day, six days per week, or from 7:00 P.M. and 6:00 A.M.
if between fourteen and sixteen years of age. If such children were employed unwittingly, that is, if the employer in good faith accepted a certificate indicating the person was of proper age, the employer was exempted
from penalties for nonpayment of the tax.[28] Again David Clark was forced
to contrive a case in order to permit the Supreme Court to answer the ques-

[26] Ibid., pp. 616, 619, 621.
[27] Ibid., pp. 3029–30, 3035, 4245.
[28] U.S., *Statutes at Large*, vol. 40.

tion of constitutionality of regulating child labor.[29] This time the contro-versy arose over an employer paying the tax under protest.

The subsequent litigation of *Bailey* v. *Drexel Furniture Company* in-volved the collector of revenue in Judge Boyd's district in North Carolina assessing the Drexel Company $6,321.79 taxes for employing child labor and the company appealing its payment under protest. Again without writ-ten opinion, Judge Boyd held the tax an unconstitutional invasion of the state-reserved powers and the case went to the Supreme Court on appeal.[30] Edward White had died the previous year so the new chief justice, Wil-liam H. Taft, spoke for a court divided only by the dissent of Justice John Clarke who failed to write an opinion.[31]

Relying upon the concept of Dual Federalism, Taft declared that if the tax were valid, Congress could then regulate practically any subject by taxation. The reserved powers were protected by the Tenth Amendment, however, and "to give such magic to the word 'tax,' " Taft observed, "would be to break down all constitutional limitation of the power of Con-gress and completely wipe out the sovereignty of the states." The Court could see no difference between this measure and the attempt to regulate child labor with the commerce power. In the present case, Taft said, "Con-gress, in the name of a tax which, on the face of the act, is a penalty, seeks to do the same thing, and the effort must be equally futile."

Taft did not wish to overturn the state bank note and oleomargarine precedents. He therefore distinguished between them and the present tax by noting that in neither of the earlier taxes "did the law . . . show on its face, as does the law before us, the detailed specifications of a regulation of a state concern and business with a heavy exaction to promote the efficacy of such regulation."[32] If child labor was beyond the reach of Congress through

29 See Wood, *Constitutional Politics*, chapt. 8.

30 *Bailey* v. *Drexel Furniture Company*, 259 U.S. 20 (1922). On the day of this de-cision Taft wrote his brother that "we can not strain the Constitution . . . to meet the wishes of . . . yankee competitors." Stanley I. Kutler, "Chief Justice Taft, National Regulation and the Commerce Power," *Journal of American History* 51 (March 1965) : 652 n. Compare with note 3 above.

31 Clarke believed a dissent based on the oleomargarine and Doremus opinions "could have been made very convincing," but one of his sisters was dying at the time and he could not write an opinion. Clarke to Woodrow Wilson, September 9, 1922, quoted in Alpheus Thomas Mason, *William Howard Taft: Chief Justice* (London, 1964), p. 166.

32 *Transcripts of Records and File Copies of Briefs*, Case #657, 1921 Term, vol. 108, U.S. Supreme Court Library; Paul L. Murphy, *The Constitution in Crisis Times, 1918–1969* (New York, 1972), pp. 52–53.

the commerce power, it was equally so in connection with the taxing power. White had said in the McCray precedent that Congress could not abolish a fundamental right through taxation. The Taft Court decided labor relations was one of the rights the regulation of which belonged to states.

Undoubtedly the most surprising aspect of the decision was the switch of McKenna, and especially Brandeis and Holmes, all of whom had supported Holmes's vigorous dissent in the first child labor case.[33] One factor, of course, that helps account for this would be Taft's particular emphasis on, and ability to achieve, unanimity which played a part in "the reactionary Child Labor Tax decision."[34] One student believed Holmes probably concluded Congress had gone too far this time with the power of taxation. Brandeis, this same scholar noted, was in company with other liberals such as Edwin Corwin, Felix Frankfurter, and Thomas Reed Powell who changed their opinions concerning congressional power to control child labor from the time of the Dagenhart decision to one of approval of the Drexel opinion.[35] Significantly, the first setback to the use of the taxing power for social and economic purposes was dealt by a nearly unanimous Court. That same day the Court delivered a second blow to the taxing power in regard to grain futures.

The Future Trading Act of 1921 required boards of trade to become "contract markets" and comply with regulations on futures contracts or pay a tax. Certain members of the Chicago Board of Trade immediately petitioned their board after passage of the act to institute a suit to have the law declared unconstitutional. The board refused, saying it would comply with the law in order to become designated as a contract market and be able to continue operations. Thus the individual members brought suit on their own insisting the law was unconstitutional because 1) it deprived them of property without due process of law by forcing acceptance of farm co-ops as members of these boards of trade, 2) it regulated commerce that was wholly intrastate in character, and 3) it violated the Tenth Amendment by superceding the reserved power of the state of Illinois to regulate the state-chartered exchanges.[36]

[33] The background of the justices and their thinking in this case is well presented in Wood, *Constitutional Politics*, chapt. 9. McKenna, it should be noted, joined the minority in 1919 in *United States* v. *Doremus* (249 U.S. 86), which insisted the narcotics tax violated the Tenth Amendment.

[34] Alpheus Thomas Mason, *The Supreme Court from Taft to Warren* (New York, 1964), p. 58.

[35] Wood, *Constitutional Politics*, pp. 286–92.

Chief Justice Taft spoke this time for a unanimous Court. He noted that it was "impossible to escape the conviction, from a full reading of the law, that it was enacted for the purpose of regulating the conduct of business of boards of trade." The sole purpose for the tax, therefore, could only be to compel boards of trade to comply with these regulations "many of which have no relevancy to the collection of the tax at all."[37]

Taft emphasized that the act's purpose, stated in the title and "so clear from the effect of the provisions," was so obviously regulatory that "it leaves no ground" upon which the measure could "be sustained as a valid exercise of the taxing power." The *Drexel* decision that just preceded this litigation, Taft announced, "completely covers this case." Furthermore, the law could not be sustained under the commerce power because the words *interstate commerce* could not be found anywhere in the act. Taft went on to cite *Ware and Leland* v. *Mobile County*[38] to explain that Congress could not regulate futures contracts—this was in the realm of state reserved powers—unless it could be found they "directly" interfered in such a manner as to become "an obstruction or burden" to the flow of interstate commerce. This could be, and was, construed as a suggestion to Congress to rewrite the law, basing the control on the commerce power.

Brandeis wrote a concurring opinion, agreeing the tax was unconstitutional but expressing doubt that the plaintiffs had sufficient standing "to require the court to pass upon the constitutional question in this case." Brandeis noted the act did not require a board of trade to become a contract market but once it did, it must then comply with the regulations. In the event a board became a contract market, its individual members might lose financially under the restrictions, but they might also gain; this, Brandeis observed, was a question "calling for the exercise of business judgment." In any event, this business decision had to be made by the board of trade. He was "unaware of any rule of law," Brandeis said sarcastically, that required any corporation, "upon the request of a minority stockholder, to play the knight-errant and tilt at every statute affecting it, which he believes to be invalid."

Congress immediately enacted this law under the commerce power following the *Hill* v. *Wallace* decision. The Grain Futures Act of 1922

[36] *Transcripts of Records and File Copies of Briefs*, Case #616, 1921 Term, vol. 3, U.S. Supreme Court Library.

[37] *Hill* v. *Wallace*, 259 U.S. 44 (1922).

[38] 209 U.S. 405 (1908).

established the same regulations, although with criminal rather than tax penalties for noncompliance. The Chicago Board of Trade just as quickly brought suit against the United States Attorney for the Northern District of Illinois, challenging the constitutionality of the law. If the Supreme Court struck down child labor laws under both the commerce and taxing powers, surely it would do likewise with the regulation of grain futures contracts.

The next year Taft, again speaking for the Court, upheld the law as a valid exercise of the commerce power.[39] Congress had found that unregulated futures contracts obstructed the flow of interstate commerce, Taft said. As substantiation of congressional power over these activities, he cited the Supreme Court validation of the Stockyards Act, by which the national government regulated the activities of livestock sales and meat-packers under the commerce power.[40] McReynolds and Sutherland dissented from the majority on the futures contract decision but did not write an opinion.

The twin decisions in 1922 on the taxing power marked a turning point in congressional use of this power for regulation. The Taft Court, with its concern over possible national regulation of labor-management relations, emphasized the constitutional interpretation of Dual Federalism to restrict any encroachment on state prerogatives. Of the two, the child labor tax was the more important in constitutional law. Here it was necessary for the Court to draw a fine line of distinction between previous endorsements of the use of the taxing power to regulate and the current increasing reliance on Dual Federalism. This the Taft Court did by determining that the "evil" was not being taxed, which was reserved to state regulation, but rather the end product of the evil that entered the stream of interstate commerce, and the purpose of the law was clearly regulatory and not to raise revenue.[41] With this determination the justices obviously felt compelled to strike down the futures tax as well, for it was clearly regulatory in nature and concealed no hint of raising revenue. In contrast the oleomargarine tax was regulatory, even prohibitive on one type of product, but taken all together, the provisions resulted in revenue.

As if to demonstrate that the McCray decision had not been overturned

[39] *Board of Trade of City of Chicago* v. *Olsen*, 262 U.S. 1 (1923). For an excellent analysis of Taft's liberal construction of the commerce power, see Kutler, "Chief Justice Taft," pp. 651–68.

[40] *Stafford* v. *Wallace*, 258 U.S. 495 (1922).

[41] In 1941, in *United States* v. *Darby Lumber Company* (312 U.S. 100), the Supreme Court upheld the prohibition of goods in interstate commerce made by child labor.

in 1922, the Supreme Court refused to hear a case ten years later involving a discriminatory tax on ticket scalping. The practice of buying in advance tickets for choice theater seats or for popular performances and then reselling them at increased prices, or scalping, is particularly prevalent in cities such as New York where successful stage plays are first presented. Scalping became so widespread, and so annoying to theatergoers, that a new procedure developed by the time of the Progressive movement to supplant the individual scalpers. Theater ticket agencies were formed to provide the services of a middleman. These agencies would purchase large blocks of tickets for performances and sell them through their agents at various locations, such as newsstands, shoe shine stations, or hotels, for cost plus fifty cents or, normally, a 20 percent profit. This arrangement proved quite satisfactory for the theater patron, because it eliminated the problem of standing in line at a box office. It also helped assure financial success for theaters to have this advanced commitment of sales.

But soon a 20 percent profit was insufficient and the agencies or their agents began scalping.[42] Finally, to control the abuse, the New York state legislature enacted a prohibition against resale of amusement tickets at a price exceeding fifty cents over the price printed on the ticket. Despite the preamble of the law declaring that this problem was "a matter affecting the public interest," the Supreme Court determined otherwise. In 1927 the High Court declared that theater tickets were not in the category of the public interest and, therefore, beyond the control of the state. To prohibit absolutely the sale of tickets above a certain price violated the Fourteenth Amendment by denying property without due process of law.[43]

Meanwhile, Congress was using the taxing power to assist states in controlling ticket scalping. During World War I numerous nuisance taxes were enacted, including an excise on tickets to places of amusement. The Revenue Act of 1926 continued this tax of 5 percent but further provided for an exactment of 50 percent on the resale of tickets on the amount exceeding fifty cents over the price printed on the ticket. In 1928 the amount of profit allowed, before the 50 percent rate went into effect, was raised to seventy-

---

[42] For this development see Walter De Leon, "Inside Box Office Stuff," *Saturday Evening Post* 197 (June 6, 1925) :24; "Are You a New Yorker?" *Nation* 125 (July 20, 1927) :51.

[43] *Tyson* v. *Banton*, 273 U.S. 418. Decisions on similar types of state legislation by the Court in the 1920s were reversed in *Nebbia* v. *New York* (291 U.S. 502 [1934]) and thus permitted a wide range of activities to be controlled by states as areas of "public interest."

five cents.[44] A ticket agency decided to test the constitutionality of the tax.

Between 1926 and 1930 the Couthoui ticket brokerage company of Chicago paid the national government $167,606.22 in taxes on ticket sales. Of this amount, $40,688.32 was paid at the usual rate of 5 percent on amusement tickets and the remainder was at the 50 percent rate for scalping, the latter being the sum the company sought to recover.[45] The Court of Claims, however, sustained the constitutionality of the scalping tax by citing the *Kollock* and *McCray* decisions. In the oleomargarine cases, the court noted, the prohibitive rates were approved by the Supreme Court as policy; the scalping tax came under this same category. In 1932 the Supreme Court refused to grant a writ of certiorari to the Couthoui company, based upon the reasoning of the lower court, and the theater tax was not litigated further.[46] The tax was finally repealed in 1965 as a part of the tax reduction program of President Lyndon B. Johnson.[47]

The refusal to review the lower court's decision on the scalping tax indicated a continued adherence to the *McCray* principle but revealed nothing about the Court's thinking in terms of Dual Federalism. If the Supreme Court were to continue the emphasis on Dual Federalism enunciated in the child labor cases and the grain futures tax, it would be difficult for Congress to expand the national police power through the taxing power. In the period of the "First New Deal," a majority of the justices gave every indication they would continue to rely upon this doctrine to restrict novel uses of national power to combat the Great Depression.

The Supreme Court of the 1930s, led by Chief Justice Charles Evans Hughes, was markedly separated into three groups. On the far right were Justices WillisVanDevanter, James McReynolds, George Sutherland, and Pierce Butler, men whose views on constitutional jurisprudence can best be described as "constitutional fundamentalism" and were known as the Four Horsemen. All had at one time before appointment to the High Bench enjoyed a lucrative corporate law practice and were staunch believers in rugged individualism and nineteenth-century laissez-faire. Viewing the increased expansion of national governmental powers during the twentieth century with alarm and abhorrence, these four justices continued to expound Dual Federalism in order to thwart the New Deal approach to eco-

---

[44] U.S., *Statutes at Large*, vols. 44 and 45.
[45] *Couthoui* v. *United States*, 54 Fed (2d) 158.
[46] 285 U.S. 548.
[47] *United States Code Annotated* 26 ss 4231.

nomic recovery as long as those judges remained on the Supreme Court.

The liberal wing of the Hughes Court was composed of Justices Louis Brandeis, Benjamin Cardozo, and Harlan F. Stone. These men were willing to exercise judicial self-restraint and to allow Congress to formulate policy unless the law was blatantly unconstitutional. Chief Justice Hughes and Justice Owen Roberts, usually referred to as the "swing men," occasionally voted with the liberals, particularly after 1936, but more often supported the Four Horsemen, especially in the crucial 1935 Term.[48] In 1935 and 1936, in a series of decisions that were normally six to three but sometimes five to four, the Four Horsemen were joined by Roberts and often by Hughes in striking down much of the First New Deal legislation. In two of these instances the statutes used the taxing power and were declared unconstitutional because they invaded the states' reserved powers. This created "the most acute constitutional crisis in the life of the nation" and precipitated Franklin D. Roosevelt's "Court Packing Plan."[49]

[48] For a good brief character sketch of these nine justices, see Fred Rodell, *Nine Men* (New York, 1955), pp. 217–29, and William F. Swindler, *Court and Constitution in the Twentieth Century* (Indianapolis, Ind., 1971), vol. 2, chapts. 1 and 2.

[49] Rodell, *Nine Men*, p. 214. For other brief but penetrating accounts of the Supreme Court and the New Deal crisis, see Robert McCloskey, *The United States Supreme Court* (Chicago, Ill., 1960), chapt. 7, and Mason, *The Supreme Court from Taft to Warren*, chapt. 3. For a more detailed account, consult Edward S. Corwin, *Constitutional Revolution, Ltd.* (Claremont, Calif., 1941).

10 The Climax of Dual Federalism

During the depression of the 1930s the taxing power was used to assist two particularly sick segments of the American economy, bituminous coal and agriculture. The first of these programs came during the Hundred Days session, from March 9 to June 16, 1933, when an overwhelmingly Democratic Congress responded enthusiastically to President Roosevelt's requests for the use of broad governmental powers to increase agricultural income. At this time farmers were suffering economically as much as any group in the United States. This was not a new development in agriculture; tillers of the soil had been economically depressed for the previous decade and the stock market crash in 1929 merely worsened their condition. By 1933 the principal problem in agriculture was depressed prices caused by overproduction and the lack of consumption by an industrialized society paralyzed by depression.

During World War I, with the insatiable demand for agricultural products, American farmers were encouraged to increase their production to the maximum. Following the recovery of European agriculture by 1920, markets for United States foodstuffs were curtailed and farmers, continuing to produce at the accelerated rate, faced the problems of overproduction and depressed prices while most other segments of the economy enjoyed "Coolidge prosperity." Republican Senator Arthur Capper of Kansas, in arguing for the first AAA (Agricultural Adjustment Administration) in 1933, graphically illustrated with statistics the plight of the American farmer during this decade. Using the index of 100 to represent the ratio of farm-selling prices in relation to farm-purchasing prices from 1909 to 1914, he noted that this ratio dropped from 99 in 1920 to 81 in 1922. The index, which represented the purchasing value of the dollar to the farmer then fluctuated from a high of 92 in 1925 down to 80 in 1930, the first year the effects of the 1929 stock market crash were felt. This deflated dollar then dropped rapidly to 47 in 1933.[1]

The worsening conditions caused by the general depression led to the Farmers' Holiday Association, an attempt by farmers in many areas to raise prices by refusing to market their commodities and using force to prevent mortgage foreclosures and delinquent tax sales. This "strike" reached its apex under Milo Reno of Iowa in 1932 and the organization threatened to renew its effort on a national basis during the congressional debates on the farm bill during the Hundred Days session.[2] A meeting of the nation's farm leaders in December 1932 endorsed the approach of restrictions on production in order to raise farm prices. Franklin Roosevelt's secretary of agriculture, Henry A. Wallace, was convinced that a workable plan must include some scheme for reducing surpluses. The most popular method being promoted, which Wallace accepted, was the domestic allotment plan nurtured by the Montana farm economist Milburn L. Wilson.[3] On March 10, 1933, Secretary Wallace called a conference of fifty leaders of the major farm organizations to receive their views on a farm program. Following this meeting, Wallace, with the assistance of his staff, especially Mordecai Ezekiel, Jerome Frank, and Rexford Tugwell, drafted a bill to present to Congress in the Hundred Days session which became the first AAA.[4]

The bill was sent to the House of Representatives on March 16, 1933. Four days later the Committee on Agriculture reported H.R. 3835 favorably to the House. Because the current agricultural situation was an emergency, the measure proposed an extensive regimentation of farmers. The principal objective was "to establish and maintain such a balance between production and consumption of agricultural commodities" as to give "farmers their pre-war purchasing power." Parity would be achieved by paying subsidies equal to the difference between current market prices and that amount

[1] *Congressional Record*, 73 Cong., 1 Sess., 1933, 77:1731–32.

[2] C. Roger Lambert, "New Deal Experiments in Agricultural Control: The Livestock Program, 1933–1935" (Ph.D. diss., University of Oklahoma, 1962), pp. 16–17; Arthur M. Schlesinger, Jr., *The Coming of the New Deal* (Boston, 1959), pp. 42–44.

[3] Gilbert C. Fite, "Farmer Opinion and the Agricultural Adjustment Act, 1933," *Mississippi Valley Historical Review* 48 (March 1962):658.

[4] For the background to drafting this bill, see Schlesinger, *The Coming of the New Deal*, pp. 38–39, and Paul L. Murphy, "The New Deal Agricultural Program and the Constitution," *Agricultural History* 29 (October 1955):160–69.

necessary for farmers to attain their purchasing power in the years 1909–1914. To alleviate the chronic problem of surpluses, the secretary of agriculture would be empowered to enter into agreements with individual producers to reduce acreages planted for which they would be compensated by rental payments. Relief from surpluses, it was believed, would result in higher domestic prices for farm commodities. This extensive program would be financed by a tax placed on the first major processors of the commodities, the amount to be determined by the secretary of agriculture and to be sufficient to establish parity. The tax would be placed only upon those products in surplus that the secretary would have previously announced would receive benefit payments.

If the processing tax were too high, processors would probably turn to substitutes which would then accentuate the surplus problem of the particular commodity. So the bill proposed giving broad, discretionary taxing powers to the secretary of agriculture, similar to the flexible provisions of the tariff that permitted the president to raise and to lower import duties. The measure authorized the secretary of agriculture to exempt from the tax "any class of products of a commodity of such a low value" that the additional tax would force the processor to turn to substitute products. Also, if the processing tax proved too burdensome for the manufacturer to pay and still compete with other products, which in turn would prevent use of the commodity, the secretary was empowered to place a compensating tax on the competing commodity to equalize the disadvantage in order to preclude surpluses. Products for home consumption, of course, were exempted from the tax, as well as those where the processor was also the producer but whose sales were less than $100 per year. The latter category was limited to hogs, cattle, sheep, and milk.[5]

In a message accompanying the legislation, President Roosevelt admitted "frankly that it is a new and untrod path, but I tell you with equal frankness that an unprecedented condition calls for the trial of new means to rescue agriculture." He was uncertain whether or not this program would work but he cheerfully told Congress that if it did not he would be the first to acknowledge it as a failure.[6] The observation that this was "a new and

---

[5] U.S., Congress, House, Report 6 (Serial 9774), 73 Cong., 1 Sess., 1933; a similar report on H.R. 3835 was submitted in the same Congress by the Senate Committee on Agriculture and Forestry, Senate Report 16 (Serial 9769).

[6] House Report 6; Samuel F. Rosenman, ed., *The Public Papers and Addresses of Franklin D. Roosevelt* (New York, 1938–1950), 2:74.

untrod path" was quite an understatement. While the taxing power had been used many times to assist certain segments of agriculture, this bill proposed using the power to uplift all American farmers. Even more revolutionary, it sought to delegate the congressional power to tax to a cabinet officer and to allow him to use it at his discretion. The measure charged the secretary of agriculture with the duty of solving the economic crisis of farmers and to achieve this, granted him broad powers with few guidelines or limitations.

Democrat Marvin Jones of Texas introduced H.R. 3835 to the House. He described the New Deal efforts to meet the economic emergency as a war in which the AAA farm program was to be a major battle. Roosevelt asked for this program, Jones declared, and that was sufficient reason for its enactment. "While this war is on," the Texan said, "I am going to follow the man at the other end of the Avenue, who has the flag in his hand." The provisions of the measure were to apply to the basic commodities of wheat, cotton, field corn, rice, tobacco, hogs, and milk, if any of these were in surplus. But the authorization to tax was discretionary, based upon probable surpluses and the need for controlling production, so Jones promised his colleagues that the processing tax would probably be small and it would possibly be applied only to one or two commodities at first. This discretionary aspect was inserted, he observed, so that the president and the secretary could "proceed cautiously," and Jones was certain they would. "Like millions of others who have pinned their faith to him [F.D.R.]," Jones stated, "I believe he will lead us out of the darkness and into the light of a new day. [*Applause*]."[7]

Not all congressmen were convinced of Roosevelt's messianic qualities, however, at least in the area of agriculture. In opposing H.R. 3835, John D. Clarke, Republican of New York, described the AAA as "a glorified sales tax." Republican Ray P. Chase of Minnesota reluctantly agreed to vote for the bill. His doubt, he said, stemmed from the current trend of giving tremendous powers to the executive branch. Referring to the Emergency Banking Act passed two weeks previously, Chase noted that Congress had "placed in the hands of a dictator supreme control of the wealth of America." Now, he said, Congress was being asked to create another dictator, "this time a subordinate dictator—and place in his hands the future and the welfare of agriculture." When asked why he would vote for such a bad bill if he be-

7 *Congressional Record*, 73 Cong., 1 Sess., 1933, 77:674.

lieved as he did, Chase replied that after repeated inquiries to his constituents on what farm program they wanted, he was told "to stand by the President."[8]

Republican Clifford Hope of Kansas, a leading agricultural expert, opposed the AAA. He agreed agricultural conditions were in an emergency state but this program would require at least a year before it would become effective. Although Hope had "high respect" for Secretary Wallace, this proposal would give him dictatorial powers which one man could not possibly administer. The secretary was kept busy running the Department of Agriculture, Hope noted, without also placing him in control of producing, marketing, and processing farm products. "You are simply going to put a tax on the American people," Hope announced, "which would be of no benefit in any way to the farmer." The American farmer was an individualist, Hope warned, and did not want this type of regimentation. The answer to the farm problem, he said, was to take much more land out of production and give farmers the relief they really desired in the form of lower taxes, freight rates, interest rates, and refinancing of farm debts.[9]

Republican Allen Treadway of Massachusetts raised the only significant question in the House concerning the constitutionality of the measure. He observed that the processing tax plan had "the earmarks of an impractical college professor." In a practical sense, he said, it would be difficult to determine the 1909 purchasing power of farmers; few farmers, for example, bought automobiles or radios in that year. Treadway particularly questioned the constitutionality of delegating the taxing power to the secretary of agriculture. He then quoted part of Chief Justice Taft's opinion in *Hampton and Company* v. *United States*,[10] that in regard to the flexibility provisions of the tariff Congress must establish "an intelligible principle" for the president and treasury secretary to follow. The AAA measure, he noted, contained no guiding principle on the processing tax. The House, however, merely voted to change the parity period on tobacco to August 1919–July 1929 and accepted the bill on the second day of debate by vote of 315 to 98.[11]

David Reed, Republican of Pennsylvania, led the fight in the Senate against the AAA which he said would place a sales tax "of more than 100 percent upon the essentials of living of the poorest people in America."

[8] Ibid., pp. 675–77.   [9] Ibid., pp. 682–83.
[10] 276 U.S. 394 (1928).
[11] *Congressional Record*, 73 Cong., 1 Sess., 1933, 77:734–35, 765.

Reed warned fellow senators that during the reign of Louis XVI a tax of 55 percent was placed on living items of the French people which resulted in "one of the most bitter revolutions in the world's history." How long would the American people submit to this proposed 100 percent sales tax, he asked, especially when they found out that the proceeds would go to "a particular group of farmers, most of them in the Upper Mississippi Valley and in Texas, . . . as a bounty on their production?" Reed further noted there was "a clearly established principle" that a legislature could not "tax one citizen in order to give the proceeds to another." To substantiate this, he cited *Citizens Savings and Loan* v. *Topeka,* in which the Supreme Court enunciated this principle with the observation that such a law "is none the less a robbery because it is done under the forms of law and is called taxation." [12] "I do not believe," Reed suggested, "that the Supreme Court is going to forget that it said that when this bill comes before it." He also mentioned *Parkersburg* v. *Brown* as a precedent in which the Supreme Court declared unconstitutional a tax law to raise revenue to pay off bonds a city had issued and loaned to manufacturers because the tax was not for a public object.[13] Delegating the taxing power to the secretary of agriculture also made the bill unconstitutional, Senator Reed said, because the amount of tax, the articles to be taxed, and cessation of the taxes were left to the secretary's discretion, without provision for appeal or any guidelines.[14]

Senator John Bankhead, Democrat of Alabama and one of the AAA's proponents, admitted Reed had raised a serious constitutional question of taxing one to give to another. But, he pointed out, the bounty paid on domestic sugar had twice gone to the Supreme Court for adjudication and had never been declared unconstitutional for that reason. Everyone also knew the oleomargarine tax was to benefit the dairyman, Bankhead said, and yet the Supreme Court had refused to inquire into congressional motives on that tax. Finally, he pointed out, Congress had delegated to the president its power over the tariff which the Supreme Court had sustained, so Bankhead could see no substantial constitutional problem with the AAA processing tax. The Senate then passed the bill 64 to 20, the House agreed to the Senate amendments, except the cost-of-production concept, and President Roosevelt signed it into law on May 12, 1933.[15]

A terrible drought in the Midwest solved the wheat surplus problem in

---

[12] 87 U.S. 655 (1875).   [13] 106 U.S. 487 (1882).
[14] *Congressional Record*, 73 Cong., 1 Sess., 1933, 77:1640–44.
[15] Ibid., pp. 1716–17, 2562, 3066, 3499.

1933, but cotton and tobacco surpluses continued to plague farmers. Thus in 1934 Congress enacted two laws to supplement the AAA program for these crops. The Cotton Control Act provided that if two-thirds of the cotton farmers approved acreage allotments for the following year a tax of 50 percent (market value) would be placed on all cotton ginned that was produced in excess of the allotment. The Tobacco Control Act of June 1934 also placed a tax of $33\frac{1}{3}$ percent on all tobacco produced in excess of quotas. Cooperating producers were given warrants from the secretary of agriculture which were acceptable in payment of the tax; if the farmer stayed within his quota he would have sufficient warrants to pay the tax.[16]

The AAA tax was soon challenged in the courts. On July 14, 1933, Secretary of Agriculture Henry Wallace established a processing tax on cotton textile millers. The United States government presented a claim to the Hoosac Mills Corporation and the company, then in receivership, refused to pay the tax. The subsequent case of *United States* v. *Butler* was decided by the Supreme Court in January 1936.[17] Not surprisingly, the Four Horsemen, joined by Chief Justice Hughes and Justice Roberts, rejected the AAA processing tax as unconstitutional in what a contemporary lawyer described as "the most important decision rendered in recent years."[18]

In a six-to-three decision, the Court, speaking through Roberts, decided the tax could be sustained only "by ignoring the avowed purpose and operation" of the law which was to "restore the purchasing power of agricultural products to a parity." The tax played "an indispensible part" in the total program, the majority held, and it was "inaccurate and misleading" to describe it as a tax. A tax, "in the general understanding of the term, and as used in the Constitution," Roberts said, denotes an exaction for the support of government; it "has never been thought to connote the expropriation of money from one group for the benefit of another."

The government brief for the case had stressed the general welfare clauses as providing power for the AAA, especially because the Supreme Court had so narrowly interpreted the interstate commerce power in invalidating the NIRA (National Industrial Recovery Act).[19] But this entailed

---

[16] U.S., *Statutes at Large*, vol. 48.

[17] 297 U.S. 1 (1936).

[18] W.J.W., "Comments," *Michigan Law Review* 34 (January 1936):366. Robert Jackson, then solicitor general and later attorney general and an associate justice, said this decision, "more than any other to that date, had turned the thoughts of men in the Administration toward the impending necessity of a challenge to the Court." Robert H. Jackson, *The Struggle for Judicial Supremacy* (New York, 1941), p. 139.

too broad an interpretation of the welfare clauses, the majority of the Court said, because farming was a local affair and the program thus invaded the reserved powers of the states. "The tax, the appropriation of the funds raised, and the direction for their disbursement," Roberts declared, "are but parts of the plan. They are but means to an unconstitutional end." The majority agreed that the taxing power could be used to carry out another delegated power, but to use the power "to effectuate an end which is not legitimate, not within the scope of the Constitution, is obviously inadmissible." The plan actually was not voluntary, as government counsel insisted, because farmers would not reject the program and thus refuse its benefits. Yet the national government cannot tax and then "buy compliance" to a program that violates the Tenth Amendment. Again Dual Federalism was invoked to restrict the national government.[20]

In an obvious reference to the extreme criticism currently being directed at the Court, Roberts called attention to the charge that the Court occasionally "assumes a power to overrule or control the actions of the people's representatives." This was a misconception, Roberts declared. The duty of the Justices was not that complicated. He then described, in what has been labeled the "Slot Machine" theory of jurisprudence, the function of the Supreme Court: "When an act of Congress is appropriately challenged . . . the judicial branch of the Government has only one duty—to lay the article of the Constitution which is involved beside the statute which

---

[19] *Transcripts of Records and File Copies of Briefs*, Case #401, 1935 Term, vol. 74, U.S. Supreme Court Library. The government brief contained sixty-eight pages on the question of delegation of power but surprisingly, in the light of the NIRA *Schechter* case, the majority opinion ignored this issue.

[20] John W. Holmes, "The Federal Spending Power and State Rights," *Michigan Law Review* 34 (March 1936) : 637–49, noted that the child labor and grain futures decisions left "handwriting on the wall" which was not heeded by the writers of the AAA. After the *Butler* opinion, he predicted, better draftsmanship of bills should result because regulatory measures must at least appear on the surface to be revenue laws or the Court would reject them. Another scholar, F.D.G. Ribble, "Conflicts Between Federal Regulation Through Taxation and the States," *Cornell Law Review* 23 (December 1937) : 131–41, made the same point. If regulatory laws were properly written, the latter observed, the Supreme Court normally sustained them through a process that he illustrated with a quote from a Kipling poem. The verse described how enlisted men kept the drunkenness of an officer from being discovered through a "shut-eye sentry":

> There was me e' 'd kissed in the sentry box
> As I 'ave not told in my song.
> But I took my oath, which were Bible truth
> I 'adn't seen nothing wrong.

is challenged and to decide whether the latter squares with the former."

In an often-quoted dissent, Justice Stone, joined by Brandeis and Cardozo, stingingly described the majority opinion as a "tortured construction of the Constitution." Stone argued that the majority had held the tax unconstitutional because they "disapproved of the use of the proceeds." He completely rejected the argument that agriculture was "a local affair," calling attention to the national scope of the depressed condition of farmers. The majority held that the tax was actually a penalty and cited the cases of *Bailey* v. *Drexel Furniture, Hill* v. *Wallace, Linder* v. *United States*, and *Constantine* v. *United States* as precedents for invalidating the processing tax. Stone repudiated this reasoning, noting that the regulations were achieved not by the tax but by the expenditure of the proceeds. The program, he declared, could be "accomplished by any like use of public funds, regardless of the source." Stone then warned his colleagues that "courts are not the only agency of government that must be assumed to have capacity to govern." In declaring laws unconstitutional, he established two guidelines for his brethren: "One is that courts are concerned only with the power to enact statutes, not with their wisdom." The other, he said, was to remember the executive and legislative branches were checked by the judiciary but "the only check upon our own exercise of power is our own sense of self-restraint."

Agricultural surpluses continued to plague farmers so New Dealers enacted the second AAA in 1938.[21] This plan met the Supreme Court's objections in the *Butler* case by providing for national farmer referendums on the annual programs and for financing them out of the general treasury. In the meantime, the New Deal recovery efforts had suffered another setback by Dual Federalism in the attempt to bring order to the economic chaos existing in the bituminous coal industry.

The bituminous coal industry was one of the really sick industries during Coolidge prosperity and had been in serious trouble for years prior to World War I. Democratic Senator Joseph F. Guffey of Pennsylvania noted in Congress in 1935 that, except for the World War I period, the coal industry had been suffering for the previous fifty years.[22] The Great Crusade stimulated increased production and, following the war, the bituminous coal industry immediately lapsed back into depression. A tremendous expansion in production, accompanied by a return to normal postwar domes-

[21] U.S., *Statutes at Large*, vol. 52.
[22] *Congressional Record*, 74 Cong., 1 Sess., 1935, 79:13947.

tic consumption, resulted in devastating effects on the coal operators and the miners. Labor's wages represented 65 percent of the costs of production. With other production expenses remaining relatively constant, this meant that any reduction by the operators would be at the expense of the miners and their families.

"Overdevelopment," the United States Coal Commission said in 1923, was the "outstanding factor" causing a depression in the soft-coal industry. In the previous twenty years miners had averaged 215 workdays per year. But there was great fluctuation among the various regions. Some miners worked as much as 300 days and in depressed areas they worked as few as 100 days annually. At this time about 400,000 of the 660,000 miners were members of John L. Lewis's United Mine Workers and lower wages were prevalent in the nonunion areas.[23]

The advent of the depression worsened these conditions. Senator Guffey found the workday averages had dropped from 187 in 1930 to 160 in 1931 and then declined to 146 the following year. But the operators also had suffered. Guffey discovered, from the income tax returns in the Bureau of Internal Revenue, that bituminous coal operators endured losses of $27 million in 1925. These losses shrank to $15,822,000 in the boom year of 1929 and then rose to over $44 million the next year and jumped to $51,944,000 in 1932. These losses, Guffey concluded, resulted from the productive capacity of the mines during this period being 100 percent greater than consumer demands.[24] It is not strange that some of the operators were willing to sell their mines to the government "at any price." "Anything," they pleaded, "so we can get out of it."[25]

Between 1913 and 1935, nineteen significant hearings or investigations were conducted by congressional committees or governmental commissions on conditions in soft-coal mining.[26] Nothing, however, was done to bring relief to this basic industry until 1933. The first Hundred Days session of Congress enacted the NIRA to revive American industry. The National Recovery Administration (NRA) was created to govern the program, the heart of which were the "codes of fair competition." Each major industry, repre-

23 U.S., Congress, Senate, "Report of the United States Coal Commission," Senate Document 195, Pt. 3 (Serial 8402), December 10, 1923, 63 Cong., 2 Sess., 1925, pp. 1043–49.

24 *Congressional Record*, 74 Cong., 1 Sess., 1935, 79:13947.

25 Quoted in Schlesinger, *The Coming of the New Deal*, p. 89.

26 Noted in Dissenting Opinion, *Carter* v. *Carter Coal Company*, 298 U.S. 238 (1936).

sented by workers, owners, and government officials, were to agree upon codes establishing minimum wages and maximum hours and other working conditions. The code for bituminous coal was approved on September 18, 1933.[27]

The soft-coal industry began to stabilize under the NRA. The code provided for miners to organize and within a few months about 90 percent were affiliated with a union. Average daily wages then rose to five dollars and even the operators enjoyed a "reasonable profit" instead of an "unreasonable loss."[28] This temporary program worked so well that many Northern operators were persuaded to join John L. Lewis and his UMW in an effort to obtain permanent legislation.[29] It was well for them that they did, for the NRA was short-lived. In 1935, in *Schechter* v. *United States*, the Supreme Court declared the NRA unconstitutional.[30] According to President Roosevelt, the Court took the United States back to the "horse and buggy days" of interstate commerce. First of all, the Court said, Congress had attempted an unconstitutional delegation of power by not defining standards and rules for the codes. More significantly, Chief Justice Hughes, speaking for the Court, revived the old "indirect effects" doctrine enunciated in the *Knight* case of 1895 in regard to interstate commerce. The activities that were controlled, in this case the sale of poultry in New York, were intrastate commerce and thus beyond the control of the national government. The details of the poultry industry in New York were "as essentially local as mining, manufacturing and growing crops" and they had only an indirect effect on interstate commerce.

Meanwhile, in early January 1935 Guffey introduced a bill drafted by the United Mine Workers which became known as the Guffey-Snyder bill. The measure, reported the following April, declared the bituminous coal industry to be affected with a national public interest. In order to stabilize the industry and to promote it in interstate commerce, cooperative marketing would be established by taxing the industry and providing for a rebate on the taxes if the operators abided by the controls. It further established a fund of $300 million for the national government to stockpile surplus bituminous coal, to retire unproductive mines, and to rehabilitate the miners thus made unemployed. The fund was to be financed by bonds which

[27] U.S., *Statutes at Large*, vol. 48.
[28] U.S., Congress, Senate, Report 470 (Serial 9878), 74 Cong., 1 Sess., 1935, p. 2.
[29] Schlesinger, *The Politics of Upheaval* (Boston, 1960), pp. 334–35.
[30] 295 U.S. 495 (1935).

would be retired by the proceeds from an excise tax on coal. The Senate report declared the bill to be essential because of recent activities. The temporary NRA had stabilized the coal industry but, in "anticipation of the expiration" of the NRA code, many operators were attempting to get contracts to sell coal at prices "substantially lower" than those established by the code.[31] Chaos threatened the industry again!

A similar bill was introduced in the House by Democrat John Snyder of Pennsylvania. Following extensive hearings, and convinced the stockpiling scheme and other provisions of the Guffey bill might be unconstitutional, the House Ways and Means Committee rewrote the bill into a "little NRA" measure and reported H.R. 9100 in August 1935. The report pointed out that the NRA wage agreement in coal had expired the previous March. Faced with the threat of a national coal strike, the president had persuaded the operators and the miners to extend voluntarily this agreement three succeeding times. This situation called for congressional action. The report conceded the "question of the constitutionality of this bill has been seriously debated" but, of course, denied the validity of the opponents' argument, particularly because many of the controversial features had been eliminated in committee. The opposition argued that recent Supreme Court decisions emphasized coal mining was local in character. The proponents of the measure cited Court decisions upholding grain futures and meat packing regulations to support their position. These controls on coal were justified, constitutionally, because of the effects of mining activities on interstate commerce. Furthermore, the report noted, striking miners had been repeatedly enjoined under the antitrust laws because such strikes interfered with the interstate commerce of coal. If it were constitutional to regulate labor struggles in the mines, Congress could also legislate on conditions causing the strikes.[32]

The bill proposed the establishment of a coal commission which would work out a code for marketing coal and would control wages, hours, and working conditions. A tax of 15 percent, based on the sale price, would be levied when the coal was brought to the surface of the mine. In the case of captive coal—coal that was owned by the producer who also consumed it, such as a railroad—the price would be based on the market value of the

[31] U.S., Congress, Senate, Report 470 (Serial 9878), 74 Cong., 1 Sess., 1935, pp. 1–5.

[32] U.S., Congress, House, Report 1800 (Serial 9889), 74 Cong., 1 Sess., 1935, pp. 3–6.

product. If the operator complied with the coal code, he would be permitted a 90 percent drawback on the tax or, in effect, would actually only pay a net tax of 1.5 percent. This feature, the report declared, met the Supreme Court's objection to the poultry code of the NRA because it was voluntary. And it was a revenue-producing bill because even if all the industry agreed to the code, it would still produce $10 million annually.[33] The minority members of the Ways and Means Committee began their report by bluntly stating, "we are opposed to this bill." They agreed that stabilization of the coal industry was "a laudable objective and . . . much to be desired," but opposed this approach because it was unconstitutional. Coal mining was intrastate in nature and therefore beyond the reach of Congress. The proposed tax features only added to its unconstitutionality, they argued, because its purpose was not to raise revenue but was "a penalty to compel through direct coercion, the submission to regulations not otherwise within the power of Congress to enforce."[34]

The Guffey-Snyder bill, according to one opponent, had an interesting background. Although introduced in early January 1935, its whereabouts was unknown until President Roosevelt included it in his must program of the second Hundred Days session. Following hearings on the measure, a majority of the committee members believed it to be unconstitutional and, despite "a number of secret meetings" and "in spite of all the pressure and intimidation the administration could exert," refused to report it favorably. Further secret meetings of the Democratic majority were held and on August 12 the committee voted. Two Democrats then withdrew their negative votes and answered present, thus permitting the bill to be reported by a one-vote majority. John McCormack of Massachusetts admitted being one of the Democrats who changed, saying he did so in order to allow the bill to be considered by the House.[35]

The issue of constitutionality was debated in as great a detail in the House as any other taxing measure creating a national police power that had previously passed Congress. To pressure the House committee to report out the bill, Roosevelt sent a letter to the chairman. This letter acknowledged the current constitutional debate over the bill but suggested the question was for the Supreme Court to settle. Roosevelt's missive concluded with the

[33] Ibid., pp. 9–11.   [34] Ibid., p. 45.

[35] *Congressional Record*, 74 Cong., 1 Sess., 1935, 79:13437, 13466. Donald Morgan, *Congress and the Constitution* (Cambridge, Mass., 1966), chapt. 8, is a good study of the Guffy-Snyder bill.

observation that he hoped the committee would "not permit doubts as to the constitutionality, however reasonable, to block the suggested legislation."[36] The letter, needless to say, was used to the utmost by the Republicans to fight the bill, especially the indiscreet phrase "however reasonable."

Samuel B. Hill, Democrat of Washington, introduced the bill on the floor by calling attention to the voluminous discussion about its constitutionality. This talk, he said, had created much prejudice against the measure because congressmen who had not read its provisions had already assumed it was unconstitutional. He asked his colleagues to approach the issue with open minds. Hill assured his listeners of the constitutionality of the proposal because the Supreme Court had many times ruled that mining directly affected the interstate commerce in coal. He substantiated this by citing the *Coronado* and *Red Jacket* cases involving striking coal miners. The laborers argued in these cases that mining was intrastate; the Courts held that it affected interstate commerce and therefore their actions were subject to restraint under the antitrust laws. On the basis of these and other decisions, Hill affirmed, there was "reasonable expectation" that the Supreme Court would sustain the Guffey-Snyder bill although there was no guarantee.[37]

Opponents of the measure, however, did not permit Hill to dispose of the constitutional question this easily. Congressman Treadway repeated his congressional oath to uphold the Constitution and stated he would not violate it by voting for this bill. He called attention to Roosevelt's letter to the committee, saying that he believed the president would not disagree with his interpretation that the bill was unconstitutional. Minnesota Republican Harold Knutson declared that "we all know that this whole bill is illegal" and even Roosevelt admitted so in his letter. Knutson strongly suspected that the New Dealers' approach was "to constantly pass bills which are unconstitutional in the hope that they will work up such a sentiment for the rewriting of the Constitution that it will be done. It is plain that the purpose of the new deal is to break down the Constitution." Knutson emphasized that Democrat Jere Cooper of Tennessee had submitted a minority report declaring H.R. 9100 to be unconstitutional which was endorsed by four other Democrats on the Ways and Means Committee. "I want the world to know," Knutson happily announced, "that the administration does not com-

[36] "A Frequently Misquoted Letter," in *The Public Papers and Addresses of Franklin D. Roosevelt*, 4:297–300.
[37] *Congressional Record*, 74 Cong., 1 Sess., 1935, 79:13442–45.

pletely dominate all the Democrats on the Ways and Means Committee [*Applause*]."[38]

Fred Vinson, Democrat of Kentucky, who was later secretary of the treasury and then elevated to chief justice by President Truman, presented a lengthy argument to prove the constitutionality of the bill. He based his defense of the measure in the Supreme Court decisions of *Stafford* v. *Wallace* and *Board of Trade* v. *Olson* whereby the stockyards and grain futures regulations were found valid because these activities had a direct effect on interstate commerce. The High Court had several times held that mining had a direct effect on interstate commerce in litigation over labor disputes. These cases, he stated, included *Coronado Coal Company* v. *United Mine Workers* and the *Appalachian Coals* case.[39] Also included in this category, he said, was the *Red Jacket* case, a circuit court opinion which the Supreme Court refused to review, thereby confirming the decision of the lower court that a labor dispute in a mine affected interstate commerce.[40] Jere Cooper cited an equally impressive list of Supreme Court decisions which had determined that coal mining was not a part of interstate commerce. These included the *Hammer* case, *Delaware, Lackawanna and Western Railroad* v. *Yurkonis*,[41] and the first *Coronado* litigation.[42] Furthermore, Cooper argued, the taxing power does not permit the national government to evade the Tenth Amendment. He substantiated this view by referring to the *Bailey* decision and *United States* v. *One Ford Coupe Automobile*.[43] The *Veazie* and *McCray* decisions did not alter this interpretation, Cooper declared, because the constitutional issue in those cases was the excessive amount of taxation, not that they were an invasion of the states' reserved powers.[44]

Congressman Treadway was one of the chief spokesmen of the opposition to the bill. Use of the taxing power, he said, would not validate invasion of the reserved powers of states. He cited approvingly the Supreme Court declaration in *United States* v. *One Ford Coupe Automobile* that "the use

38 Ibid., p. 13447.

39 268 U.S. 295 (1925). *Appalachian Coals* v. *United States*, 288 U.S. 344 (1933).

40 18 Fed (2d) 840.

41 238 U.S. 439 (1915). In this litigation a miner was refused damages for injuries sustained in blasting in a coal mine.

42 *United Mine Workers* v. *Coronado Coal Company*, 259 U.S. 344 (1922).

43 272 U.S. 32 (1927). This case involved seizure and confiscation of an automobile used in evading the national revenue on liquor during Prohibition.

44 *Congressional Record*, 74 Cong., 1 Sess., 1935, 79:13460–65.

of the word 'tax' in imposing a financial burden does not prove conclusively that the burden imposed is a tax." Pennsylvania Democrat Denis J. Driscoll responded to Treadway's charge that the bill was hasty and ill-considered legislation by reciting a long list of investigations into the coal industry beginning with the creation of a coal commission in 1914. As a result of these studies, Driscoll recalled, Treadway had introduced regulatory legislation in 1924 and again in 1926. These bills, he noted, were similar to H.R. 9100 and had one of Treadway's proposals reprinted in the *Congressional Record* as evidence. He expressed confusion over Treadway's thinking that national controls over the coal industry would be valid in the 1920s but not in the 1930s and wondered if the answer lay in which party controlled the presidency at those times.[45]

Following a two-day debate the House accepted H.R. 9100 by a relatively close vote of 194 to 168.[46] There was little constitutional debate in the Senate, compared to that in the House. Attention, of course, was called to the current arguments, pro and con, on the constitutional issue, and to Roosevelt's letter. Democratic Senator Maury Maverick of Texas noted that "some people blat and roar about the Constitution for their own benefit," but when "human liberty [was] at stake these reactionaries keep quiet." Millard Tydings, Democrat of Maryland, led the opposition to the measure. He did not think the law would "hold water 3 minues after it gets to the Supreme Court" especially because of the provision to suspend the antitrust laws only for operators who complied with the code. Tydings conceded he was in a very embarrassing position because coal mining was a big industry in his state. "Practically all the miners" and "most of the operators" in his state were pressuring him to support the Guffey-Snyder bill, but he was forced to oppose it because it was unconstitutional and would suffer the same fate as the NRA. Tydings offered to support the measure if the tax were struck out, but his amendment to do so was defeated by vote of 29 to 44. Expressing concern that the proposed 15 percent tax would result in higher coal prices for consumers, Tydings then offered a motion to reduce the rate to 5 percent. This also was rejected 36 to 40. The Senate then passed the bill, with minor changes, by vote of 45 to 37.[47] A conference committee adjusted the differences in the two versions and President Roosevelt signed the Guffey-Snyder Act on August 30, 1935.

[45] Ibid., pp. 13484–87.
[46] Ibid., pp. 13666–67.
[47] Ibid., pp. 13516, 13771–74, 13982, 13985, 14084.

The Bituminous Coal Conservation Act of 1935 declared the soft-coal industry to be affected with a national public interest and the industry contained conditions that burdened and obstructed the flow of interstate commerce. To alleviate the situation, the law created a Bituminous Coal Commission of five members with power to fix coal prices. The Commission was to establish a code to govern the industry. The code would include price agreements based on 1934 production and prices, to be determined by twenty-three boards in each of the coal districts of the nation. Most important, the code had to contain a guarantee of the right of miners to organize and bargain collectively. When the operators of two-thirds of the annual tonnage production and representatives of a majority of the workers agreed to the terms, minimum wages and maximum hours were to be promulgated. All operators had to pay a tax of 15 percent of the market value of their mined coal; if they complied with the provisions of the coal code, they would receive a drawback or rebate of 90 percent of the tax paid. The law also contained the usual separability provisions.[48]

Soon after the Guffey-Snyder Act was passed the American Liberty League issued a pamphlet declaring it to be invalid on several counts. The law was unconstitutional, the organization said, because it sought to regulate activities "inherently local in character," and it "capriciously and arbitrarily infringes upon the individual liberties of producers and employees." Furthermore, neither a "pretended exercise of the taxing power" nor a congressional declaration that the coal industry was "affected with a national public interest" would make it constitutional. The pamphlet contained a long list of the Supreme Court cases cited by the opposition in the House debates to substantiate the argument.[49] The League was also fighting the National Labor Relations Act at this time. When that law was enacted in 1935, the League issued a similar pamphlet declaring it unconstitutional and urged manufacturers to violate it so as to get a decision quickly from the Supreme Court striking it down.

The day after Roosevelt signed the Guffey-Snyder Act into law, and before a code was agreed upon and put into operation, a man brought suit to enjoin his own coal company from complying with the coal code on the grounds of unconstitutionality of the law. The subsequent case of *Carter* v.

[48] U.S., *Statutes at Large*, vol. 49.

[49] National Lawyers Committee of the American Liberty League, *Report on the Constitutionality of the Bituminous Coal Conservation Act of 1935* ("Issued" December 9, 1935).

Carter Coal Company reached the Supreme Court and was decided the following year.[50] Justice Sutherland, joined by the other Four Horsemen and Roberts, agreed with the appellee. Despite the labor provisions not yet having become operable, and ignoring the separability clause, the justices found the tax to be "clearly not a tax but a penalty." The entire purpose of the exaction was "to coerce what is called an agreement—which, of course, it is not, for it lacks the essential element of consent," Sutherland said. The Constitutional Convention had not made a "grant of authority to Congress to legislate substantively for the general welfare." This could be done only indirectly through use of an expressly delegated power.

The regulations could not be sustained under the interstate commerce power, Sutherland observed, because interstate commerce meant intercourse for the purposes of trade and "plainly the incidents leading up to and culminating in the mining do not constitute such intercourse." In an interpretation quite similar to the *Knight* case, the majority noted that working conditions relating to mining, such as wages and hours, constituted "intercourse for the purposes of production, not trade." Mining merely brought "the subject matter of commerce into existence. Commerce disposes of it." The justices, though hard pressed to do so, were able to distinguish the previous antilabor decisions in coal mining from the present case. The earlier issues were also local in character, but the intent of the strikers was to restrict the flow of interstate commerce directly and the current conditions affected interstate commerce only secondarily and indirectly. Apparently labor conditions affected interstate commerce directly if miners sought to protect their rights, but indirectly when the producers had a complaint. In a concurring opinion Chief Justice Hughes agreed on the invalidity of the labor provisions of the law but disagreed with the majority, based on the separability clause, that this invalidated the entire act.

Cardozo, Brandeis, and Stone dissented. These three justices noted that 97.5 percent of all coal mined went into interstate commerce one way or another. With such a massive and direct impact on interstate commerce, the dissenters argued, Congress had power to fix prices on coal. In regard to the labor provisions, Cardozo said, the separability provision made the *Carter* case a premature one, because they had not gone into effect, so the "complainants have been crying before they are really hurt."

The next year Congress passed the Bituminous Coal Act of 1937, which

[50] 298 U.S. 238 (1936).

reenacted the program, but deleted the labor section and declared instead that the national government would not purchase coal from companies not complying with National Labor Relations Board rulings. This act also levied a 19.5 percent tax on coal operators who were not members of the Coal Code, a provision not dissimilar to the 1935 tax. The section establishing the Coal Code, however, was specifically based on the commerce power.[51]

The "Roosevelt Court" upheld this tax in 1940.[52] Justice William O. Douglas, a Roosevelt appointee, wrote the opinion sustaining the tax because its purpose was to enforce the code which was a constitutional exercise to control interstate commerce. McReynolds, the only one of the Four Horsemen still on the Supreme Court, was the lone dissenter. He wrote no opinion, merely observing that he disagreed because the act was "beyond any power granted to Congress."

The first AAA and the 1935 coal law both illustrate that New Dealers first viewed overproduction as a basic factor retarding recovery. Both acts were revolutionary in approaching a major economic problem with the taxing power. All previous taxes that built a national police power were levied on a specific item or were to benefit a particular group such as dairymen. These New Deal programs were designed to revive and to regulate entire segments of the economy. When this unique approach met the opposition of Dual Federalism endorsed by a majority of Supreme Court justices, it met the same fate as the Child Labor Tax. Congress enacted other "little NRAs" but not through use of the taxing power. Wright Patman introduced several measures during this period to control chain retail stores by taxing them, but none of his bills were reported by the House Ways and Means Committee.[53] The only other significant tax New Dealers were able to enact which affected the police power was on a specific item, dangerous firearms, the use of which during the decades of the 1920s and 1930s was becoming increasingly a menace to society.

[51] U.S., *Statutes at Large*, vol. 50.

[52] *Sunshine Coal Company* v. *Adkins*, 310 U.S. 381.

[53] *Congressional Record*, 75 Cong., 3 Sess., 1938, 83:1921; 76 Cong., 1 Sess., 1939, 84:22; 77 Cong., 1 Sess., 1941, 87:11.

11 Efforts to Control Firearms

Many elements contributed to the tradition that the possession and use of firearms is the birthright of every American. The frontier environment, in which guns were vital for self-protection and procurement of food, aided, as did the concept of the citizen soldier in time of war. Myths evolved that the Second Amendment, designed to stimulate militias of states and thus avoid a standing national army, actually guaranteed every citizen the right to bear arms. In the twentieth century, with the passing of the frontier and the Old West, Hollywood, with its emphasis on the gunslinger cowboy and the criminal protagonist, did not ameliorate this tradition. It was further accentuated following World War II by television programs which featured violence through firearms. As a result, American children, from the toddler up, are introduced to guns in the form of toy pistols or rifles and from that point on until physical maturity permits use of real ones, games consist in large part of "cowboys and Indians" and "cops and robbers" in which weapons play a major role. The subsequent passion of many Americans for guns resulted in the widespread belief that any governmental controls over firearms violated the fundamental right, or even duty, of the self-reliant, individualistic American male to possess a weapon to protect himself, his family, and his property.

The emergence of a highly industrialized, urban society in the twentieth century and the lack of controls over the indiscriminate possession and use of firearms, led to problems of deaths by guns, due to accident, their use to commit murder, or by criminals to perpetrate deeds of crime. From 1900 to 1970, more than 800,000 people in the United States were killed by guns, or more than the total killed in all American wars. By 1970 this slaughter was continuing to claim some 20,000 lives annually. In addition, in 1968 guns were involved in 44,000 serious assaults, 50,000 robberies, and 100,000 nonfatal injuries each year, according to President Lyndon Johnson.[1] The problem became particularly acute following World War I with the return of veterans, availability of surplus weapons, and, especially, the rise of organized crime during the Prohibition era with subsequent wars among gangs using the latest automatic weaponry.

Gangland wars of organized crime reached a crest in the 1920s and 1930s. These internecine battles added substantially to the growing crime and murder rate in the United States. It was not until 1930 that attempts were made to record crime statistics on a national level. At that time the Federal Bureau of Investigation began publishing the Uniform Crime Reports. The mechanics of collecting and reporting these statistics were rather rudimentary until 1933; thus the figures for that year are usually the ones used to begin charts or graphs which indicate crime trends. These graphs show a high point in crime in 1933 which then declined until after World War II. But it has been estimated that crime rates for "a sizable number of individual cities" were even higher for the years 1930–1932 than for 1933 and the rates for many offenses in the 1920s were higher yet in certain large cities such as Boston, Chicago, and New York.[2] Crimes involving firearms reached such alarming proportions during the depression that an overwhelming percentage of citizens began demanding some controls over these lethal weapons.

The first Gallup poll on this subject, in 1938, noted that 84 percent responded yes to the question "Do you think all owners of pistols and revolvers should be required to register with the government?"[3] The percentage of citizens expressing similar views on this issue remained around 75 to 80 percent in all subsequent polls on firearms legislation. A Gallup poll taken in 1967 indicated 83 percent agreed that pistols and revolvers should be registered and 73 percent expressed the same opinion about rifles and shotguns. Perhaps more significantly, a Harris poll in 1967 showed that 66 percent of the white gun owners in the United States favored registration.[4]

---

[1] "A Question of Guns," *Newsweek* 71 (June 24, 1968):81; Carl Bakal, *No Right to Bear Arms* (New York, 1968), p. 1.

[2] Report of President's Commission on Law Enforcement and Administration of Justice, "The Challenge of Crime in a Free Society" (Washington, D.C., 1967), p. 24.

[3] *Public Opinion Quarterly* 2 (July 1938):394.

[4] Many of the more recent polls are reprinted in U.S., Congress, Senate, Subcommittee on Juvenile Delinquincy, *Hearings on S. 1*, 90 Cong., 1 Sess., 1967, pp. 520–27.

In the face of such massive opinion favoring controls, it seems strange at first glance that there have been only two significant national laws on the subject before 1968 and these were so weak they proved practically worthless in curtailing the gun menace. The reason lies in one of the most powerful and amazingly successful American lobbies, the National Rifle Association (NRA).

The NRA was first organized in 1871 by a group of New York Civil War veterans and militiamen who wished to improve their marksmanship. It later was chartered nationally and moved its headquarters to Washington, D.C. With approximately 900,000 members in 1970, and an annual income of about $6 million, the NRA occupies a $3 million building located within gunshot of the White House. The NRA, a nonprofit organization, states that it is devoted to a program of educating its members and the public concerning firearms and safety in their use and performs a service for the national government; because it is a nonprofit organization, it has a tax-free status and, in addition, is not required to register as a lobby. Yet it has proved to be one of the most aggressive lobbies in the Capital and has successfully defeated every significant legislative effort to enact reasonable controls over guns that has appeared in Congress until 1968.[5]

NRA governmental services began in 1903 when the organization persuaded Secretary of War Elihu Root to establish the National Board for the Promotion of Rifle Practice in conjunction with other army reforms he was instituting. This board loaned guns and provided ammunition for target practice for gun clubs affiliated with, and approved by, the NRA. In addition, the NRA, in cooperation with the National Board, sponsored the annual shooting matches at Camp Perry, Ohio, and the NRA selected the rifle and pistol teams that represented the United States in the Olympic Games, the Pan American Games, and other international marksmanship competitions. Throughout the history of firearms legislation, NRA lobbying proved vital as this organization spearheaded the opposition of gun buffs against all proposed controls.

It was not until the New Deal that Congress enacted the first truly effective firearms law. With the crime rate peaking in the early 1930s, and

[5] "T.R.B.," *New Republic* 152 (June 19, 1965) : 4. A great deal has been written in recent years about the NRA and its activities. See, e.g., Bakal, *No Right to Bear Arms*; Bakal, "The Traffic in Guns: A Forgotten Lesson of the Assassination," *Harpers* 229 (December 1964) ; Robert G. Sherrill, "The Big Shoot," *Nation* 202 (March 7, 1966) ; Robert Sherrill, "A Lobby on Target," *New York Times Magazine*, October 15, 1967; "A Question of Guns," *Newsweek* 71 (June 24, 1968).

particularly with the attempted assassination of President-elect Franklin D. Roosevelt in 1933 by a demented man, Attorney General Homer Cummings launched an anticrime crusade which included stringent controls over guns. By this time criminal use of the Thompson submachine gun in the United States was making world headlines so Congress used the effective power of taxation to restrict this deadly type of weapon.

On October 14, 1926, a United States mail truck was robbed at Elizabeth, New Jersey, by bandits armed with Thompson submachine guns. Two months later it was reported that "the press of other nations has not yet ceased discussing" the crime.[6] *Collier's* sent a reporter to check on the difficulty of a person securing such a weapon. The reporter discovered he, and thus he assumed anyone, could buy one without question for $175 plus an additional $20 for an ammunition magazine. This instrument would fire a maximum of 400 bullets per minute, a weapon that obviously should be possessed only by military personnel.[7] While some states, especially New York with its strict Sullivan Law of 1911, had regulations requiring a police permit before possession of handguns, there were no restrictions on these terrible weapons, a problem that greatly concerned Attorney General Cummings.

The Justice Department wrote a bill and sent it to Congress in 1934 where it was referred to the House Ways and Means Committee. Attorney General Cummings was the first witness and he explained the background and features of his proposal. He declared that twice as many criminals (500,000) currently were armed with deadly weapons as there were personnel in the United States armed forces. His department had begun a study of the problem in 1933 and had decided that use of the taxing power would be the best approach because of the need to identify weapons and keep records of their transfer from person to person. He proposed, therefore, a bill which embodied the principles of the Harrison Narcotic Act. If any firearm—"a pistol, revolver, shotgun having a barrel less than sixteen inches in length, or any other firearm capable of being concealed on the person, a muffler or silencer therefor, or a machine gun"—were sold or transferred, it must be registered and taxed. Cummings's proposal did not state the amount of tax and, upon questioning, he suggested a $5,000 annual tax for manufacturers and importers of firearms and a $200 tax on transfer of

---

[6] William G. Shepherd, "Machine Gun Madness," *Colliers* 78 (December 11, 1926) : 8.

[7] Owen P. White, "Machine Guns for Sale," *Colliers* 78 (December 4, 1926) :11–12.

machine guns, or 100 percent because they sold for approximately that amount. He also stated that President Roosevelt authorized him to say he was "strongly in favor of this measure," as well as several other anticrime bills the Department of Justice was recommending which would use the interstate commerce power.[8]

Cummings called the attention of the committee to the omission of rifles and shotguns used for sporting purposes. This, obviously, was because criminals very seldom used this type of weapon and because no politician who was in favor of gun controls would want to antagonize the large number of voters who were also hunters. But one provision of his bill—that buyers of firearms must be fingerprinted and photographed—drew the particular attention of Arkansas Democrat Claude Fuller. This congressman thought the requirement would "cause an awful revolt . . . amongst private citizens" and suggested eliminating pistols and revolvers from the bill. Cummings, however, expressed the belief that "it would be a terrible mistake to adopt any half-way measures about this." He believed the sooner Americans accepted "the fact that the possession of the deadly weapons must be regulated and checked, the better off we are going to be as a people." Under questioning he admitted that even if the bill became law criminals would still obtain guns. But with this regulation the Department of Justice would be able to convict them. As he pointed out, Al Capone was imprisoned not for alleged criminal activities but for income tax evasion. The Justice Department also submitted a memorandum on the British firearms law to illustrate the need for the proposal. In 1920 Great Britain began requiring citizens to obtain a permit from their local police chief before purchasing guns or ammunition; this requirement was more rigorous than the Cummings measure. To illustrate the efficacy of the British regulation, the Department of Justice noted that in 1930 the United States statistics on murder and manslaugher ran 1 to 11,000 population; in France, with controls, the ratio was 1 to 72,500, and in England, with its strict controls, it was 1 to 165,000. This memorandum also noted a steady increase in United States homicide statistics from 6,205 in 1920 to 11,160 in 1931.

Cummings had not reckoned with the NRA. Representatives of this organization testified after him and subsequently persuaded the committee to emasculate his bill. The adjutant general of Maryland, Milton Reckord, who was also an NRA executive vice president and Karl T. Frederick, pres-

[8] U.S., Congress, House, Committee on Ways and Means, *Hearings on H.R. 9066*, 73 Cong., 2 Sess., 1934, pp. 1–12.

ident of the NRA, presented the views of their association to the committee. Reckord declared the NRA was not obstructionist "in any way," but they were extremely disappointed that they were not consulted in the drafting of the bill. They had heard the Department of Justice was working on this problem and had offered to help. The attorney general had failed to take advantage of their generous offer, however, and they were subsequently surprised to hear the bill had been introduced; therefore the NRA officers had not had time "to completely formulate" their views on the measure because they had not studied its provisions.[9]

Some of the committeemen expressed puzzlement over the "stream of telegrams" they had received in the previous two days. These telegrams insisted the committee should "give all possible consideration" to NRA suggestions on gun controls; but how could NRA members know what their officers were going to recommend if they did not know what provisions the bill contained? Under questioning Reckord admitted that he had wired some state affiliates that the proposed legislation was bad and had probably "intimated" they should wire their congressmen. When asked if NRA members then blindly followed instructions, Reckord lamely replied, "I would not say blindly."[10]

Committeemen soon discovered that the NRA objected principally to the inclusion of pistols and revolvers in the measure. Joseph B. Keenan, assistant attorney general who attended the committee hearings of both houses of Congress on firearms legislation, charged that Reckord had previously said the NRA would never agree to regulations on handguns. When Reckord replied that such had never been the NRA position, committee chairman Robert Doughton, Democrat of North Carolina, adjourned the hearings for one month, telling the NRA and the Department of Justice to get together and agree on a bill.[11]

During the interim the Department of Justice remained adamant in the desire to obtain strict controls on all guns except rifles and shotguns, but did yield on two significant points. The compromise version retained the original provision for firearms registration but omitted the requirement to photograph and fingerprint current owners; this would be done only when guns were purchased or transferred in the future. Also pistols and revolvers of .22 caliber rimfire, used for target practice, were excluded and a shotgun

9 Ibid., pp. 22, 28–31.
10 Ibid., pp. 62–64.
11 Ibid., p. 82.

would not be considered a firearm unless the barrel was less than eighteen inches in length. Apparently the NRA was active during the hearings recess in appraising its members of the threat posed to the complete freedom of access to weapons. Joseph Keenan, in presenting the compromise bill, noted the NRA had sent messages asking its members "to bombard this committee with objections" to the proposed legislation and these communications regretably contained "misrepresentations." J. Weston Allen, chairman of the National Anti-Crime Commission, quoted a letter sent to NRA members from the national office. The missive, in part, suggested that the compromise version, H.R. 9741, was merely the beginning. If it became law, it warned, the next year the Department of Justice would ask for more stringent regulations which would result in "every rifle and shotgun owner in the country ... paying a special tax and having himself fingerprinted and photographed for the Federal rogues' gallery, every time he buys or sells a gun of any description." [12]

Reckord testified that the NRA was still dissatisfied with the changed bill; he wanted the controls to cover only machine guns because the remaining provisions contained "nothing worthwhile." Reckord expressed particular alarm over the registration requirement, insisting this would make the law "another Volstead Act." [13] The NRA would be satisfied with regulation of only the deadliest of weapons. The bill, reported to the House, was in the form acceptable to the NRA. [14]

Democrat Royal Copeland of New York, chairman of the Senate Subcommittee on Commerce which also held hearings on the firearms bill, was pressed for time because he was trying to report out other Department of Justice anticrime proposals, considered equally important, in time for enactment before Congress adjourned. General Reckord, who expressed extreme apprehension to Copeland's committee over the registration feature of the original proposal, tried to take advantage of the time factor. When he suggested Copeland report the House-emasculated version in order to get it passed before adjournment, the senator said, "If I did not believe in firmarms legislation, I would think this [H.R. 9741] is the best bill in the world." If Reckord wanted to omit pistols from coverage in the law, Copeland was "not interested." Copeland was particularly distressed over someone creating the impression that Congress was "trying to embarrass the

---

12 Ibid., pp. 83–100, 129.
13 Ibid., pp. 109–23.
14 U.S., Congress, House, Report 1780 (Serial 9776), 73 Cong., 2 Sess., 1934.

farmer so that he cannot use a revolver or shotgun, or leave one with his wife, or take a pistol along in his automobile." He then had reprinted in the hearings some current NRA literature describing the original bill. The NRA condemned the Cummings proposal because their "constructive suggestions . . . were utterly disregarded." The NRA, in this literature, expressed no doubt that, if enacted, it would be "of greater benefit to the criminals of this country than to the law enforcement officials" and concluded that the proposal was "simply an effort to disguise as a revenue bill a Federal police measure."[15] The NRA, however, was successful in its tactics. The full Senate Committee on Commerce reported H.R. 9741 favorably but lowered the licensing tax on manufacturers and importers to $500.[16]

At this time the General Federation of Women's Clubs held its annual meeting at Hot Springs, Arkansas. Joseph Keenan sadly announced to the audience that the National Rifle Association had "proved more powerful than the Department of Justice" in the fight for firearms controls. This caused one delegate to jump to her feet and declare that if 1,000,000 NRA members (there were actually 250,000 at this time) could get handguns deleted from controls, "two million American club women are strong enough to lick them to a frazzle" and restore pistols and revolvers to the bill. They adopted and sent a resolution to congressional leaders expressing their outrage over the deletion. *Field and Stream* editors telegraphed the women that the original proposal was "a vicious measure that would affect only honest citizens . . . believed by many people" to be part of an effort to deny ultimately the right to possess any type of firearms. The magazine editors explained that it was necessary to omit handguns from controls because "the security and safety of the homes and families of all the people of this country demand it."[17]

The women lost the struggle in Congress. Doughton described the watered-down version in the House. When asked why handguns were deleted in the face of protests from women's clubs throughout the country, he explained that "the ordinary law-abiding citizen" desiring a pistol for protection should not be fingerprinted, registered, and "classed with criminals, racketeers and gangsters." A two-thirds vote to suspend the rules was

[15] U.S., Congress, Senate, Subcommittee of Committee on Commerce, *Hearings on Bills to Regulate Commerce in Firearms and to Tax Firearms*, 73 Cong., 2 Sess., 1934, pp. 58–63, 72–75.

[16] U.S., Congress, Senate, Report 1444 (Serial 9770), 73 Cong., 2 Sess., 1934.

[17] "Club Women Mapping War on Gangsters," *Literary Digest* 117 (June 16, 1934) :19.

achieved and the bill passed the House without a roll call vote. The Senate also accepted it, with the lower fee on licenses, without recorded vote and the House agreed to the Senate change.[18] President Roosevelt signed the National Firearms Act on June 18, 1934. The law defined firearms as being rifles or shotguns with barrels shorter than eighteen inches in length, weapons capable of concealment on the person other than pistols and revolvers, machine guns, silencers, and mufflers. Importers and manufacturers of such weapons must pay an annual tax of $500, dealers $300, and pawnbrokers $200. Each transfer of these firearms must be accompanied by a special form, with a copy sent to the commissioner of Internal Revenue along with a $200 tax payment. In sixty days possessors of such firearms had to register them and have them identified with a mark. Exceptions were made for all governmental agencies and peace officers and for firearms that were unserviceable. Violations would be punished with a $2,000 fine and/or five years in prison.[19]

Homer Cummings did not abandon the fight. His philosophy was "show me a man who doesn't want his gun registered, and I will show you a man who shouldn't have a gun."[20] His proposal to control pistols and revolvers was approved in 1935 by the Senate Committee on Commerce.[21] This measure included a provision requiring a gun owner to show his state gun-permit in order to buy ammunition for licensed weapons if his state law had a permit system. The bill was passed over in the Senate and then received approval in 1936 but was never reported out of House committee.[22]

It was not until 1938 that Congress again enacted a gun control law. Congressmen, Senator Copeland informed his colleagues, had the assistance of the NRA and the American Pistol Association in "perfecting" the new law. It passed the Senate without recorded vote and won House approval without roll call vote the following session. President Roosevelt signed it on June 30, 1938.[23] The Federal Firearms Act of 1938 invoked the interstate commerce power to require manufacturers and dealers in firearms to obtain a national license. The annual fee was twenty-five dollars for the manufacturer and one dollar for the dealer. The licensing requirement was to serve the purpose of helping enforce the remaining provisions of the law.

18 *Congressional Record*, 73 Cong., 2 Sess., 1934, 77:11400, 12400, 12555.
19 U.S., *Statutes at Large*, vol. 48.
20 Quoted in Bakal, *No Right to Bear Arms*, p. 173.
21 U.S., Congress, Senate, Report 997 (Serial 9880), 74 Cong., 1 Sess., 1935.
22 *Congressional Record*, 74 Cong., 2 Sess., 1936, 80:2427.
23 Ibid., 75 Cong., 1 Sess., 1937, 81:1257; 75 Cong., 2 Sess., 1938, 82:9659.

Firearms could not knowingly be shipped or sold in interstate commerce in violation of state laws or to persons convicted of a crime of violence or fugitives from justice. Records of sales had to be kept, and penalties for violation included a $2,000 fine and/or five years imprisonment.[24]

The 1934 tax and the 1938 regulations were challenged in the Supreme Court as, among other things, an infringement on the Second Amendment. This declares in full that "a well regulated Militia being necessary to the security of a free State, the right of the people to keep and bear Arms shall not be infringed." It was designed to preserve militias.[25] The Supreme Court had first pronounced judgment on this amendment during Reconstruction. In *United States* v. *Cruikshank,* several persons appealed their conviction for having violated the Enforcement Act of 1870 by denying rights to citizens. Among the charges was an indictment for denying certain citizens [Negroes] the "right to keep and bear arms." The Supreme Court reversed the convictions on the grounds that these guarantees stemmed from state citizenship, not national, and the victims must look to their state governments for protection of these rights. The prerogative of having arms, the Court said, "is not a right granted by the Constitution."[26]

Despite this pronouncement, gun advocates continued to emphasize the myth that every citizen has the right to have firearms. In 1937 the Supreme Court passed judgment on the 1934 law that taxed this right. Max Sonzinsky was arrested and convicted for dealing in firearms without paying the required license tax. He had sold one sawed-off shotgun which, he argued, did not make him a dealer and he was thus not subject to the license requirements. The petitioner also claimed that it was not a "true tax, but a penalty imposed for the purpose of suppressing traffic in a certain noxious type of firearms."[27] Speaking through Justice Harlan Stone the Court rejected this argument, again enunciating the broad scope of the taxing power. In exercising this power, Stone declared, "Congress may select the subjects of taxation, choosing some and omitting others. On its face it is only a taxing measure," the decision continued, and every tax is in some manner a regulation. "But a tax is not any the less a tax because it has a regulatory effect." Stone noted it had been well established that as long as the tax is an exercise

24 U.S., *Statutes at Large,* vol. 52.
25 See especially Irving Brant, *The Bill of Rights,* Mentor ed. (New York, 1967), p. 478.
26 92 U.S. 542 (1876).
27 *Transcripts of Records and File Copies of Briefs,* Case #614, 1936 Term, vol. 110, U.S. Supreme Court Library.

of the taxing power "on its face," it is no less a tax because it is "burdensome or tends to restrict or suppress the thing taxed." "Inquiry into the hidden motives" of Congress in the exercise of the taxing power, he concluded, "is beyond the competency of courts." [28]

A case testing the constitutionality of the 1938 law reached the Supreme Court two years later. In *United States* v. *Miller* the Supreme Court stated its most comprehensive analysis to date of the intent of the framers of the Second Amendment.[29] Jack Miller and Frank Layton were convicted of violating the Federal Firearms Act by transporting a sawed-off twelve-gauge shotgun from Claremore, Oklahoma, to Siloam Springs, Arkansas, without having registered it. They appealed on the grounds that this law infringed upon their right to bear arms. The decision, significantly, was written by Justice James McReynolds, one of the Court's Four Horsemen. McReynolds traced the history of the colonial development of militias, with each man supplying his own firearm, through the Revolutionary Minutemen, to the framing of the Second Amendment. The Court determined that the right to bear arms was intended to apply only to the preservation of state militias. In this instance a sawed-off shotgun could not be considered part of the equipment of "a well regulated Militia." Because the defendants failed to produce evidence that possession of this type of shotgun had "some reasonable relationship to the preservation or efficiency" of a state militia, their conviction was sustained. "We cannot say," McReynolds concluded, "that the Second Amendment guarantees the right to keep and bear such an instrument."

During the next three decades the 1938 act proved practically worthless while the 1934 tax, although nearly as meaningless as the Federal Firearms law because of its limited coverage, did eliminate the most dangerous of weapons. In addition, several loopholes in the laws were closed in the succeeding years. In 1947 Congress amended the 1938 act to correct an oversight. A letter from Attorney General Tom Clark, later a Supreme Court justice, called attention to a circuit court of appeals freeing a man sentenced for transporting a firearm, although he had previously been convicted for robbery.[30] So the Eightieth Congress included robbery as a crime of violence in the 1938 regulations.[31] But the amendment sponsors were warned

---

[28] *United States* v. *Sonzinsky*, 300 U.S. 506 (1937).

[29] 307 U.S. 174 (1939).

[30] U.S., Congress, House, Report 48 (Serial 11118), 80 Cong., 1 Sess., 1947.

[31] U.S., *Statutes at Large*, vol. 61.

in the House debate that the measure had better not include gun registration "or it would not get very far."[32] In 1950 Congress again amended the 1938 law to provide for disposition of seized weapons so they would not be returned to the original owners. Finally the 1938 act was amended in 1961 to eliminate the section on crimes of violence and inserted instead the national standard for a felony, that is, anyone indicted, convicted, or fleeing from a crime punishable by more than one year in prison could not obtain or carry a firearm in interstate commerce.[33]

A new development in guns led sportsmen to demand a change in the tax law in the 1950s. A combination rifle and small gauge shotgun, sometimes called an "over and under," had been developed but, to keep down its weight, had a barrel length under that proscribed by the National Firearms Act. Gun collectors had also been hampered by the "other weapons" category. A congressional report noted these people desired the "gadget type" or "unique" weapons that the gangsters would not be interested in.[34] Both houses of Congress acquiesced in amendments to the tax without roll call vote.[35] The change permitted the combination guns as long as they were single shot models with barrels over twelve inches long and imposed a five-dollar tax on their transfer. Any type of modified weapon had to be at least twenty-six inches in overall length or it would be considered a "firearm" within the meaning of the 1934 law. It also raised the dealers tax from one dollar to ten for the "other weapons" category but permitted acquisition of any kind of weapon by collectors if they were deactivated.[36]

The inefficacy of these meager gun controls was repeatedly demonstrated in the period following World War II. After 1945 there was a tremendous upsurge in the manufacture and importation of guns, as well as an increase in war surplus armaments. This increase in weaponry was accompanied by a significant rise in the crime rate, juvenile delinquency, and violence of the civil rights movement, particularly in the 1960s. Total crimes against persons had dropped from 155 per 100,000 population in 1933 to 93 during World War II. But the rate then rose to 145 by 1960 and to 185 in 1965.[37]

Concern over the increase in juvenile delinquency led the Senate to

[32] *Congressional Record*, 80 Cong., 1 Sess., 1947, 93:1629.

[33] U.S., *Statutes at Large*, vols. 64 and 75.

[34] U.S., Congress, House, Report 914 (Serial 12163), 86 Cong., 1 Sess., 1959.

[35] *Congressional Record*, 89 Cong., 1 Sess., 1959, 111:16203; 89 Cong., 2 Sess., 1960, 112:9534.

[36] U.S., *Statutes at Large*, vol. 74.

[37] President's Commission, "The Challenge of Crime in a Free Society," p. 22.

create a special subcommittee to investigate this phenomenon. In 1961 the subcommittee turned its attention to the problem of easy availability of firearms to juveniles. The committee chairmanship was taken over by Senator Thomas Dodd, Democrat of Connecticut, who began several years of intensive investigation of the firearms traffic and a long, frustrating attempt to achieve some controls, especially over mail-order guns.[38] Dodd had introduced a bill to control this type of gun traffic when the nation was stunned by the assassination of President John F. Kennedy on November 22, 1963, through use of a mail-order rifle.

Dodd's committee discovered that the one-dollar license fee for dealers had been meaningless. In fact, advertisements in gun magazines urged customers to become dealers and outlined the necessary steps. For the one-dollar fee the "dealer" could avoid the gun permit requirements in those few states where they existed; could avoid arrest for carrying guns in automobiles in violation of state laws or city ordinances; could purchase guns at wholesale prices; and could avoid sales taxes.[39] By becoming a dealer anyone could circumvent local, state, and national laws—juveniles, criminals, insane persons—merely by using a mail order to purchase weapons.[40]

The committee also discovered a huge traffic in deactivated weapons. Many of these were called "Dewats" or deactivated war trophies. The committee reprinted in the hearings an article from the *Saturday Evening Post* of February 8, 1958. The author of the article had a two-year old daughter who received a gun advertisement through the mail. He answered in her name and in the return mail received a machine gun deactivated by having the barrel welded shut. He then answered another advertisement and received a new barrel with which he replaced the original using ordinary tools "of a dimestore variety." Also an advertisement from the *Los Angeles Times* was reprinted with its caption "Submachine Gun for Father's Day?"[41] Anyone could purchase one of these weapons and with a smattering of knowledge about firearms could easily make it operable.

[38] This broad problem of gun controls is admirably detailed in Bakal, *No Right to Bear Arms.*

[39] U.S., Congress, Senate, Subcommittee on Juvenile Delinquincy, *Hearings on Interstate Traffic in Mail Order Firearms*, 88 Cong., 1 Sess., 1963, pp. 3218–23. Hereafter cited as *Dodd Hearings* with appropriate year.

[40] In 1965 Secretary of the Treasury Henry Fowler testified that of the 99,544 "dealers," less than half were legitimate dealers, *Dodd Hearings*, 1965, p. 33.

[41] *Dodd Hearings*, 1963, pp. 3597, 3303–7.

The development in the 1960s of extreme right-wing guerrilla groups such as the Minutemen and the Paul Revere Associated Yeomen added to the gun menace. Public attention was focused on the NRA marksmanship program when it was discovered that Robert DePugh, head of the Minutemen, urged all his followers to join the NRA in order to qualify for free rifles and ammunition. Adding to this public alarm was the discovery that, when captured, a former Minuteman had in his possession one hundred submachine guns, a flame-thrower, a 75 mm recoilless cannon, five .50 caliber machine guns, several 25-pound aerial bombs, automatic pistols and ammunition—all bought from the Department of Defense as Dewats and restored to working order.[42]

These activities increased the public interest in the marksmanship program. Anyone who would pay five dollars and declare himself to be eighteen years old and not have been convicted of a major crime, could join the NRA if recommended by another member, an officer of the armed forces, or a reputable citizen. This statement was accepted at face value and did not have to be notarized; apparently the NRA made little effort to ascertain the truth about applicants.[43] This membership qualified the person to buy surplus .45 caliber pistols at cost—$17.50—and M1 rifles for twenty dollars and receive guns on loan and free ammunition. Any group of ten or more people could form a gun club, receive NRA affiliation, and qualify for these benefits. From 1959 to 1964 this program cost the American taxpayer $12 million.[44] The chief justification for the program was the improvement of marksmanship for those who would later serve in the armed forces. With the bad publicity engendered by disclosure of Minutemen activities, the army ordered an investigation of the program, the first since its founding in 1903. Critics were not reassured by the report of this investigation which stated that it was difficult to be absolutely sure that club officers of NRA affiliates "do or do not have police records."[45] Equally distressing to some was the disclosure that 42 percent of the participants in the marksmanship program were over draft age and only 3 percent of army recruits had ever participated in the program.[46]

[42] "Don't Wait, Buy a Gun Now," *New Republic* 150 (June 6, 1964) : 9–10.

[43] "Be Strong, Carry a Gun," *New Republic* 149 (December 14, 1963) :7; Carl Bakal, *No Right to Bear Arms*, declares he joined by having his brother-in-law, who fits none of these requirements, recommend him, p. 142.

[44] Bakal, *No Right to Bear Arms*, p. 139.

[45] Sherrill, "A Lobby on Target," p. 129.

[46] *Dodd Hearings*, 1967, p. 742.

A presidential commission, following an exhaustive study of crime in the United States, pointed to further firearms problems. It was noted that in the 1960s approximately 1,000,000 cheap surplus rifles were being imported into the country annually. One of these, a Mannlicher-Carcano from Italy, was purchased by mail order when Lee Harvey Oswald clipped an advertisement from the *American Rifleman* and mailed it to a Chicago firearms company. When captured following the assassination of President Kennedy, Oswald was carrying a pistol bought by mail order from a Los Angeles company. The commission further noted that only eight states had gun permit requirements and even these lost their efficacy because of the interstate nature of the gun trade. For instance, Massachusetts had a strict permit law but 87 percent of the firearms used to commit crimes in that state came from another state. As the commission noted, "almost every industrialized nation in the world" had some type of firearms registration law; only four states in the United States did. The commission made several recommendations including outlawry of possession of military weapons by citizens, or any firearms by dangerous people, and national prohibition of mail order and interstate shipment of guns. Perhaps the strongest suggestion was the urging of state laws requiring registration of all firearms and, after five years, a national firearms registration requirement applicable to states that failed to act.[47]

All these postwar developments led to a tremendous public demand to control firearms, a sentiment that crystallized when President Kennedy was assassinated. To counteract this massive public support for gun controls, as indicated by public opinion polls, the NRA, a nonregistered lobbying organization, conducted the most successful lobbying campaign probably ever witnessed in recent United States history. The NRA, through its journal the *American Rifleman* and news bulletins to its members, began a massive education program to oppose all threatened controls. Emphasizing the right to bear arms, the organization insisted that "Guns do not kill people; People kill people" and argued that heavier penalties should be enacted for crimes committed with guns, rather than any further regulations on firearms.[48]

The NRA claimed to be able to deluge Congress with 500,000 letters from its members within a 72-hour period and, according to one source, this

[47] President's Commission, "The Challenge of Crime in a Free Society," pp. 241–43.

[48] See, e.g., *Dodd Hearings*, 1963, pp. 3473, 3481, for such NRA arguments.

was "probably not a cheap boast."[49] Using the slogan "Register Communists, Not Guns," the organization stressed the theme that any gun controls
would lead to registration which was part of a Communist plot to have an
available list of firearms owners. The specter of Communist hordes seizing
one's gun was sufficient stimulation to any firearms advocate to write his
congressman. The mere suggestion of a registration law aroused an immediate response from sportsmen.[50] With the NRA campaign, firearms
controls became an either-or proposition in the minds of many gun advocates; one was either pro-gun or anti-gun. As one NRA critic has suggested,
the NRA had a financial stake in this problem. In the 1960s the advertising
by firearms manufacturers and dealers in the *American Rifleman* constituted approximately one-fourth of its almost $6 million annual income.[51]
The NRA itself estimated that the shooting industry was worth $2.5 billion
a year when hunters' gasoline, motel bills, equipment, and all the expenses
connected with hunting are included.[52] In any event, NRA expenses for
"legislative and public affairs" rose 100 percent from 1962 to 1964.[53]

Other gun magazines joined the NRA crusade, often displaying even
more vehemence against anti-gun people than the *American Rifleman*. In
one issue *Guns & Ammo* informed its readers that anyone favoring gun
registration or the "overly restrictive laws" then being considered by Congress was "a fool, a Communist or one with a guilty conscience who is
afraid of getting his just desserts."[54] This attitude, of course, does not permit pursuit of any middle course of action or much latitude for compromise.

[49] Sherrill, "The Big Shoot," p. 261.

[50] Perhaps it should be noted there are exceptions. I have been an enthusiastic
hunter for years and, from personal conviction, believe a registration law is an absolute
necessity in contemporary American society. This should also be accompanied by an
annual physical and mental test before a permit to use firearms is granted. Oddly
enough, supporters of registration laws are assumed to be anti-gun by the pro-gun
people and the apparently few sportsmen who adopt this middle ground feel comelled
to apologize for this betrayal. For a different view see Paul Good, "Blam! Blam!
Blam!," *New York Times Magazine*, September 17, 1972.

[51] Bakal, *No Right to Bear Arms*, p. 138.

[52] "A Question of Guns," p. 83.

[53] Sherrill, "The Big Shoot," p. 262.

[54] *Guns & Ammo* 12 (October 1968) :16. Dodd was forced to subpoena the editor
of this magazine in order to question him about misrepresenting proposed controls in
his journal. Dodd charged that in one editorial in *Guns & Ammo*, twenty-seven of
twenty-eight paragraphs were not "anywhere nearly truthful" about his proposal. The
editor explained this as "editorializing"; Dodd described it as "lying." *Dodd Hearings*,
1965, pp. 618–22.

But the opposition to any and all controls was quite successful. Following President Kennedy's assassination, some twenty gun control bills were introduced in Congress all of which, the NRA happily informed its members, were "either turned back or gutted." [55]

The NRA adopted a clever strategy in opposing these controls. Its officials worked quite closely with the Dodd Committee and consistently gave testimony in the hearings in order to work out acceptable compromises. Then when the legislation was ready for consideration by Congress, NRA members were urged to flood congressmen with letters and telegrams demanding that the right to bear arms be protected and to vote against any firearms controls. Or, as one source described the process, they "cozy up to a reform politician and get him to cripple his own legislation; then when the malformed bill is introduced, crush it the rest of the way." The same technique was also employed successfully on state legislatures. [56] The NRA was assisted in this endeavor by approximately thirty congressmen who were members of their organization, including Democrat Robert Sikes of Florida, a ranking member of the House Appropriations Subcommittee on Defense which handled the budget requests of the National Board for the Promotion of Rifle Practice. Other congressmen friendly to NRA principles included Senator Warren Magnuson, Democrat of Washington and chairman of the Committee on Commerce; Republican Roman L. Hruska of Nebraska, a member of Dodd's committee; Wilbur Mills, Democrat of Arkansas and chairman of the House Committee on Ways and Means; and Cecil King, Democrat of California, also a member of this committee and an NRA director. [57] Even liberal Democratic senators from Western hunting states such as Frank Church of Idaho, George McGovern of South Dakota, and Gale McGee of Wyoming had to be careful of their position on firearms controls because of their constituents. [58]

Although the NRA was successful in preventing any meaningful controls for several years, 1968 marked a turning point, for two significant

[55] Sherrill, "A Lobby on Target," p. 27.

[56] Sherrill, "The Big Shoot," p. 261. Often the NRA badly misrepresented to its members legislation it helped the Dodd committee perfect. See, e.g., *Dodd Hearings*, 1965, pp. 33–35, 40–41, for such charges by Attorney General Nicholas deB. Katzenbach, pp. 207–15; *Dodd Hearings*, 1967, pp. 546–57.

[57] Bakal, *No Right to Bear Arms*, pp. 145–46.

[58] Church and McGee, for example, voted against the Senate version of the Gun Control Act of 1968; McGovern was absent and not paired. *Congressional Record*, 90 Cong., 2 Sess., 1968, 119:S10986 [unbound].

political assassinations took place in that year. Martin Luther King, Jr., the nation's most prominent civil rights leader, was shot to death on April 4 and Senator Robert F. Kennedy of New York was gunned down on June 4 in the middle of his quest for the Democratic party's presidential nomination. These actions stunned the nation and congressmen who had opposed fire-arms legislation, such as Magnuson and Senate Majority Leader Mike Mansfield, Democrat of Montana, were converted. The Johnson administra-tion sponsored a bill which would require registration, licensing, and strict controls, pledging "a total effort." [59] As a result, on October 22 President Johnson signed into law the most comprehensive firearms act in United States history, the Gun Control Act of 1968. [60]

Again the NRA managed to have registration and licensing struck from the bill. The new law, however, imposed strict controls on interstate move-ment of firearms and ammunition by banning such sales by mail except for manufacturers, dealers, importers, and collectors licensed by the national government. Out-of-state persons could buy a rifle or shotgun, but not hand-guns, in other states if it were legal in both states; but a seven-day waiting period for delivery was required to provide time for a police check. The same cooling-off period was applied to in-state mail orders. Sales of guns and ammunition were prohibited to mental incompetents, drug addicts, felons, and fugitives from justice or people under indictment. Eighteen-year-olds could buy rifles and shotguns but the minimum age of twenty-one was established for purchase of other guns. Dealers were required to keep records of sales, including name, age, and residence of customers. These restrictions became effective on December 16, 1968. An immediate ban was placed upon importation of military weapons.

These provisions replaced the Federal Firearms Act of 1938. In addi-tion, the 1968 law amended the National Firearms Act of 1934 by extending the regulatory taxes to destructive devices such as bombs, grenades, anti-tank guns, and bazookas. After thousands of deaths by means of guns the Congress finally overrode the gun lobby and enacted legislation similar, although not as restrictive, to that imposed by most civilized nations several decades earlier. [61] The desire of a great majority of citizens was at least

[59] "A Question of Guns," pp. 84–85.

[60] Public Law 90–618.

[61] Robert Sherrill, "The Saturday Night Special and Other Hardware," *New York Times Magazine*, October 10, 1971, points out a major loophole in the 1968 law which banned importation of gun frames but not other parts. A thriving business soon de-

partially met through the use of the taxing and commerce powers and brought some semblence of control over these deadly devices. These efforts, however, were blocked for a half-century by a powerful lobby that was uncertain if it were really representing the wishes of a majority of its members.[62] When Congress used the taxing power in recent United States history two other times for social purposes, to control gambling and drug abuse, there was no such powerful lobby to oppose it.

---

veloped of importing parts costing one dollar and producing so-called Saturday Night Specials selling for about fifteen dollars.

[62] In 1967 Dodd asked NRA President Harold Glassen if his organization had ever considered polling its members on the question of gun controls. This was after several congressmen had received letters from NRA members complaining they had never been asked. Glassen replied, "We never felt the need for it." *Dodd Hearings*, 1967, p. 516.

12 *The Continuing Problem of Drugs*

The period from World War I to the Nixon administration brought many additions to the United States program for drug control. Much of this resulted from internal developments, including an alarming increase in the use of narcotics; part of it stemmed from the continuing international crusade to control the traffic in narcotics.

With many nations involved in the First World War, the world crusade against opium, and attempts to prevent smuggling, halted until hostilities ceased. Then the Treaty of Versailles placed continuation of the work of The Hague Convention in the League of Nations. But the United States refused to become a member of this world organization and participated in League activities only in an unofficial capacity. As a result, the United States relinquished its leadership of the narcotics reform movement.

By the end of World War I, the United States, because of weaknesses in its narcotics control legislation, was an unwilling accessory to the revival of the world opium trade. As John Dewey wrote in 1919, the holier-than-thou attitude of the United States had to be abandoned because of complicity in this traffic.[1] The new trade involved the transshipment of narcotics from Great Britain to Japan, or from the United States to Japan; the drugs were then sent into Japan's leased territory of Manchuria or smuggled directly into China proper.[2] One Chinese authority estimated that the amount of morphine smuggled into China increased from five and a half tons in 1911 to twenty-eight tons in 1919.[3] Much of this was imported into the United States from Turkey or Persia, two nations that never ratified The Hague Convention, processed into morphine and then legally shipped to Japan.[4] Despite Japan's strict domestic regulations over opium and the 1909 law requiring United States exports to conform to regulations of the country the drug was exported to, Japan had no regulations on drugs trans-shipped to that country and thence to another. Japanese prohibitory laws applied only to imports to be consumed domestically. Thus the loophole in the 1909 American law permitted this traffic.

The British attempted to control this new development by enacting the Dangerous Drug Act in 1920, which placed strict regulations upon the exportation of drugs through a license system. The United States soon responded with a similar law which tightened the restrictions in the 1909 act. A bill was introduced in Congress in December 1920 and extensive hearings were held, including testimony and the favorable reaction from members representing the departments of State, Treasury, and Commerce.[5] H.R. 2193 was then reported to the House in March 1922, passed without a roll call vote, and sent to the Senate. The upper house agreed to the bill a few days later with no debate or roll call vote.[6] This act established a Federal Narcotics Control Board composed of the secretaries of State, Treasury, and Commerce. The board was empowered to determine the legitimate drug needs of the United States for medicinal and scientific purposes and also to investigate the regulatory laws of other nations. The board could regulate the shipment and consumption of drugs anywhere in the United States and could strictly control exportation of drugs to countries that ratified The Hague Convention, thus limiting the traffic to legitimate trade.[7]

With the creation of this control board in 1922 the regulatory system of the United States was basically complete. There remained only the problems of eliminating weaknesses when discovered and extending regulations to new drugs as they were developed. Thus in 1924 the 1909 prohibitory law was extended to exclude the importation of opium for the purpose of manufacturing heroin.[8] The Federal Narcotics Control Board was replaced in 1930 by a new agency, the Bureau of Narcotics in the Department of Trea-

[1] "Our Share in Drugging China," *New Republic* 21 (December 24, 1919) : 116.

[2] Ibid.; see also "Poisoning the Chinese," *Literary Digest* 68 (February 26, 1921) : 30.

[3] Taraknath Das, "The Menace of Opium," *Nation* 116 (June 20, 1923) : 729.

[4] John Campbell, "India and the American Opium Supply," *Living Age* 320 (February 23, 1924) : 362–63; Ellen M. LaMotte, "America and the Opium Trade," *Atlantic* 129 (June 1922) : 735–36.

[5] U.S., Congress, House, Report 852 (Serial 7956), 67 Cong., 2 Sess., 1921, pp. 1–20.

[6] *Congressional Record*, 67 Cong., 2 Sess., 1922, 67:4669, 6341, 6835.

[7] U.S., *Statutes at Large*, vol. 42.

[8] Ibid., vol. 43.

sury, in order to facilitate control and administration of the narcotics laws.[9] The interstate commerce power was used in 1939 to exert greater control over the transportation of narcotics. A law enacted that year forbade the hauling of any contraband article in the United States (narcotic drugs, firearms, and counterfeit coins) in any "vessel, vehicle or aircraft."[10] This act was amended in 1950 to permit the carrying of drugs if the person had paid the required taxes or was an employee of one who had fulfilled the revenue requirements on narcotic drugs.[11]

A major extension was made in 1937 to control the increased use of another drug, marijuana. Prior to the 1930s there was little traffic in "grass" or "pot," as it is also known, outside the southwestern part of the United States. Then during the Great Depression, there was a widespread growth and use of the drug. Marijuana, which is produced from the flowering tops, leaves, and seeds of the hemp plant and usually smoked in the form of a cigarette, could be grown almost anywhere in the United States. Congressmen, in debating a proposal to control the drug, called attention to the widespread marijuana addiction among criminals. But of greater concern was the increased traffic in the form of sales of marijuana cigarettes to the youth, "especially those of highschool age."[12] Because the Supreme Court had sustained the Harrison Act, the House Committee on Ways and Means introduced a bill to apply the principles of this law to marijuana. The committee report noted that during 1935, "195 tons of marijuana destined for illicit use" were seized and destroyed by state officials. The committee had considered the constitutionality of the proposal. They found that "the law is well settled" that a regulatory tax, although controlling a subject reserved to state jurisdiction, would be valid "if it appears on its face to be a revenue measure."[13]

No congressman opposed this bill; the only question presented during the debates was to ascertain that the regulations would not interfere with the legitimate hemp industry in Kentucky. The proposal quickly passed both houses of Congress without a roll call vote on June 14 and July 22, 1937, respectively.[14] The Marijuana Tax Act of 1937 required registration

[9] Ibid., vol. 46.
[10] Ibid., vol. 53.   [11] Ibid., vol. 64.
[12] *Congressional Record*, 75 Cong., 1 Sess., 1937, 81:5689–90.
[13] U.S., Congress, House, Report 792 (Serial 10084), 75 Cong., 1 Sess., 1937, pp. 2–3. Michael Schaller, "The Federal Prohibition of Marijuana," *Journal of Social History* 4 (Fall 1970):61–74, is an interesting account of the enactment of this law.
[14] *Congressional Record*, 75 Cong., 1 Sess., 1937, 81:5692, 7398.

with the Bureau of Internal Revenue of any person who handled the drug at any stage. Importers and manufacturers had to pay twenty-four dollars per year; producers, researchers, and physicians had to purchase a one-dollar annual license. All registered people had to keep records of sales or transfers. Any exchange of marijuana by such people was taxed at the rate of one dollar per ounce. Any transfer of marijuana by nonregistered persons was subject to a levy of $100 per ounce.[15]

Two years later, the Food, Drug, and Cosmetic Act empowered the secretary of the treasury, after public hearings, to add new drugs to the list of illicit or habit-forming drugs as they were developed.[16] Finally, Congress enacted the Opium Poppy Control Act of 1942 to regulate further the domestic production of opium. This law forbade production of the opium poppy without a special license which could be obtained annually from the secretary of the treasury. The secretary was authorized to license only that production which was necessary "to supply the medicinal and scientific needs of the United States for opium or opium products." There would be a presumption of guilt if any person were found in possession of opium poppy without the required license.[17] With these laws, American control of narcotics served as a model for other nations to emulate in efforts between the world wars to control illicit traffic in drugs.

Unfortunately, this legislation did not end the drug problem in the United States. Violations of the laws continued, especially smuggling, as did the world problem of controlling illicit drug traffic. A meeting was called by the United Nations in 1953, and again in 1961, in fruitless attempts to achieve complete world agreement on drug control and to consolidate all existing agreements. During the Cold War, however, in an ironic twist of history, the People's Republic of China became the chief villain in supplying narcotics to the illicit traffic. For decades, civilized nations endeavored to help China eliminate its opium problem; in the post-World War II crisis China supplied opium to its former benefactors. The United States was one of the chief targets in this drive.

[15] U. S., *Statutes at Large*, vol. 50. In 1950, in *United States* v. *Sanchez* (340 U.S. 42), the Supreme Court upheld the tax because, although it "closely" resembled a penalty, it was fundamentally a revenue measure. There is an excellent annotation of the scope of the taxing power following this case in 95 L. E. 50–52. Appellant had appealed on the grounds the tax was actually a penalty. See *Transcripts of Records and File Copies of Briefs*, Case #81, 1950 Term, vol. 44, U.S. Supreme Court Library.

[16] U.S., *Statutes at Large*, vol. 52.

[17] Ibid., vol. 56.

The problem of illicit use of drugs in the United States increased alarmingly after 1945. Drug smuggling had almost ceased during the war and then accelerated significantly immediately after hostilities ceased. The Mafia, with its international organization, assumed a dominant position in this trade. Charles "Lucky" Luciano, deported from the United States for criminal activities, gained control of the Italian operations and became the link in the traffic from the Middle East. The Senate Subcommittee on Investigations, chaired by Arkansas Democrat John McClellan, received wide publicity in 1964 and 1965 through the investigation of organized crime in the United States.[18] These hearings revealed, among other underworld business engagements, the extensive drug activities of the Cosa Nostra, the United States branch of the Mafia, with Luciano controlling the Italian end of the trade and Vito Genovese dominating the United States outlets for narcotics.[19]

American public attention, however, was first called to an increase in the drug problem in a dramatic way when Senator Estes Kefauver, Democrat of Tennessee, conducted his headline-drawing investigation of organized crime in the United States during the Truman administration. As a result of this publicity, Louisiana Democrat Hale Boggs introduced a bill in June 1951 from his Committee on Ways and Means to increase penalties for violations of narcotics laws. The House, by two-thirds vote, suspended its rules and passed the measure. The Senate, also with little debate and no roll call vote, accepted the proposal and President Truman signed it in November 1951. As Kefauver noted, the "Boggs Law" carried out a major recommendation of his investigating committee.[20] The law increased the penalties for handling illegal narcotics by requiring a mandatory prison sentence of two to five years for the first offense, five to ten years for the second offense, and ten to twenty years for offenses thereafter.[21]

With the rapid rise in influence of Wisconsin Republican Senator Joseph McCarthy and the Second Big Red Scare, congressmen discovered an additional culprit in the narcotics traffic. A Senate committee conducted a major investigation of the illicit drug traffic in 1955, taking testimony for

[18] The development of organized crime is traced in Chapter 13.

[19] U.S., Congress, Senate, Report 72 (Serial 12664), 89 Cong., 1 Sess., 1965, pp. 118–19. Genovese died in 1969 at the federal prison in Springfield, Mo., while serving a narcotics conviction sentence.

[20] *Congressional Record*, 82 Cong., 1 Sess., 1951, 97:8211, 13676.

[21] U.S., *Statutes at Large*, vol. 65.

thirty-seven days in major cities of the United States, and submitted an 8,667-page report of findings. This committee discovered that, at the time, there were 60,000 drug addicts in the United States, or more than in any other country in the Western world, both in numbers and percentages. The committee was especially concerned with the statistic that 13 percent of these addicts were under twenty-one years of age. This number of addicts represented a significant increase; at the end of World War II there was a ratio of one addict per 10,000 population while the new figure represented a ratio of one to 3,000. This increase in addiction, the report said, resulted in an average of 2,000 arrests per month for narcotics violations. The committee also concluded that drug addiction was responsible for 25 percent of the crimes committed in the United States and for 50 percent of all crimes committed in metropolitan areas.

Not only was there an increase in drug traffic from Italy at this time, the committee believed, but more important, the People's Republic of China had launched a major program of a "vicious illicit traffic" to drug the non-Communist world, with the United States as one of its "principal targets." There was a twofold purpose in this campaign of the Peking regime: "(1) to obtain dollars to purchase strategic materials and to pay foreign operatives and (2) to demoralize susceptible individuals in our military services and in the general population." The report further pointed out the lucrative aspects of this trade with the statistics that an amount of heroin worth $3,000 abroad, sold in the United States for $300,000 when processed.[22]

Armed with the additional motive of national security Congressman Boggs then sought further restrictions on narcotics violators. His Committee on Ways and Means recommended H.R. 11619, which would increase again the penalties for violating the drug laws. "Experience with the Boggs Law," the committee report declared, "has clearly demonstrated the efficacy of severe punishment in reducing the illicit commerce in drugs." With the increased traffic in narcotics from Italy and a "deluge of heroin from Red China," the report continued, the problem by 1950 had "approached grave proportions," but the Boggs Law had brought a decrease in the traffic.[23]

The Senate Judiciary Committee also considered the problem of addict treatment. The national government had established special hospitals in

[22] U.S., Congress, Senate, Report 1440 (Serial 11886), 84 Cong., 2 Sess., 1956, pp. 1–5.
[23] U.S., Congress, House, Report 2388 (Serial 11899), 84 Cong., 2 Sess., 1956, pp. 12, 58.

Lexington, Kentucky, and Fort Worth, Texas, in 1929 to treat drug addicts. The Senate committee decided this program was insufficient in scope because one of every three addicts treated in these hospitals returned to their addiction. Forty percent returned to the national hospitals for repeated treatment. Particularly disturbing to the committee was the statistic that 75 percent who volunteered for this treatment (it was entirely voluntary) demanded to leave before being cured and in some cases a few individuals returned to the hospitals as many as thirty times. The committee, therefore, recommended giving district courts the authority to commit addicts for mandatory periods of time for treatment and after three unsuccessful cures commit the addict to some type of farm.[24] Congress, however, did not approve this drastic step for another decade.

Instead, the House of Representatives passed without a recorded vote the bill being promoted by Hale Boggs. The Senate amended the measure to increase even more the penalties and approved it without a roll call vote. President Dwight D. Eisenhower signed it into law on July 18, 1956.[25] This law raised the mandatory penalities for drug offenses to five to ten years for the first offense, ten to thirty years for the second offense, and life imprisonment for the third offense. The Narcotic Control Act of 1956 also required life imprisonment for any conviction for sale of heroin to anyone under eighteen years of age "except that the offender shall suffer death if the jury in its discretion shall so direct."[26]

Four years later Congress enacted a law to carry out United States treaty obligations. By a protocol agreement in 1946, the United Nations agreed to continue the work of the League of Nations on narcotics. A 1948 protocol expanded the scope of these efforts to include new drugs not covered by the League of Nations in the 1930s. The United States entered into these agreements which required legislation for implementation.[27] On September 9, 1959, the House of Representatives approved the Narcotics Manufacturing Act of 1960 without a roll call vote and the Senate passed the measure the following March 28, without a recorded vote. President Eisenhower affixed his signature to the proposal on May 2, 1960.[28] This law implemented

[24] U.S., Congress, Senate, Report 1850 (Serial 11887), 84 Cong., 2 Sess., 1956, pp. 14–21.

[25] *Congressional Record*, 84 Cong., 2 Sess., 1956, 102:10686, 10809, 13527.

[26] U.S., *Statutes at Large*, vol. 70.

[27] See U.S., Congress, House, Report 1053 (Serial 12163), 86 Cong., 1 Sess., 1949.

[28] *Congressional Record*, 86 Cong., 1 Sess., 1959, 105:18819; 86 Cong., 2 Sess., 1960, 106:6611, 9078.

previous statutes by adding all new drugs to the list of those controlled for export and import purposes. It also established a license system for manufacturing drugs and provided for a quota for production, to be administered by the secretary of health, education, and welfare. Production of drugs in the United States was to be limited to the domestic "medical and scientific needs" and to "lawful export requirements" and stockpiling needs. All manufacturers licensed to produce drugs would receive an annual quota determined by the Department of Health, Education, and Welfare.[29]

The continuing illicit traffic in drugs in the United States prompted President John F. Kennedy to call a White House Conference on Narcotics in 1962.[30] By the 1960s there were two phases to the problem. First of all, a congressional committee report noted that the severe penalties enacted in 1951 and 1956 were not curtailing the illicit use of drugs as Congressman Boggs had promised. Although the 1956 act was "one of the harshest penal laws ever placed in our statute books," the Senate Judiciary Committee reported in 1964, "statistics and other data suggest that it has failed in its deterrent purpose and has been most costly to the Government." In 1956, there were 1,189 convictions for narcotics violations; by 1962 the number had dropped only to 1,071. More important, the percentage of narcotics violators, of the total population in national prisons, had increased significantly. In 1950, the 2,017 prisoners convicted of drug violations represented 11.2 percent of the total prison population. After the first Boggs Law was enacted, this percentage increased to 15.1 percent in 1956; by 1962, under the second Boggs Law, the percentage was up to 17.7. The 4,368 prisoners convicted in 1962, the committee reported, cost the national government $8,824,000 annually to maintain in prison.[31] Congressmen were beginning to conclude that more severe punishment was not the answer to drug-abuse controls.

[29] U.S., *Statutes at Large*, vol. 74.

[30] For a brief account of this and other postwar developments in narcotics, see Arnold, "The United States and the International Movement," postscript. The entire issue of *Law and Contemporary Problems* 22 (Winter 1957) is devoted to this problem, both legally and socially.

[31] U.S., Congress, Senate, Report 1519 (Serial 12618), 88 Cong., 2 Sess., 1964, pp. 4–5. "Seizure of illegal narcotics and Marihuana," said President Lyndon Johnson in 1965, "rose 62 percent from 1962 to 1965." *Public Papers of the Presidents of the United States, 1965* (Washington, D.C., 1966), 1:296. These papers of presidents from Truman through Johnson will be cited hereafter as *Public Papers* with appropriate year.

In the mid-1960s the widespread use of barbiturates (depressants) and amphetamines (stimulants) was reaching incredible proportions. By 1965 over 9 billion of these tablets were being produced annually and 50 percent of these were distributed through illicit channels.[32] In addition, the practice of taking hallucinogenic, or psychedelic, drugs was beginning to receive national publicity in a sensational form.

Some of these drugs, like marijuana, are not addictive but are considered by many persons to be a danger to the user and, subsequently, to society. There are numerous such drugs, some of which have been known and consumed by men for centuries. These include psilocybin, extracted from a certain Mexican mushroom, hashish and marijuana from hemp, and mescaline or peyote from cactus. Peyote is legally used by the Native American Church (predominantly American Indian) in religious ceremonies.[33] But the psychedelic drug that received prominent publicity at this time was lysergic acid diethylamide (LSD), derived from rye-rot.

LSD was discovered in 1938 by a chemist in the Sandoz laboratories in Switzerland. Produced in the United States solely by Sandoz Pharmaceuticals of New Jersey, LSD remained in the laboratory for several years as an interesting research tool. Experiments were quietly conducted which seemed to demonstrate that LSD might be helpful in treating psychosis, alcoholism, and sexually frigid women by acting as a release to the mind when used in conjunction with psychiatry.

Then in the 1960s Timothy Leary, a professor of psychology at Harvard University, began experimenting with LSD. His use of students in his research led to his being fired from Harvard in 1963.[34] He subsequently received widespread publicity through his efforts to have legalized the use of LSD as a part of the religious ceremony in his cult which, he argued, should be protected by the First Amendment.[35] With this campaign, "al-

[32] U.S., Congress, House, Report 130 (Serial 12665–1), 89 Cong., 1 Sess., 1965, p. 1.

[33] In 1959 in *Native American Church* v. *Navajo Tribal Council*, the Tenth Circuit Court of Appeals (272 Fed [2d] 131) held the Native American Church to be entitled to First Amendment protection thus legalizing its use of peyote. See Peter Nabokov "The Peyote Road," *New York Times Magazine*, March 9, 1969, for a good description of the religious ceremony of this church.

[34] The most thorough, although popularized account of this drug is John Cashman, *The LSD Story* (Greenwich, Conn., 1966). Leary's experience at Harvard is described on page 58.

[35] Edward J. Weintraub, "Constitutional Law: (Freedom of Religion) + (LSD) = (Psychedelic Dilemma)," *Temple Law Quarterly* 41 (Fall 1967) :52–80, is a good account of the current legal status of this issue.

most singlehandedly, Leary transformed LSD from a medical curiosity into the most controversial drug since opium." Early in 1966 Sandoz company stopped producing LSD because of "unforeseen public reaction."[36] Production and consumption of LSD, however, continued at an ever-increasing rate because it is relatively easy to manufacture illegally and because many students on college campuses adopted the drug as part of their movement.

Users take LSD by dropping it in liquid form on a cube of sugar and swallowing it. This is called taking a "trip." A trip was described in a publication by the Medical Society of the County of New York in this way:

After the cubes, containing 100–600 mcg. each, are ingested a startling series of events occurs with marked individual variation. All senses appear sharpened and brightened; vivid panoramic visual hallucinations of fantastic brightness and depth are experienced as well as hyperacusis. Senses blend and become diffused so that sounds are felt, colors tasted; and fixed objects pulsate and breathe. Depersonalization also occurs frequently so that the individual loses ego identity; he feels he is living with his environment in a feeling of unity with other beings, animals, inanimate objects and the universe in general. The body image is often distorted so that faces, including the user's, assume bizarre proportions and the limbs may appear extraordinarily short or elongated. The user is enveloped by a sense of isolation and often is dominated by feelings of paranoia and fear. If large doses are ingested (over 700 mcg.) confusion and delirium frequently ensue. During LSD use, repressed material may be unmasked which is difficult for the individual to handle. Duration of the experience is usually 4 to 12 hours but it may last for days.[37]

The tremendous increase in the illicit use of psychedelic drugs, barbiturates, and amphetamines led President Lyndon B. Johnson to emphasize repeatedly to the Ninetieth Congress the need for additional legislation to regulate these drugs. Because the consumption of these drugs was believed to be related to an increase in crime, Johnson's efforts were closely connected with a national drive to control crime. Early in January 1965 President Johnson asked Congress for legislation "to bring the production and distribution of barbiturates, amphetamines and other psycho-toxic drugs under more effective control." On March 8, 1965, in a special message on law enforcement, Johnson further recommended a law to provide for

[36] Cashman, *The LSD Story*, pp. 10, 52, 115.
[37] Quoted in Report of President's Commission of Law Enforcement and Administration of Justice, "The Challenge of Crime in a Free Society" (Washington, D.C., 1967), p. 215.

"civil commitment" of addicts to a rehabilitation program if they appeared "likely to respond to treatment." [38]

The House Committee on Interstate and Foreign Commerce then recommended passage of H.R. 2 to amend the 1939 Food, Drug, and Cosmetic Act to include control over these drugs. The committee report acknowledged that LSD was legitimately "used as an adjunct to psychotherapy and as a research tool in psychiatry." But its use "by amateurs and drug abusers can cause some terrifying experiences for the victims," particularly when a psychiatric problem is already present and thus "can precipitate the acting out of an antisocial behavior problem." Drug abuse was considered by the committee to be the taking of drugs in such amounts as to create a health hazard to the user or safety to the community, or if obtained through illicit channels, or if taken through personal initiative rather than by medical prescription. The committee report stated that the Bureau of the Budget strongly endorsed H.R. 2.[39]

The Drug Abuse Control Amendments of 1965 was the only drug bill during this period to receive a recorded congressional vote. The House of Representatives approved the measure with no dissenting votes, and the Senate accepted it without a roll call vote. President Johnson signed it on July 15, 1965.[40] This law authorized the Department of Health, Education, and Welfare to decide if drugs were dangerous and to control their use if so determined. All manufacturers and distributors of barbiturates, amphetamines, or hallucenogenic drugs must keep records of transactions. The secretary of health, education, and welfare could designate current and future drugs as depressant or stimulant drugs and these regulations would automatically apply to them. Possession of such drugs was illegal except for personal medical use by the owner or members of his household or pets. The law further enlarged enforcement powers by authorizing drug officials to carry firearms and "make arrests without warrant in certain cases."[41]

The next year Congress complied with President Johnson's request for a compulsory rehabilitation program. Following the testimony gathered by the McClellan committee on crime and narcotics, the Senate Judiciary Committee suggested commitment of addicts for a minimal period of one year.[42]

[38] Lyndon B. Johnson, Special Message to Congress, January 7, 1965, *Public Papers, 1965,* 1:20–21, 226.

[39] U.S., Congress, House, Report 130 (Serial 12665–1), 89 Cong., 1 Sess., 1965, pp. 6–7, 26.

[40] *Congressional Record,* 89 Cong., 1 Sess., 1965, 111:2701, 14611, 17917.

[41] U.S., *Statutes at Large,* vol. 79.

In 1966 this committee recommended passage of S. 2191.[43] Congress enacted the measure which established a program permitting commitment of addicts to medical treatment if they habitually used narcotics "so as to endanger the public morals, health, safety, or welfare."[44]

Although early in 1968 it was reported that use of LSD was "waning among college students and hippies," the use of marijuana was rising, as was amphetamines. College students at this time reported LSD was "too dangerous."[45] LSD was also creating a problem for Congress in terms of proposals to control it. In March 1968 a House committee considered making mere possession of LSD an offense, which was desired by the Bureau of Drug Abuse Control. The Department of Health, Education, and Welfare, however, argued that harsher measures such as this would only "crowd jails with students and other young people experimenting with LSD on a one-time 'kicks' basis." Health, Education, and Welfare preferred to continue its attempts, through educational means, to deter such experiments and thus curtail the spreading use of LSD.[46]

By 1970 the increased use of marijuana had reached alarming proportions. During the decade of the 1960s, smoking marijuana was confined primarily to "hippies" and to newcomers to the "drug culture." At the end of that decade, however, many middle-class Americans had tried it and the habit was spreading rapidly downward from college students to the secondary level and even to elementary students. As a result, the National Institute of Mental Health estimated in October 1969 that five million juveniles and adults had tried marijuana at least once. In June 1970 the director of the Institute quadrupled this figure to twenty million.[47] As increasing millions of "respectable" Americans experimented with pot, there was a proportionate increase in public pressure for the legalization of marijuana.[48]

---

[42] U.S., Congress, Senate, Report 72 (Serial 12664), 89 Cong., 1 Sess., 1965, p. 126.

[43] U.S., Congress, Senate, Report 1667 (Serial 12710–15), 89 Cong., 2 Sess., 1966, p. 11.

[44] U.S., *Statutes at Large*, vol. 80.

[45] *New York Times*, March 3, 1968.

[46] *Newsweek* 71 (March 11, 1968) :85–86. Gertrude Samuels, "Pot, Hard Drugs and the Law," *New York Times Magazine*, February 15, 1970, is a good description of the views of Stanley Yolles, director of the National Institute of Mental Health, who opposed punitive legislation for drug control.

[47] For a story on the rising respectability of marijuana, see Sam Blum, "Marijuana Clouds the Generation Gap," *New York Times Magazine*, August 23, 1970.

[48] This development has stimulated, among other things, further experiments to determine the effects of marijuana on the user. See "Marijuana: Is It Time for a

The return of veterans from the Vietnam conflict undoubtedly contributed to the widespread use of pot in the United States. It was estimated in 1971 that over 60 percent of American servicemen in Vietnam smoked marijuana. Obviously, many continued the habit upon their return home.[49] The widespread violation of drug laws calls to mind a parallel development of the "Roaring Twenties" during the era of Prohibition when the idea grew that the best way to get rid of an unpopular sumptuary law was to violate it on a large scale.

The regulations to control illicit drug traffic marked a major step in the development of a national police power. They were rooted in the concept of a light tax (except marijuana) to require registration and, subsequently, control. When compared to the previous regulatory or prohibitory taxes on such products as oleomargarine, mixed flour, and matches, the moral aspects of this crusade become obvious. Although the earlier tax bills either failed to pass Congress or were enacted by a divided vote, none of the drug laws except one were submitted to a roll call vote and this one did not receive a dissenting vote. Public opinion and congressional approval was apparently so overwhelming that few congressmen allowed their constitutional scruples against extension of a national police power to intrude in the debates on these measures. The morality of suppressing the narcotics vice apparently was not debatable—the course of congressional action was clear.

Drug addiction itself has never been considered a national crime. One state's attempt to make it so was struck down by the Supreme Court as con-

---

Change in Our Laws?" *Newsweek* 76 (September 17, 1970) :20. In 1970 Congress made possession of marijuana a misdeameanor rather than a felony; U.S., *Statutes at Large*, vol. 84. For a description of efforts to "decriminalize" marijuana on all levels of government, see Patrick Anderson, "The Pot Lobby," *New York Times Magazine*, January 21, 1973.

[49] *Newsweek* 77 (January 11, 1971) :34. In 1971 the Nixon administration declared war on drugs. Returning veterans who were heroin addicts received methadone treatments. Attempts were also made to dry up the source of heroin from France and opium from Turkey. But as this source was cut off, the United States was increasingly supplied from Southeast Asia; one-half the world's supply of 1,500 annual tons of opium are grown in the Golden Cresent. See review of Alfred W. McCoy, *The Politics of Heroin in Southeast Asia* (New York, 1972), in *New York Times Book Review*, September 3, 1972. In September 1972 President Nixon called home United States narcotics control agents in American embassies for a three-day conference on the drug problem. He asked them to warn the countries to whom they were certified that he would comply with United States law and cut off foreign aid to nations that illicitly supplied the United States with addictive drugs. See *New York Times*, September 19, 1972.

stituting a "cruel and unusual punishment" which violated the Fourteenth Amendment due-process clause.[50] American policy of drug control, though, has resulted in treating addicts as criminals, rather than as sick people, and almost guaranteed a flourishing illicit traffic. As long as the demand for drugs remains great and profits in illicit drugs are enormous, the United States policy of narcotics control demonstrates vividly that smuggling and illicit manufacturing of drugs will continue. Without complete international cooperation the sources of supply cannot be dried up. But the enforcement of drug laws has fallen most heavily on the user or consumer. This, unfortunately, is natural because the addict is constantly exposed to surveillance and, because of his weakness, is a potential informant. The United States, therefore, has done little to cure the sickness for these people. Perhaps the narcotics policy of England, which is typical of that followed by many Western European countries, is a wiser one. Beginning in 1920 Great Britain allowed addicts to have legal, but closely regulated, access to low-cost drugs. As a result, in 1955 there were a reported 335 drug addicts in the United Kingdom compared to an estimated 60,000 in the United States.[51]

While Congress was wrestling with the great drug problem of the post-World War II period, it was also attempting to control another major social concern, illegal gambling. Because illicit drugs and illegal gambling are both dominated by organized crime, the two issues are closely related. Congress determined that regulatory taxes on drugs was the best approach to that social question and, similarly, Congress decided during the Truman administration that a regulatory tax would provide the best means of controlling gambling. Taxing illegal gambling was the last use Congress made of the taxing power to create a police power and, significantly, it was a Supreme Court decision on this tax that further called into question the entire policy of creating a national police power through regulatory taxation.

[50] *Robinson* v. *California*, 370 U.S. 660 (1962).

[51] Alfred R. Lindesmith, "The British System of Narcotics Control," *Law and Contemporary Problems* 22 (Winter 1957) :1938. Alfred R. Lindesmith, *The Addict and the Law* (New York, 1967), is an excellent sociological study of how United States narcotic laws affect the addict and society. Rollo May, in his review of Timothy Leary's *High Priest* and *The Politics of Ecstacy* in *New York Times Book Review*, January 26, 1969, states that "the blind opposition to drugs in Washington serves only to drive control of them into the hands of the Mafia," p. 28.

13 *Attempts to Curtail Gambling*

Gambling is probably as old as civilized man. Taking financial risks seems to be an inherent part of man's nature and is found in various economic and political systems. This activity was considered by Communist doctrine to be "the root and branch of capitalist instability and injustice" and was abolished in their communal societies "in which the only permissible source of income is work." Soon, however, all East European Communist countries introduced state-operated gambling and it became so popular that some of the regimes are wondering how to curtail this "craze" which "distracts the masses" from their "socially useful" occupations.[1] Gambling appears equally popular in capitalistic countries, and in the United States it is one of the principal activities of organized crime.

Following the assassinations and gangland warfare of the 1920s, the nation's leading criminals met in Atlantic City in May 1929 and agreed to organize on a national basis by dividing up territory and establishing a group of directors to govern the various syndicates. This organization was still in existence over three decades later. With repeal of Prohibition, the criminal syndicates moved into other endeavors during the depression, particularly the illegal activities of gambling, narcotics, extortion, loan sharking, and labor racketeering. Soon gambling became "the core activity" that provided organized crime with money to finance other illicit operations.[2]

The lack of information was one of the fundamental shortcomings in efforts to control criminal syndicates. "Criminologists have long been at fault," one source has declared, "in regard to empirical and theoretical investigations into the workings of organized crime."[3] As a result, authorities were forced to rely chiefly upon journalists until 1951. After World War II, newspapers and magazines increasingly published articles describing criminal activities, stressing the marked rise in the crime rate. In May 1950 the Senate adopted a resolution, "based largely on averments contained in various newspaper articles, editorials, magazine articles, and materials from crime commissions," to conduct a national investigation.[4] This resulted in a series of hearings and reports, which received widespread publicity, by the Special Committee to Investigate Organized Crime in Interstate Commerce, better known as the Kefauver Committee. Because of the enormity of its task the committee's life was extended twice and from May 1950 to September 1951 testimony was taken from more than eight hundred witnesses, both law enforcement officials and gangsters, some of which was televised. The nation acquired its first actual knowledge of the scope of criminal activities from these hearings.

The Kefauver Committee found that simultaneously with the adoption of the Twenty-first Amendment a turning point came in the depression and money became "more plentiful." The depression psychosis engendered an increase in gambling–the desire to risk a little and perhaps receive a lot– and organized crime was quick to exploit this penchant. The committee believed that "a continuity of identity" existed in the following three decades, both in terms of gangs and individuals within the organizations. Individual members were attracted to gangs because of certain advantages. When in trouble with police, the group helped the culprit with bondsmen, expensive and able counsel, and, if necessary, bribery and intimidation of witnesses. In return, the individual took orders and adhered to the strict code of silence in regard to syndicate activities.

There was "no doubt," the Kefauver Committee declared, that two major syndicates controlled all organized crime in the United States. One had an axis between Miami and the Capone gang of Chicago, which in 1950 was led by Tony Accardo, the Fischetti brothers, and Jake Guzik. The other had an axis between Miami and New York City, headed by Frank Costello and Joe Adonis. In case of frictions or disputes between the two elements, Charles "Lucky" Luciano served as arbiter. Although Luciano had been

---

[1] Free Europe Committee, "The Jackpot: Gambling in the Soviet Bloc," in *Gambling*, ed. Robert D. Herman (New York, 1967), pp. 69–76.

[2] Herbert A. Block and Gilbert Geis, *Man, Crime and Society* (New York, 1962), pp. 225–28; President's Commission, "The Challenge of Crime in a Free Society," p. 188. Donald R. Cressey, *Theft of the Nation* (New York, 1969), pp. 37–47, says a treaty signed in 1931 ended the warfare.

[3] Block and Geis, *Man, Crime and Society*, pp. 216–17.

[4] U.S., Congress, Senate, Report 1317 (Serial 11367), 81 Cong., 2 Sess., 1950, p. 2.

deported to Italy, the committee noted, he still maintained "associations
with both groups through his former racketeer affiliates." The committee
found that all leading criminals made business arrangements with each
other, got together in resort areas such as Miami and Hot Springs, and occasionally performed "each other's dirty work when a competitor must be
eliminated, an informer silenced, or a victim persuaded." Having an out-
sider render these services made detection more difficult.[5]

Authorities have long speculated over the existence of a Mafia in the
United States.[6] It was not until the McClellan Committee heard testimony
from Joseph Valachi in 1964 and 1965, however, that substantial proof was
obtained of the existence of such a group known as the Cosa Nostra.[7] Then
in 1967, the President's Commission on Law Enforcement and Administration of Justice described the structure of the American Mafia, the Cosa
Nostra. This commission believed it was composed of twenty-four groups,
combining about 5,000 people into a loose confederation. Coordinating the
operation was a "commission" of the leaders of nine to twelve of the groups
which "serves as a legislature, supreme court, board of directors, and arbi-
tration board; its principal functions are judicial." Five of these people
came from New York City and thus dominated national organized crime.
Philadelphia, Buffalo, Detroit, and Chicago had one member each.[8]

One of the features of this development causing alarm among government authorities was the increasing infiltration of organized crime into legitimate business. Kefauver found that after World War II criminals were
particularly attracted to businesses which handled large sums of money or
which had black market potential. These included hotels, restaurants, night
clubs, meat and provision companies, liquor stores, beer and whiskey distributorships, automobile dealerships and distributorships, small steel companies, and even some banks.[9] Owning these businesses also permitted

[5] U.S., Congress, Senate, Report 141 (Serial 11491), 82 Cong., 1 Sess., 1951, pp.
2–10. By the mid-1950s, Vito Genovese had wrested control of the New York syndicate
from Costello.

[6] This issue is discussed and authorities cited in Block and Geis, *Man, Crime and
Society*, pp. 247–48.

[7] For a good sociological discussion of this organization, see Robert T. Anderson,
"From Mafia to Cosa Nostra," *American Journal of Sociology* 71 (1965) :302–10.

[8] Report of President's Commission on Law Enforcement and Administration of
Justice, "The Challenge of Crime in a Free Society" (Washington, D.C., 1967), pp.
192–96. Cressey, *Theft of the Nation*, p. 111, states there are eight "commissioners."

[9] U.S., Congress, Senate, *Interim Report from Kefauver Committee*, Senate Report
2370 (Serial 11371), 81 Cong., 2 Sess., 1950, p. 16.

criminals to have a source of legal funds on which to pay taxes and thus evade income tax prosecution for failing to report their illicit income. Unfortunately, this harmed legitimate businessmen because the same methods of force and violence were used by the criminal in both his illegal and legal activities and the ordinary businessman was unable to compete.[10] But the "most shocking revelation" to the Kefauver Committee was the testimony describing "official corruption and connivance" between organized crime and public officials. This reached all levels—from national agents who did not enforce the income tax laws to state and local officials who accepted bribes and political contributions and succumbed to political pressure, with some even participating "directly in the business of organized crime."[11]

As its final report indicated, the Kefeauver Committee had "served as a powerful spotlight" in exposing the national scope of organized crime. The committee had experimented with the relatively new medium of television and some of the hearings were brought into the homes of millions of citizens. The public reaction was immediately apparent. Previous reform efforts had required organization, collection and dissemination of information, and an indefinite period of public gestation before sufficient pressure could be brought on officials to take action. The impact of the revelations of the Kefauver Committee, by contrast, was revolutionary. An aroused citizenry immediately demanded that criminal activities be curbed. Because the Kefauver Committee found that illegal gambling was the most important criminal activity—which the committee conservatively estimated at $20 billion annually—demand for action focused on this problem.[12] Illicit gambling, the committee discovered, was particularly widespread in horse racing and the numbers game.

Although only Nevada and two counties in Maryland had legalized gambling by 1951, the numbers racket, or "policy," was extremely popular in most large cities, especially in slum areas, because of the small amount wagered and the large return to winners. Policy is played by purchasing a slip with three numbers on it which the buyer hopes will be chosen that day. The numbers are selected in various ways, usually from a large drum containing seventy-six numbered balls. The odds against winning are high, but

[10] President's Commission, "The Challenge of Crime," pp. 189–90. An interesting chart showing organized crime and its legal and illicit operations is presented on page 194.

[11] U.S., Congress, Senate, Report 141 (Serial 11491), 82 Cong., 1 Sess., 1951, p. 26.

[12] Ibid., p. 13.

a lucky ticket, purchased for ten cents will win twenty dollars.[13] At one time in Chicago twenty-six large "policy wheels" were in simultaneous operation taking in $150 million annually. They required a virtual army of 5,000–6,000 workers to operate them.[14]

Illegal gambling on racing had an even more elaborate organization and, because it was a nationwide operation, required the services of interstate communications. "Horse racing," a Senate committee noted, "is an old sport, probably 2,000 years older than the Christian era." It had a modern revival in England under the patronage of the later Tudor and early Stuart monarchs, becoming known as "the sport of kings." It was early introduced into the American colonies and throughout United States history remained a popular sport. By 1920 Kentucky and four other states had regulated horse racing. Then during the depression, with declining state tax income, many states decided to legalize race gambling as a source of revenue. By 1951, twenty-seven states licensed and regulated horse race tracks and taxed legal betting on them.[15]

Betting on races on a large scale was made possible when Pierre Oller of Paris invented the "totalizer" in 1865, a mechanical process for determining odds. In 1927 the dial telephone system was adapted to this principle and in 1933 "the first completely electrical totalizer" was put into operation at Arlington Park, Chicago, for pari-mutuel betting. This process divides the total money wagered on the horses to win, place, and show. After deducting the track costs and the state gambling taxes, the remaining amount determines the odds on the horses. The cost and taxes range from 10 to 20 percent and the remainder is paid back to bettors. If many bettors chose horse A, its odds might be 2 to 1; if few chose horse B, the odds on it winning might be 50 to 1. If horse B won, the total would be divided among the few winners and if A won the same amount would be divided among many. The betting odds on the horses (or dogs) then, is a reflection of the collective bettors' views on the outcome of the race rather than the merits of the animals. If it were ever possible for bettors always to pick the correct win, place, and show horses, this would force the odds down so low and would result in such large numbers of winners that pari-mutuel betting would be

---

[13] There is a good description, complete with jargon, in St. Clair Drake and Horace Clayton, " 'Policy': The Poor Man's Roulette," in *Gambling*, ed. Herman, pp. 3–10.

[14] *Congressional Record*, 82 Cong., 1 Sess., 1951, 97:12230–35.

[15] U.S., Congress, Senate, Report 925 (Serial 11490), 82 Cong., 1 Sess., 1951, p. 10.

uneconomical. It thrives because a large majority of bettors guess wrong.

This form of gambling had become so popular by 1948 that 25 million Americans attended horse races that year and bet over $1.6 billion, with states collecting $96 million in taxes from the twenty-six race tracks in the nation. Horse racing is a respectable business particularly from the standpoint that improvement of the horses is a concern to "the Nation's first citizens of wealth, position and public esteem." The fact that horse racing contained the elements of credulous and naive bettors, high political and social standing of those connected with the business, a great deal of money, and the financial interests of state and local governments, made certain, a Senate committee decided, that legalized horse racing would continue to expand "in the foreseeable future."[16] No attempt was made nationally to curtail this legitimate business, but reformers were determined to curb the illicit betting on races.

All states that legalize horse racing permitted only on-track betting; all states in the Union, except Nevada, forbade off-track betting. The illicit activity had reached the estimated volume of $3 to $5 billion annually in 1948 and it was this category the reformers wished to control. Not only was this gambling illegal but, in addition, the bookmakers were a part of organized crime and those who placed a bet with them had even less chance to break even than in legal gambling. Illegal bookies protected themselves from loss in a number of ways. Invariably they set a limit on their maximum liability payoff to 20 to 1 on winners, 8 to 1 on place horses, and 4 to 1 on show horses. If betting were relatively heavy in any particular race, bookies would also "lay off" part of their bets to other bookies to hedge and spread the chance of loss. If all else failed, a bookie could telephone an agent at the track to place part of the bet on horses in the race in order to run it through the pari-mutuel machine to lower the odds.

Off-track betting depended upon track information for its existence. As organized crime took over this illegal gambling on a nationwide basis, interstate communications became necessary to the operation and wire services soon played a vital role. During the 1930s racing news was disseminated by Nationwide News Service owned by M. L. Annenberg and his partners Arthur McBride of Cleveland and James Ragen of Chicago. The Annenberg family left the business in 1939, but McBride and Ragen continued it under the name Continental Press Service. Then after World War

16 Ibid., pp. 10–13.

II the Capone syndicate decided to take over the operation. Ragen in Chicago refused to abdicate the field, so the Capone mob set up a rival news service, Midwest News, and the Illinois Racing Commission refused to let Continental Press send out racing news until thirty minues after each race. Despite this impossible competition, Ragen remained adamant until he was shot. While recuperating from his wound in the hospital he was mysteriously poisoned. McBride then bought Ragen's share of the business from his widow, proved to be more tractible with the syndicate, and by 1949 Continental Press was again the lone wire service handling racing news.

The Kefauver Committee found in 1951 that Continental Press was "controlled . . . by the gangsters who constitute the Capone syndicate."[17] The company sold its services to twenty-four independent regional distributors who in turn dealt with subdistributors and bookies. The news was carried principally by 23,000 miles of leased Western Union lines and, to a lesser degree, by telephone. In 1949 Continental Press Service had a gross income of $2,366,648 and net profits before taxes of $692,207. The wire service was vital in continuing off-track betting because of the need for prompt track information just prior to the race, which could change the bookies' odds. This information included last-minute scratches of horses for the race, late jockey changes, and the rapidly changing odds as the last-minute bets were placed. The influence of organized crime and the importance of wire services to its gambling activities was indicated when a plane crash disrupted telegraphic services in Bakersfield, California, in 1942. It took fifteen minutes for Continental Press to have its services restored and yet, at a time when a Japanese attack was momentarily expected, it required two or three hours to renew telegraphic communications for the Fourth Army.[18] This use of the means of interstate communications prompted the Kefauver Committee to recommend controls through the exercise of the commerce power.[19]

Although Kefauver and other congressional leaders decided the commerce power would be the best approach to curb gambling, suggestions of using the taxing power also were bruited about. And the national govern-

[17] U.S., Congress, Senate, Report 141 (Serial 11491), 82 Cong., 1 Sess., 1951, p. 17.

[18] U.S., Congress, Senate, Special Committee to Investigate Organized Crime in Interstate Commerce, *Hearings*, Pt. 2, 81 Cong., 2 Sess., 1950, pp. 229–30.

[19] For the development of Continental Press, see Senate Report 141 (Serial 11491), pp. 17–21; Senate Report 925 (Serial 11490), pp. 19–26. See also John Bartlow Martin, "Al Capone's Successors," *American Mercury* 68 (June 1949) : 728–34, who told the story two years before the Kefauver Committee did.

ment had a precedent here. In the Revenue Act of 1941, an annual tax of ten dollars was levied on the operation of pinball machines and fifty dollars per year on slot machines. The following year the slot machine excise was doubled and the Revenue Act of 1950 increased it to $150. In 1948 Congress prohibited gambling ships or any type of gambling in the territorial waters of the United States.[20]

The final report of the Kefauver Committee on organized crime in 1951 strongly recommended controlling gambling through use of the commerce power. The committee had "rejected numerous proposals to impose direct, confiscatory taxes on various types of criminal enterprises," the report stated, because this direct approach was not "a suitable general device" for curbing these activities. In addition, the committee believed there was "force in the argument that recognizing gangsters and hoodlums directly for tax purposes tends to compromise the dignity of the Federal Government." Finally, the committee noted, this type of tax "might be subject to grave questions on constitutional grounds." To substantiate this possibility, *United States* v. *Constantine* was cited which struck down a national license tax imposed on liquor dealers who operated in violation of state law. On the other hand, the committee did believe that use of the taxing power should be made "to require disclosures and information incidental to the imposition and collection of . . . taxes" when used as an adjunct to general taxes, "both to protect the Federal revenues and to expose illegal operations."[21] The committee, then, would support a tax on gambling only if it were indirect such as an income tax on illegal gains, and the reporting of this income would serve the purposes of disclosure. As a result, Congress in 1950 used the power over interstate commerce to control crime.[22]

A gambling tax, however, was imposed late in 1951, despite the efforts of the Senate crime committee, because of the urgent need for additional revenues. With prosecution of the Korean police action requiring additional money, President Truman asked Congress to enact a "Pay as We Go" tax program. This entailed a $10 billion tax increase which, he observed, would also be healthy for the economy as it would help check the wartime inflation.[23] The House Ways and Means Committee began a long series of

[20] U.S., *Statutes at Large*, vols. 55, 56, 62, and 64.

[21] U.S., Congress, Senate, Report 725 (Serial 11491), 82 Cong., 1 Sess., 1951, p. 93.

[22] Slot machines were prohibited in interstate commerce if shipped to states where they were illegal; U.S., *Statues at Large*, vol. 64.

[23] "Special Message to the Congress," February 2, 1951, *Public Papers, 1951*, pp. 134–38.

hearings on proposals to increase income taxes and to levy excises on additional commodities. In May 1951 the committee considered a series of excise taxes proposed by its staff. Taxes on golf and tennis fees, pleasure boats, and china and glassware were rejected. Instead the committee voted to impose a levy on gambling despite the protests of officials from the Bureau of Internal Revenue that such a tax would be extremely difficult to collect.[24]

The committee report on the revenue bill stressed that gambling was "a multi-billion-dollar Nationwide business that has remained relatively free from taxation." Yet, the report noted, this business was "particularly suitable as a subject for taxation." The committee believed continuation of this tax immunity was inconsistent with the current need for additional revenue, particularly when "many consumer items of a seminecessity nature" were going to be taxed even more heavily. The committee admitted that proposed national gambling taxes were criticized because this appeared in effect to sanction an activity that was illegal in most states. But, in response, the committee observed that the national income tax applied uniformly to income whether legal or illegal, and this had "never been generally supposed" to authorize illegal activities. Moreover, the report stated, the excise on coin-operated gambling devices had been levied without regard to the legality of these machines under state or local law. The Ways and Means Committee, therefore, recommended a fifty-dollar annual occupation tax on all persons who were in the business of accepting wagers. This tax would not apply to pari-mutuel gambling licensed by states and lotteries of tax-exempt organizations. This wagering tax, the report estimated, would yield $400 million annually.[25]

Democrat Robert Doughton of North Carolina, chairman of the Ways and Means Committee, had charge of the revenue bill on the House floor. In presenting the measure, Doughton called attention to the numerous new items to be taxed, including gambling. One congressman interrupted with the observation that gambling was illegal; Doughton replied that illegality of activities did not preclude their being taxed. Clare Hoffman, Republican of Michigan, asked if this clause would carry any implication that the occupation stamp would license gambling activities and received the reply that there was no "intention to condone these activities in any sense."[26]

[24] *New York Times*, May 17, 1951; *Washington Post*, May 17, 1951.
[25] U.S., Congress, House, Report 586 (Serial 11497), 82 Cong., 1 Sess., 1951, pp. 55–60.

Opposition to the Revenue Act of 1951 came from leading Republicans. The minority Republicans, led by Daniel Reed of New York, expressed extreme criticism over Truman's request for additional revenues. These congressmen believed that the Democratic administration should attempt first to cut expenditures and, espousing a traditional party principle, that high taxes would not curb inflation. After denouncing the entire tax bill, Reed then called attention to "probably the only constructive new tax contained in this bill." Noting that the American public had been "shocked by the recent congressional revelations of the appalling extent of this multi-billion-dollar business," the Republican leader gave his approval to the gambling tax. He believed it would be "unconscionable" not to tax this activity and while critics said it would be difficult to enforce, Reed thought that failure to try would be "far more difficult to explain . . . to the American people."[27]

Edgar Jonas, Republican of Illinois, however, construed the tax as a license that would lend color to the view that a gambler could violate state laws openly. Republican Congresswoman Katherine St. George of New York described the proposal as "hypocritical and absurd." When Jonas continued to attack the tax as "a sop" to the public desire to "stamp out gambling," Reed defended the tax on the grounds that the registration feature would be "of material assistance" to investigating groups and would help the Bureau of Internal Revenue to make "a more accurate audit of gamblers' income tax returns." Following this exchange no further opposition to the gambling levy was voiced in the House. The bill passed by vote of 233 to 160.[28]

The Senate Finance Committee submitted a report favoring the revenue act which was almost verbatim of the House report. In addition, though, several amendments had been proposed to the Senate committee. One change would terminate the allowance of gambling losses as income tax deductions and another would require gambling houses to keep records of their activities for seven years. It was also recommended to the committee that anyone with a gross income of more than $2,500 acquired from illegal activities in each of the preceding five years be required to file "a net worth statement." These changes, the committee report declared, required detailed study and so they were not endorsed at that time.[29]

---

[26] *Congressional Record*, 82 Cong., 1 Sess., 1951, 97:6891.

[27] Ibid., p. 6896.

[28] Ibid., pp. 6906, 6967, 6971–72, 6998.

[29] U.S., Congress, Senate, Report 781 (Serial 11489), 82 Cong., 1 Sess., 1951, pp. 112–20.

Immediately after the revenue bill was reported out of committee, Senator Kefauver attended a meeting of the American Bar Association. The gambling tax received considerable attention at this gathering and Kefauver assured the lawyers he would attempt to amend the gambling tax out of the revenue proposal.[30] When the Senate debated the measure, Kefauver offered an amendment on behalf of himself, Democrats Herbert O'Conor of Maryland and Lester Hunt of Wyoming, and Republicans Charles Tobey of New Hampshire and Alexander Wiley of Wisconsin—the members of the Kefauver Committee. The amendment would strike out the gambling tax and registration and insert instead the suggestions rejected by the Senate Finance Committee. Kefauver declared that the gambling tax was morally offensive and unenforceable. It would simply drive the bookies "underground and . . . discourage local and State officials from enforcing their laws against gambling." Taxing this activity was "not in keeping with the best instincts of our people," Kefauver insisted, because it "purports to accept the existence of an evil and accept it as a way of life." He called attention to the twenty-six large policy wheels that were operating at one time in Chicago alone, using from 5,000 to 6,000 "runners" to conduct them. On this basis it would take "a veritable army" of agents to enforce a gambling tax, he said.

If Congress wanted to suppress gambling, Kefauver insisted, it should attack the problem directly. His substitute proposals—gambling records, disallowance of gambling losses as deductions, and net worth statements of criminals—were unanimously recommended by the American Bar Association's Commission on Organized Crime, and he urged their enactment. Democrat Robert Kerr of Oklahoma remarked that the registration requirement should help to uncover gamblers and asked Kefauver if he believed his investigations, which identified criminals, had discouraged local and state law enforcement officials in their efforts. Kefauver, of course, refused to concede that his committee had retarded progress of the fight against crime. Kerr further pointed out that federal taxes on tobacco, guns, narcotics, and pastel mink coats did not, in themselves, constitute congressional approval of these items and this closed the debate. The Senate then rejected Kefauver's amendment 29 to 49 and approved the revenue bill by vote of 57 to 19. President Truman signed the Revenue Act of 1951 on October 20.[31]

[30] *New York Times*, September 20, 1951.
[31] *Congressional Record*, 82 Cong., 1 Sess., 1951, 97:12230–41, 12244, 12382, 13785.

This law raised the slot-machine tax to $250 annually, required a $50 license stamp for gamblers, and levied a 10 percent tax on all wagers. All people engaged in accepting wagers had to register their names and business addresses and identify all persons who received wagers for or on their behalf. This section was amended in 1958 to require the same information of gamblers concerning their employers.[32]

With this tax law, as with the narcotics registration acts, "a gambler was damned if he registered and damned if he didn't."[33] If the number of federal stamps purchased is any indication, gamblers soon discovered they had a better chance escaping damnation if they did not register. In 1952, almost 20,000 gamblers bought the stamps. This number steadily declined and ten years later only 8,230 registered. By 1967 this number had declined to 5,917.[34] Ten years after the tax went into effect Republican Paul Fino of New York, in arguing for a national lottery, pointed out that the gambling tax had raised a total of $75 million. This fell far short of the annual $400 million predicted by the sponsors of the measure and yet Fino estimated gambling to be currently a $50 billion annual business.[35]

The 1951 gambling tax was quickly litigated and soon reached the Supreme Court. Joseph Kahringer of Philadelphia was in the business of accepting wagers but failed to buy the fifty-dollar occupation stamp. He defended this failure to comply with the law on the grounds that the tax was a penalty, rather than a way to raise revenue, and that it violated the Tenth Amendment by regulating an activity reserved to state control. In addition, Kahriger argued, the registration requirement violated the Fifth Amendment by compelling him to be a witness against himself. The District Court for Eastern Pennsylvania sustained his request for dismissal of charges, holding the tax to violate the Tenth Amendment according to the precedent established in *United States* v. *Constantine*.[36] The United States appealed this particular decision, on the grounds that seven other district courts had

---

[32] U.S., *Statutes at Large*, vols. 65 and 72.

[33] Lester Velie, "What Are the Gamblers Doing Now?" *Saturday Evening Post* 224 (May 3, 1952) : 26.

[34] These figures are taken from the *Annual Report*, Commissioner of Internal Revenue, for each year.

[35] *Congressional Record*, 87 Cong., 2 Sess., 1962, 108:4049. He tried again, unsuccessfully, two years later for a national lottery. See ibid., 88 Cong., 2 Sess., 1964, 110: 4253–54. For a survey of earlier attempts to establish a national lottery, see John S. Ezell, *Fortune's Merry Wheel* (Cambridge, Mass., 1960), pp. 276–78.

[36] *Transcript of Records and File Copies of Briefs*, Case #167, 1952 Term, vol. 57, U.S. Supreme Court Library.

previously held the gambling tax to be a valid one in similar cases.

The Supreme Court, in a six-to-three decision, sustained the law. The majority opinion observed that "regardless of its regulatory effect, the wagering tax produces revenue" the majority opinion concluded it was not solely a penalty. The majority agreed that statutes rooted in the commerce power were "generally sustained" whereas "a greater variation in the decisions has resulted" when the taxing power was employed. But, in regard to this tax, all the provisions of the law were adapted to collection of revenue. Even the registration requirement was not offensive; it was a normal procedure employed in collecting many types of taxes.

Kahriger's raising the incrimination issue created greater problems for the majority. The government brief argued that the Fifth Amendment had not been violated because there was no national law against gambling, except in the District of Columbia. The Supreme Court majority held that the Fifth Amendment protection against self-incrimination applied "only to past acts, not to future acts that may or may not be committed." So the registration did not invade this privilege; it merely required a stamp whether or not the purchaser subsequently engaged in gambling. Justice Robert Jackson, in a concurring opinion, agreed this tax "approaches the fair limits of constitutionality," but insisted the Fifth Amendment should not be construed so as "to impair the taxing power conferred . . . especially by the Sixteenth Amendment, further than is absolutely required."

Justice Hugo Black, joined by Justice William O. Douglas, disssented. Black was certain the gambling tax created "a squeezing device contrived to put a man in prison if he refuses to confess himself into a state prison" and thus violated the privilege of nonincrimination. Justice Felix Frankfurter also dissented, but it was on the basis of the Tenth Amendment. He noted that "constitutional issues are likely to arise whenever Congress draws on the taxing power not to raise revenue but to regulate conduct." Gambling, he insisted, was controlled by states and the Court could not "shut its eyes" to this "merely because Congress wrapped the legislation in the verbal cellophane of a revenue measure." Frankfurter saw a parallel between this tax and the child labor tax which, he noted, even the liberal Oliver Wendell Holmes and Louis Brandeis had opposed.[37]

Two years later a District of Columbia gambler, Frank Lewis, challenged the tax as violating the Fifth Amendment because gambling was

[37] *United States* v. *Kahriger*, 345 U.S. 22 (1953).

prohibited in the District. He also argued that it was a penalty, not a revenue measure.[38] The Supreme Court again divided along the lines of the *Kahriger* case. The majority held the law to be a valid tax and declared there was "no constitutional right to gamble. If they elect to wager, though it be unlawful, they must pay the tax." Black, again joined by Douglas, dissented sharply, stating that this decision "reduces the Fifth Amendment protection still more." Kahriger had to confess to violating state law, Black noted, but Lewis had to "file a written confession . . . for . . . which . . . he could be convicted of a felony . . . . If this would not violate the Fifth Amendment's privilege against self-incrimination, it is hard to think of anything that would," he said. Frankfurter also dissented but did so because the gambling tax was "a spurious use of the taxing power as a means of facilitating prosecution of federal offenses."[39]

The willingness of the Supreme Court to sustain state gambling convictions that were obtained through the national law was early demonstrated. A California gambler was convicted of violating state gambling laws. His national gambling stamp was part of the evidence presented by the state, in addition to records he had prepared for the Bureau of Internal Revenue in payment of the 10 percent tax on wagers. By a five-to-four decision the Supreme Court upheld his conviction. The majority observed that the national tax did not "make such records or stamps confidential or privileged but, on the contrary, expressly requires the name and place of business of each such taxpayer to be made public." Black, with Douglas, dissented on the basis of their reasoning in the *Kahringer* case, that the law violated the Fifth Amendment. Frankfurter, joined by Harold Burton, dissented for the same reason he stated in his dissent in the *Kahriger* decision. In a separate dissent, Douglas stingingly denounced the search-and-seizure methods used in this case, saying they "smack of the police state, not the free America the Bill of Rights envisaged."[40]

It was not until the following decade that the Black-Douglas view prevailed. In the meantime the emphasis of the Warren Court decisions was changing. Increasingly, from 1957 on, the Supreme Court demonstrated a greater concern for the freedoms and privileges of the individual in protection against government action. In 1957 the Supreme Court handed down

[38] *Transcript of Records and File Copies of Briefs,* Case #203, 1954 Term, vol. 59.

[39] *Lewis* v. *United States,* 348 U.S. 419 (1955).

[40] *Levine* v. *California,* 347 U.S. 128 (1954).

several decisions that promised a break with the philosophy of the Vinson Court and the decisions of the early Warren years. In that year the Court began altering its previous convictions of Communists and gradually extending the protection of the Bill of Rights to these political dissenters. The more liberal interpretation of these guarantees were also applied to criminal convictions.[41]

The first step in altering the *Kahriger-Lewis* opinions came when a Connecticut gambler, while on probation after conviction on a gambling misdemeanor, declined to testify in a state gambling investigation. He refused, was convicted for withholding testimony, and appealed to the Supreme Court for a writ of habeas corpus. In 1964 the Supreme Court, by a five-to-four decision, granted the writ. The majority agreed that the privilege against self-incrimination applied also to states through the Fourteenth Amendment due-process clause. This privilege, the Court determined, is available in a statutory inquiry as well as in criminal prosecutions.[42] The following year the Supreme Court unanimously held the registration requirement of the Subversive Activities Control Act of 1950 infringed on the right not to incriminate oneself. Admission of membership in the Communist party, the Court said, might be used as an investigatory lead to, or evidence in, a criminal prosecution under the subversive activities law or the 1940 Smith Act.[43]

By the time Chief Justice Earl Warren tendered his resignation in the summer of 1968, the Supreme Court members had polarized into two blocs with differing constitutional theories.[44] The activists, led by Black and Douglas, were convinced that the Court must assume a positive role in extending the Bill of Rights guarantees to individuals even at the expense of restricting the role of the legislatures in formulating public policy. This libertarian viewpoint was usually supported by Warren and another Eisenhower appointee, William Brennan, and also by Abe Fortas, appointed by President Johnson in 1965, and Thurgood Marshall, appointed in 1967.

---

[41] See the excellent discussion of these decisions in Walter F. Murphy, *Congress and the Court* (Chicago, Ill., 1962), sec. 3; also G. Theodore Mitau, *Decade of Decision* (New York, 1967), chapt. 1, on the Communist issue and chapt. 5, on criminal law; Paul Murphy, *The Constitution in Crisis Times* (New York, 1972), pp. 372–75, on the Communist issue.

[42] *Malloy* v. *Hogan*, 378 U.S. 1 (1964).

[43] *Albertson* v. *SACB*, 382 U.S. 70 (1965).

[44] This development is ably discussed in William F. Swindler, *Court and Constitution in the Twentieth Century* (Indianapolis, Ind., 1970), vol. 2, chapt. 14.

John Marshall Harlan and Potter Stewart, appointed in 1954 and 1958 respectively by Eisenhower, and Byron White, the first Kennedy appointee in 1962, represented the conservative wing of the Court. Emphasizing the concept that the justices should exercise judicial self-restraint, these men attempted to continue the role propounded by Frankfurter and the Vinson Court. To these justices, the legislative branch of government should be allowed a maximum flexibility to determine public policy. For years this bloc had predominated; by 1968 the Johnson appointees completed the solid majority that would support the Black-Douglas approach and make a major impact on the practicality of the use of regulatory taxation, especially the gambling tax.

In 1967 the Supreme Court granted certiorari to two gambling cases and a violation of the firearms tax to determine if the *Kahriger* and *Lewis* opinions should be "reconsidered in the light of recent decisions"—the *Malloy* and *Albertson* cases.[45] Anthony Grosso and James Marchetti had their gambling operations raided in Connecticut. They appealed their conviction on the grounds the national tax violated the Fifth Amendment. Seven of the Supreme Court justices now found the *Kahriger-Lewis* "reasoning no longer persuasive."[46] The Fifth Amendment, the majority decided, "was intended to shield the guilty and imprudent as well as the innocent and foresighted." The *Kahriger* and *Lewis* conclusions that the privilege against self-incrimination protected only past and present acts, the Court reasoned, was "twice deficient: first, it overlooks the hazards here of incrimination as to past and present acts; and second, it is hinged upon an excessively narrow view of the scope of the constitutional privilege." The registration requirement enhanced the possibility of discovery of past and present gambling offenses, even those which violated national law such as transporting gambling paraphernalia. And, the majority insisted, "the hazards of incrimination . . . as to future acts are not trifling or imaginary." The Court noted that Alabama and Georgia laws, for example, provided that purchase of the national gambling stamp was prima facie evidence of guilt in violating the states' gambling laws.[47]

[45] *Transcript of Records and File Copies of Briefs*, Case #2, 12, 1967 Term, vols. 6 and 7.

[46] Justice Thurgood Marshall took no part in these decisions because he was solicitor general when they were initiated.

[47] *Marchetti* v. *United States*, 390 U.S. 39; *Grosso* v. *United States*, 390 U.S. 62 (1968).

The seven justices did not hold the wagering tax to be unconstitutional —they merely said the national government could not enforce registration, which, of course, removed enforcement power. The same opinion was applied to both litigations. In both cases Chief Justice Warren dissented, sustaining the reasoning in *Kahriger* and *Lewis*. The power to tax gambling was constitutional, Warren insisted, and the information demanded was "no more than is necessary to assure that the tax-collection process will be effective." He distinguished the gambling issue from the Communist-registration principle by noting that First Amendment freedoms were involved in the latter. Warren concluded his dissent with a warning to his brethren that they were "opening the door to a new wave of attacks on a number of federal registration statutes whenever the registration requirement touches upon allegedly illegal activities." Among these, he suggested the narcotics laws and particularly the firearms registration could be challenged. He specifically called attention to the *Hayne* decision handed down that same day. The same majority that wrote the gambling opinions also held the National Firearms registration violated the Fifth Amendment on the basis of the *Grosso* and *Marchetti* decisions. Warren dissented here, too, for the same reasons he made his previous dissents.[48]

The use of the commerce power to prohibit certain gambling activities, in conjunction with the taxing of gambling, now seems incompatible with the 1968 Court decisions. It is apparent Congress will have to choose one power or the other to control gambling and abandon the attempt to use both approaches. In the light of Supreme Court decisions, it is obvious the commerce power would have the better chance of being sustained. The forced registration under the tax laws, which are vital, permit gamblers now to invoke the Fifth Amendment to avoid facing criminal penalties for violating gambling laws rooted in the interstate commerce power. The *Marchetti-Grosso* opinions demonstrate that the national effort to curb illegal gambling through the taxing power has been a failure.

---

[48] *Haynes* v. *United States*, 390 U.S. 85 (1968). Warren's forebodings materialized in 1969 when the Supreme Court freed Timothy Leary from a marijuana tax-evasion charge on the grounds that registration for the tax violated the Fifth Amendment; *Leary* v. *United States*, 395 U.S. 6. Yet later that year the Court sustained the conviction of sellers of marijuana and heroin because the danger of self-incrimination applied only to the purchaser who had to obtain the necessary order form. *New York Times*, December 9, 1969. Murphy, *The Constitution in Crisis Times*, p. 436, erroneously states that in the *Haynes* decision the Court held registration not to be compulsory self-incrimination.

In addition, the gambling tax has apparently not curtailed the activities of organized crime to any appreciable extent. As a means of raising revenue it certainly has not fulfilled the expectations of its sponsors. From 1952 to 1967 the tax yielded $105,988,000; Internal Revenue costs of enforcing the tax during this same period were $18,651,000.[49] The 1968 decisions, the chief of the section on organized crime in the Department of Justice stated, "will reduce the effectiveness of the Federal organized crime drive by about 20 percent."[50]

More importantly, the basic philosophy behind the gambling tax is open to question. Obviously, the primary purpose was to force registration and thus assist states in enforcing their prohibitory laws. As one judge has stated, "the standard that makes a bet at a race track morally and legally superior to one placed on a street corner is dubious to say the least."[51] Finally, the 1968 decisions that registration requirements for gamblers violate the Fifth Amendment could have far-reaching effects on all the other national laws that require registration of the taxpayer. The way now appears open for successful challenging of all national tax laws controlling activities that are also illegal under other statutes, if registration requirements are part of those acts.[52]

[49] These figures were supplied by Solicitor General Marshall in response to Justice Black's request during the oral argument of *Grosso* v. *United States*; *Transcript of Records and File Copies of Briefs*, Case #12, 1967 Term, vol. 7.

[50] *New York Times*, February 4, 1968. But in 1969, in *United States* v. *Knox* (396 U.S. 77), the Supreme Court, Black and Douglas dissenting, held that the Fifth Amendment did not protect *failure to comply* with the registration requirements. See Arthur C. Eads, "Wagering Tax Law," *Baylor Law Review* 19 (Winter 1970) : 154–56.

[51] Judge John M. Murtagh, "Gambling and Police Corruption," in *Gambling*, ed. Herman, p. 241. See also Donald R. Cressey, "Bet Taking, Cosa Nostra, and Negotiated Social Order," *Journal of Public Law* 19 (1970) : 13–22.

[52] Early in 1969 Senator Roman Hruska, Republican of Nebraska, introduced a gambling bill to meet the objections of the Court in the *Marchetti-Grosso* cases. The Hruska proposal would require gamblers to file with the Internal Revenue Service but the information could not be divulged for any purpose other than enforcement of the gambling taxes. This restriction, however, seems to be negated by a later clause requiring the gambler to "place and keep conspicuously in his establishment or place of business all stamps denoting payment of such special tax." It appears this would violate the self-incrimination protection. The bill is reprinted in *Congressional Record*, 91 Cong., 1 Sess., 1969, 115:S2995–96 (unbound edition).

14 *An Evaluation of Regulatory Taxes*

The development of taxes to regulate, control, or abolish commodities or activities followed in many respects the pattern of national constitutional trends from the late nineteenth century to the mid-twentieth century. During the Gilded Age, industry dominated American society and, with modern chemistry, was threatening the "pure food" of the farm. Dairy farmers responded by asking Congress to curtail production of "fraudulent" foods, just as other interests were increasingly expecting the national government to act for them. Russel B. Nye has described rural "radicalism" of this era as "a series of perfectly logical attempts to find some sensible method of removing certain threats to Midwestern interests."[1] Although oleomargarine was a good, cheap table food for poorly paid urban laborers, it threatened to drive off the market the poorer grades of butter. So the dairy farmers' response was simple: Congress should penalize the "artificial" product to the point that it could not offer this competition. The first group of regulatory taxes on foods followed this pattern.

Although they were not effectively organized politically, which thus limited their numerical superiority, agriculturalists were able to achieve many goals in the late nineteenth century through efforts of some outstanding rural leaders in Congress. This was particularly true in those politically stable areas, such as the Democratic South and the predominantly Republican Midwest, where congressmen were reelected year after year, built up seniority, and became chairmen of key committees such as Ways and Means, Appropriations, and Agriculture. The result was a series of discriminatory taxes on oleomargarine, filled cheese, mixed flour, and futures contracts, all designed to improve the well-being of farmers.

Seen in a broad perspective, these taxes on oleomargarine, flour, and cheese of the 1880s and 1890s foreshadowed the breakdown of laissez-faire that came with the Progressive movement. In the early years of the twentieth century the demand for reform came primarily from "those who wanted government aid for their own benefit."[2] But this selfish motivation soon broadened into an altruistic desire by reform groups to mitigate certain evils that infected American society. The result was a tax levied on dangerous matches which drove them out of existence, taxes to compel registration in order to eliminate drug addiction which threatened the welfare of individuals, and a prohibitive tax on child labor to help those too helpless to protect themselves.

With the advent of the depression and the New Deal there emerged a firm commitment to use the massive power of the national government to control and direct society. Out of this development, which was accentuated in the post-World War II era, came taxes to regulate segments of the economy such as agriculture and coal mining and a major assault on organized crime with regulatory taxes on firearms, illegal gambling, and further controls on the narcotics traffic. The goals of all these taxes were achieved in one manner or another except those on firearms, gambling and narcotics. The national government was able to master a powerful and unruly industrialism but has failed markedly in subduing organized crime.

The origin of these taxes also follow the pattern of legislative development in recent United States history. The early taxes on food products were initiated by individual congressmen or congressional committees, followed by pressure placed on Congress by farm organizations, some of which were for enactment such as the National Dairy Union and others, such as the Southern Alliance, opposed them. Then, particularly in the Progressive period, regulatory tax proposals generally were initiated by reform groups which also generated the necessary public opinion required for congressional action. In either instance it was Congress that took action first, rather than the executive branch, with the possible exception of taxes on narcotics. As one revisionist scholar of the Progressive movement has stated, one "must concede a much larger importance to the role of Congress than has hitherto been granted" by those who study this period.[3] From the New Deal

---

[1] *Midwestern Progressive Politics* (New York, 1965), p. 14.

[2] Harold U. Faulkner, *The Decline of Laissez-Faire* (New York, 1951), p. 366.

[3] Gabriel Kolko, *The Triumph of Conservatism* (Chicago, Ill., 1967), p. 280.

on, however, the regulatory taxes were initiated by the executive branch except for the levy on gambling which apparently was a caprice of the staff of a congressional committee.

The taxes and controls imposed in the 1950s and 1960s, regardless of their origin, reflect the tremendous impact of television. Prior to the advent of television, legislation required the organization of interest groups formulating policy and educating public opinion. These efforts were usually in conjunction with a relatively long incubation period in congressional committees and consideration by a deliberative Congress, unless an emergency required prompt enactment. The influence of television has certainly modified the traditional legislative process. When the horrors of assassinations of leading political figures, the contemptuous attitude of underworld criminals for society, or the debilitating effects of narcotics on youth are brought into the home of millions of television viewers, the result is almost instant molding of public opinion. While its impact and influence are difficult to measure, this medium of communication, if properly used, could be of tremendous assistance to those who desire to reform society through governmental direction and control.

In terms of political parties and their policies, no particular pattern emerges from a study of regulatory taxes. Democrats sponsored the oleomargarine tax of 1886 and controlled the House of Representatives (which originates revenue measures) when all the taxes were passed, except the child labor and grain futures laws, from the Match Act in 1912 through the gambling tax of 1951. Republicans controlled the House when Congress enacted the cheese, flour, and second oleomargarine taxes. The issue of using the revenue power for regulatory purposes, in effect, cut across party lines and in some instances created intraparty conflict. Southern states'-rights congressmen opposed this development, except when their constituents were directly affected as was the case with cotton futures and the first Agricultural Adjustment Administration, even when the Democratic party sponsored the legislation. Liberal Democrats with hunter-constituents rejected party leadership when firearms controls were debated. Republicans from meat-packing districts, on the other hand, voted against their political colleagues from farm areas when the dispute was drawn between dairy commodities and products from packinghouses, as did Democrats in the same situation. Constituents' interests came first, usually, before party principle. Taxes on the "evil" activities of organized crime, where the moral indignation of the public and congressmen was aroused, are exceptions as these laws acquired near unanimity in Congress. All in all, the party in power enacted these laws in response to the pressure from certain groups, an interested public, or the requests of a strong president.

It is ironical, however, that Democratic policy has been one of condemnation of Republican demands for a protective tariff which, if high enough to satisfy the pleas of manufacturers, would preclude any collection of revenue. Yet the Democratic-sponsored taxes on matches, narcotics, firearms, and gambling were enacted with the obvious desire of elimination of the "evil" which would then provide no income. The same purpose, of course, was evident in all the regulatory taxes regardless of party sponsorship. The cotton futures and match taxes produced no revenue because they immediately brought about their objective of eliminating certain practices. The levies on flour and cheese produced very little revenue and ultimately abolished almost completely these impure foods. The oleomargarine and firearms taxes produced some revenue, despite expectations of their sponsors, but were a disappointment in regard to the objective of destruction. The oleomargarine tax was the only regulatory tax to be repealed by Congress. Finally, the various laws on narcotics and the gambling tax, while producing more revenue than any of the other regulatory taxes, have been noticeable failures in curtailment. The child labor, grain futures, AAA, and coal taxes were found to violate the Tenth Amendment by encroaching upon the realm of state-reserved powers.

Imposing taxes for regulating or abolishing products or activities constituted a part of the larger picture of constitutional development from the Industrial Revolution to the present. It was but one segment of the tremendous increase in national governmental powers through a loose interpretation of the Constitution. States'-rights congressmen, especially Southerners, fought bitterly this enlargement of federal powers, except when their constituents' interests were involved. States' righters on the Supreme Court opposed this trend also until the demise of the doctrine of Dual Federalism in the "Roosevelt Court."

Supreme Court interpretations of regulatory taxes offer an interesting illustration of the trend in national constitutional growth. In the latter part of the nineteenth century the Supreme Court showed "a marked disposition to enhance the powers of the National Government by a liberal construction of the Constitution, and to widen the scope of the jurisdiction a. l powers of the National Judiciary."[4] This interpretation was quite apparent in the 1904 oleomargarine case when the Court sustained an obviously regulatory tax because, "on its face" it was a revenue measure and the justices refused "to inquire into the motives of Congress" as to why this policy was adopted. During this period, and continuing to the New Deal years, the High Court followed a course of "judicial dualism" whereby the decisions alternated between halting the national regulatory efforts and moderating governmental regulation.[5]

In sustaining the first regulatory tax in 1904, though, the Supreme Court significantly accepted the "objective-subjective" interpretation of taxes posed by Justice Edward White. Regulatory taxes would be approved if they were revenue measures on their face, but if they clearly regulated or prohibited a fundamental right they would be rejected. With this subjective criterion the existence of the tax laws would depend upon whether or not the individual justices agreed or disagreed with the purpose of the regulation. The subsequent course of Court interpretations of the tax laws lent credence to the concept that judicial review is little more than "another step in the legislative process."[6] The justices either approved or vetoed the tax policies enacted by the peoples' representatives.

The Harrison law came close to being subjectively unconstitutional when a bare majority agreed that this "evil" needed to be controlled. Three years later the Court determined that regulation of child labor and grain futures encroached upon fundamental rights and, based on the concept of Dual Federalism, invaded the exclusive jurisdiction of states to regulate labor conditions and individual contracts. More than a decade later, as a result of the same reasoning, the AAA and coal tax regulations succumbed to the doctrine of Dual Federalism. The narcotics-control taxes, and for several years the taxes on firearms and gambling, met the subjective test of the Court. These were evils that should be regulated, the justices believed. The purpose of the oleomargarine tax, as enunciated in and out of Congress, could not have been more obviously regulatory and was sustained as a policy of Congress. Yet the evil conditions of labor in terms of children or

[4] Charles Warren, *The Supreme Court in United States History* (Boston, 1926), 2:625.

[5] Robert G. McCloskey, *The American Supreme Court* (Chicago, Ill., 1960), pp. 136–44.

[6] Ibid. See also Carl Brent Swisher, *The Growth of Constitutional Power in the United States*, 2d ed. (Chicago, Ill., 1963). pp. 92–93, for a brief discussion of the Court interpretation of regulatory taxes.

coal miners or the deplorable economic condition of farmers in the Great Depression could not be alleviated by a congressional policy because the regulatory effects of these taxes were too direct an encroachment upon state authority. In short, the Supreme Court has been inconsistent in inquiring, or refusing to inquire, into the motives of Congress on tax policy.

On the other hand, the Supreme Court has been far more lenient if the purpose of the regulatory tax was to assist in carrying out some other power or to force registration, such as the narcotics laws. In comparing Court interpretations of the taxing and commerce powers, wider latitude has always been given to the commerce powers. Nowhere is this better illustrated than the grain futures legislation. The Supreme Court could not sustain the futures tax and be consistent with the striking down of the child labor tax on the same day, because both, when put to the subjective test, violated the Tenth Amendment. Acting on the suggestion of the High Tribunal that futures should be controlled under the commerce power, Congress reenacted substantially the same program through its power over interstate commerce. The justices then endorsed the grain futures regulations. Use of the taxing power to regulate futures markets invaded state authority; one year later, use of the commerce power to achieve the same purposes was constitutional, according to these same justices.

With the passing of Dual Federalism the Supreme Court was more consistent in interpreting regulatory taxes—until the gambling tax created a dilemma in regard to the protection against self-incrimination. Despite strong dissents from three justices, the Court first determined the registration provisions of the wagering tax to be consistent with the normal procedure for requiring information for revenue purposes. Then with the increasing concern of a majority of the justices during the 1960s over protection of individual rights, the dissenters, and the views of Black and Douglas in particular, finally prevailed. The Supreme Court eventually determined the registration requirement unconstitutionally forced the gambler to testify against himself which could lead to prosecution for violation of other gambling laws enacted under the commerce power. By so holding, the Supreme Court reversed a long history of judicial precedents in which the taxing power had been sustained, even though the revenue provisions themselves were open to constitutional doubt, as long as they assisted in carrying out some other delegated power.

The 1968 decisions holding tax registration requirements to violate the Fifth Amendment certainly invite litigation that would challenge all other similar revenue laws. Any commodity or activity that is taxed, and also controlled in other ways through the commerce power, is now open to question if criminal penalties are attached to violation of the subsidiary commerce power statutes. If the 1968 decisions become *stare decisis* Congress should use either the taxing power or the interstate commerce power, but never both in conjunction with each other, in any future extension of the national police power in order to have them validated.

Congress has not used the taxing power to extend the police power since the 1951 gambling tax, although opportunities to do so have arisen. The surgeon general of the United States issued a controversial report in 1964 following extensive investigation of the possible connection of cigarette smoking and lung cancer. This official report declared there was definite scientific evidence to substantiate this theory. In the ensuing public and congressional debate the tobacco interests discovered their best protection lay in the chairmanships of key committees of Congress being controlled by Southern congressmen.

Senator Robert F. Kennedy introduced a bill in the Senate in 1967 to meet the cigarette-lung-cancer crisis by taxing the more dangerous cigarettes heavily. His proposal sought to keep the current national levy of four dollars per thousand, or eight cents per package, on cigarettes containing less than ten milograms of tar and eight-tenths milograms of nicotine. This amount would then be graduated up to a maximum of fifteen dollars per thousand, or thirty cents per package, on cigarettes containing more than thirty milograms of tar and one and six-tenths milograms of nicotine. This tax measure, he said, was intended to "discourage the sale of the more lethal brands of cigarettes."[7] The Senate, however, cannot originate revenue bills and Kennedy's proposal was never reported out of committee. Instead, Congress used the commerce power to authorize the Federal Trade Commission to require all cigarette packages to bear a label warning the consumer of the health danger of the product. This was a wiser approach although far less effective than a prohibitory tax. Throughout the history of the Supreme Court in the twentieth century the justices have interpreted the commerce power far more broadly than the taxing power when Congress has imposed a police power regulation or prohibition.

Seen in their broad perspective, the regulatory taxes that created a national police power can be categorized into two types. The first group, those

---

[7] *Congressional Record*, 90 Cong., 1 Sess., 1967, 113:S12817, S12821 (unbound edition). See also the story in *Newsweek* 70 (November 6, 1967) :64–65.

that abolished or regulated adulterated foods and futures contracts can be evaluated as successful. These items required national regulation or control and the taxes achieved this end—although it could have been done through the commerce power. Those taxes on firearms, gambling, and narcotics have been almost entirely unsuccessful. They have not achieved their purpose of abolishing, or even of controlling effectively. The narcotics taxes, in fact, have brought about quite deleterious effects. The controls on narcotics have made criminals out of sick people. If Congress wanted to abolish the narcotics traffic, the commerce power should have been used exclusively and in a prohibitory manner. Concurrently, programs should have been instituted to cure and rehabilitate addicts and to educate the uninitiated to the dangers of drug addiction. In fact, in regard to both narcotics and gambling, sound programs of education would be far more sensible to alleviate these social ills than is the use of force.

The gambling and narcotics tax laws also serve as good illustrations of sumptuary legislation. Certain moral questions should be left to ecclesiasticals and the individual conscience, not to politics, as was discovered with the national experiment in Prohibition. It is difficult to make a distinction, morally speaking, between use of legal alcohol and illegal narcotics. Both can affect health adversely. Both can lead to antisocial actions if used immoderately. It is likewise awkward to differentiate morally between legal on-track gambling and illegal off-track wagers. If gambling and the use of narcotics can be judged immoral, education should be used to curtail them. Morals can best be taught, not imposed.

In a comparison of the use of the power to control interstate commerce and the taxing power, opposition to the former has been less, both in the Supreme Court and Congress. All the activities and commodities Congress has taxed in building a police power could have been more easily regulated or abolished through the commerce power. Judged from this viewpoint, regulatory taxation must be deemed a failure in policy. In the future Congress would be better advised, and receive less opposition, if the national police power is rooted in the commerce power.

Index to Cases Cited

Index

AAA. *See* Agricultural Adjustment Administration
A. B. Gwatheny and Company, 87
Abernathy, Thomas B., 29 n
Accardo, Tony, 195
Adonis, Joe, 195
Agricultural Adjustment Administration, 142, 145, 147–48, 150, 160
Agricultural Appropriations Act of 1909, 81
agriculture, 142–50
Agriculture and Forestry Committee (Senate), 71, 84
Agriculture Committee (House), 84–85, 88; debates compound lard, 31–37; debates Grout bill, 49–52; discusses commodity futures, 64–65, 72; and surplus foods, 143
Agriculture Department, 31, 37–38, 59, 86
Albert, Jose, 111
Allen, J. Weston, 167
Amalgamated Association of Iron and Steel Workers, 53
American Association for the Advancement of Science, 116
American Butter Institute, 58
American Liberty League, 158
American Pistol Association, 169
American Rifleman, 175
Ameris, Alexander, 121
amphetamines, 188
Andrews, John B., 93–94, 97 n, 101
Annenberg, M. L., 199
Arlington Park (Chicago), 198
Armour, Philip, 23
Armour Company, 19–20, 30, 52
Articles of Confederation, 4
Atlantic City, 194

Babcock test, 13
Bailey, Joseph W., 40, 53, 103, 114

Bailey, Willis, 50–51
Bakersfield, Calif., 200
Bankhead, John, 147
barbiturates, 188
Bartlett, Charles, 102–3
Bartlett, Franklin, 45
Bate, William B., 53
Bathrick, E. R., 103
Beach, Lewis, 20
Bennet, William, 87
Beveridge, Albert J., 127–28
bituminous coal, 142–60
Bituminous Coal Act of 1937, 159
Bituminous Coal Commission, 158
Bituminous Coal Conservation Act, 158, 160
Black, Hugo, 206, 217
Black Pepsin. *See* casein
Boatner, Charles, 66
Boggs, Hale, 184–87
Boyd, James Edmund, 129, 135
Bradley, Joseph, 9 n
Brandeis, Louis, 120, 130, 136, 141, 150, 159; on grain futures, 137
Breckinridge, Clifton, 21
Brennan, William, 208
Brent, Charles H., 111, 114, 116, 117
Brewer, David, 24–25, 54
Brosius, Marriot, 34
Brown, Henry, 54, 57
Brown and Fitts, 52
Brumm, Charles N., 46
Bureau of Internal Revenue, 119, 151, 182, 202–3, 211
Bureau of Labor, 93–94, 98, 127
Bureau of Narcotics, 181–82
Bureau of the Budget, 59, 190
Burton, Harold, 207
Butler, Pierce, 140
butter, process, 48–49. *See also* oleomargarine
Butterworth, Benjamin, 65

Date Due

JAN 29 '92			